ROYAL POETRIE

ROYAL POETRIE

MONARCHIC VERSE
AND THE POLITICAL
IMAGINARY OF EARLY
MODERN ENGLAND

PETER C. HERMAN

CORNELL UNIVERSITY PRESS
Ithaca and London

Publication of this volume was made possible by a generous grant from the Critical Thinking Grant Program of the College of Arts and Letters, San Diego State University.

First published 2010 by Cornell University Press

Printed in the United States of America

Library of Congress Cataloging-in-Publication Data

Herman, Peter C., 1958–
  Royal poetrie : monarchic verse and the political imaginary of early modern England / Peter C. Herman.
      p. cm.
  Includes bibliographical references and index.
  ISBN 978-0-8014-4835-5 (cloth : alk. paper)
  1. English poetry—Early modern, 1500–1700—History and criticism.   2. Kings and rulers as poets—Great Britain—History.   3. Kings and rulers in literature.
4. Monarchy in literature.   5. Politics in literature.
6. Great Britain—History—Tudors, 1485–1603.
7. Great Britain—History—Early Stuarts, 1603–1649.
I. Title.
  PR535.K56H47 2010
  821'.3—dc22   2009042858

Cloth printing   10 9 8 7 6 5 4 3 2 1

For Anne Lake Prescott

❧ CONTENTS

List of Illustrations   *ix*
Acknowledgments   *xi*
Abbreviations   *xiii*

Introduction: The Protocols
of Royal Poetrie   1

1. Henry VIII and the Political Imaginary
   of Early Tudor England   15

2. Mary, Queen of Scots and the Poetics
   of Monarchy   52

3. Elizabeth I, Privacy, and
   the Performance of Monarchic Verse   99

4. King James VI/I and the Scene
   of Monarchic Verse   157

5. Charles I and the End(s)
   of Monarchic Verse   196

Works Cited   209
Index   225

🐌 ILLUSTRATIONS

1. *Henry VIII MSS.,* fol. 40   12
2. *Henry VIII MSS.,* fol. 32v   13
3. *Henry VII,* c. 1505   19
4. Holbein the Younger, *Henry VIII,* 1537   21
5. *Henry VIII,* c. 1509   22
6. Silver ryal, Henry VII   24
7. Silver ryal, Henry VIII   25
8. *Henry VIII,* 1520   46
9. Miniature of Henry VIII by Lucas Horenbout, 1526   48
10. François Clouet, Mary "en deuil"   59
11. François Clouet, Mary "en deuil blanc"   61
12. Woodcut from Peter Frarinus, *An Oration against the Unlawfull Insurrections of the Protestants* (1566), sig. K7r   74
13. Silver ryal, 1565   78
14. Silver medal, 1565   79
15. "Rainbow" portrait, c. 1600–1603   115
16. George Gower, "Sieve" portrait, c. 1579   121
17. Detail from woodcut in *The Historie of Jacob,* 1578   154
18. Title page, *The Essayes of a Prentise,* 1584   180
19. Title page, *His Majesties Poeticall Exercises,* 1591   181
20. Title page, *Lepanto,* 1591   182
21. Title page, *Lepanto,* 1603   184
22. Running header, *Lepanto,* 1591   185
23. Running header, *Lepanto,* 1603   186
24. Woodcut from Gilbert Burnet, *Memoires of the Dukes of Hamilton,* 1677   205
25. Woodcut from John Gauden, *Eikon Basilike,* 1649   206

✒ ACKNOWLEDGMENTS

Many people have been very kind to me during the long writing of this book. I first want to thank David Richardson of Cleveland State University for asking me so long ago to write the entry on Henry VIII for the *Dictionary of Literary Biography*. That assignment led directly to my interest in Henry VIII's verse and subsequently, monarchic verse generally. Next, I must thank Ray Siemens, who graciously agreed to cowrite an article on Henry VIII for *Reading Monarchs Writing,* and who has been an invaluable (and patient) source of information on Henry VIII ever since. I remain grateful to Bob Bjork of MRTS for their decision to publish that anthology. The staffs of the University of Arizona reference desk, the British Museum, the National Portrait Gallery, the British Library, the Folger Shakespeare Library, the Royal Collection, the Huntington Library, Hatfield House, the Fitzwilliam Museum, the Burke Library of Columbia University, Art Resource, Bridgeman Art Library, and the Denver Art Museum were all very generous with their time and expertise, as were Mary Robertson of the Huntington Library as well as Ben Alsop and Kristen Wegner of the British Museum. Ben Bertram, Joseph Black, Peter Davidson, Sarah Dunnigan, Raphael Falco, Daniel Fischlin, Susan Frye, Michael Grattan, John Guy, Constance Jordan, David Scott Kastan, Roger Kuin, Leah Marcus, Steven W. May, James V. Mirollo, Janel Mueller, James C. Nohrnberg, François Rigolot, Kevin Sharpe, Helen Smailes, Donald Stump, Michael Ullyot, and Kristen Walton all provided aid and counsel, as did receptive audiences at the Renaissance Society of America Convention, the Columbia University Seminar in the Renaissance, and the University of Maine. Also, I am glad to publicly acknowledge my debt to Brad Cook, my colleague at San Diego State University, for his translation of Mary Stuart's Latin. Special thanks go to Louis A. Montrose for his support and for writing *The Subject of Elizabeth: Authority, Gender, and Representation,* a book that showed me just what interdisciplinarity really means and how to unfold the cultural resonances of monarchic verse. I am also deeply indebted to Peter J. Potter and the two anonymous readers for the Press for their enthusiasm and their perceptive comments.

Ange Romeo-Hall and Marian Rogers together transformed (magically, it seemed) a typescript into a book. My wife, Meryl Maneker, and my kids, Alison and Jon, improved everything by continually drawing me back to the world.

Earlier versions of the chapters on Henry VIII, Mary, Queen of Scots, and James VI/I appeared in *Reading Monarchs Writing: The Poetry of Henry VIII, Mary Stuart, Elizabeth I, and James VI/I,* the journal *Renaissance Quarterly,* and *Royal Subjects: Essays on the Writings of James VI and I.* I am very grateful to the editors for permission to reprint.

Finally, I dedicate this book to my dissertation advisor, mentor, and teacher, Anne Lake Prescott, whose erudition is matched only by her grace and wit. I am privileged to have been, and to continue to be, her student, and I thank her for all her help and encouragement over many years. I offer this book as small recompense for all she has done.

❧ Abbreviations

The following sources are cited parenthetically in an abbreviated form in the text and notes.

CA   *The Compleat Ambassador*, ed. Sir Dudley Digges. London, 1655.

CLSP   *Calendar of Letters and State Papers Relating to English Affairs, Preserved Principally in the Archives of Simancas: Elizabeth, 1580–1586,* ed. Martin A. S. Hume. 4 vols. London: Her Majesty's Stationery Office, 1896.

CSPD   *Calendar of State Papers, Domestic Series, Edward VI, Mary, Elizabeth, 1547–1580, ed.* Robert Lemon. London: Her Majesty's Stationery Office, 1856.

CSPF   *Calendar of State Papers, Foreign Series, of the Reign of Elizabeth,* ed. Joseph Stevenson. London: Her Majesty's Stationery Office, 1865.

CSPS   *Calendar of State Papers Relating to Scotland and Mary, Queen of Scots 1547–1603,* ed. Joseph Bain. Edinburgh: H. M. General Register House, 1898.

HMC   *Historical Manuscripts Commission: Calendar of the Manuscripts of the Marquis of Salisbury Preserved at Hatfield House.* Series 9, part 2. London: Her Majesty's Stationery Office, 1888.

LP   *Letters and Papers, Foreign and Domestic, of the Reign of Henry VIII,* ed. John Brewer. 2nd ed. London: Her Majesty's Stationery Office, 1920.

MMR   Elizabeth I. *Elizabeth I: Collected Works, ed.* Leah S. Marcus, Janel Mueller, and Mary Beth Rose. Chicago: University of Chicago Press, 2000.

ROYAL POETRIE

Introduction

The Protocols of Royal Poetrie

This book examines the intersection between a body of verse that has received surprisingly little attention—the poetry produced by the Tudor and Stuart monarchs Henry VIII, Mary Stuart (better known as Mary, Queen of Scots), Elizabeth I, and James VI/I—and the various fields of cultural meanings surrounding these rulers. To be sure, an investigation of the politics of courtly verse is nothing new, and, indeed, the concept that "love is not love," but politics, has become something of a cliché, albeit one that has produced many powerful, highly influential studies.[1] Yet for all their insights, including a sense of how thematically capacious and various Petrarchism can be,[2] students of courtly verse hold two assumptions in common. The first is that Sir Thomas Wyatt and Henry Howard, Earl of Surrey, both of whom wrote during the 1540s, constitute the beginning of this tradition in early modern England. The second is that the courtly lyric is

---

1. See, for example, Marotti's influential article "'Love is not love'"; Montrose, "'Eliza, Queen of Shepherds,'"; Greenblatt's chapter on Wyatt in *Renaissance Self-Fashioning,* 115–56; Jones and Stallybrass, "Politics of *Astrophil and Stella*"; Hedley, *Power in Verse;* Halasz, "Wyatt's David"; Klein, *Exemplary Sidney;* Walker, *Writing under Tyranny,* 279–95; Warley, *Sonnet Sequences and Social Distinction;* and Distiller, *Desire and Gender,* 43–79.

2. On the varieties of Petrarch and Petrarchism, see Greene, *Post-Petrarchism;* Estrin, *Laura;* Kennedy, *Authorizing Petrarch;* Kennedy, *Site of Petrarchism;* Dubrow, *Echoes of Desire;* Greene, *Unrequited Conquests;* and Braden, *Petrarchan Love.*

always written from the perspective of the courtier. "Love lyrics," as Arthur Marotti puts it in his seminal article, "'Love is not love,'" "could express figuratively the realities of suit, service, and recompense with which ambitious men were insistently concerned as well as the frustrations and disappointments experienced in socially competitive environments."[3] Natasha Distiller makes a different point but takes Marotti's position as her foundation: "The courtier's impossible position of self-assertion and submission is accommodated in a language which enables him to perform his frustration at this situation while insisting simultaneously on his loyalty and devotion."[4]

Both assumptions require nuance. First, the use of chivalric language to express politics does not begin with Wyatt's translations of Petrarch, but with the chivalric entertainments created by William Cornish for Henry VII, and Henry VIII is the first poet to adapt the language of courtly verse to reflect his position in the court. Moreover, he does so in the early years of his reign—c. 1508–1515 (more on these topics below). Second, monarchic verse provides a very different perspective on the commonly held assumption that Petrarchan or courtly verse served as a vehicle for articulating the problems of courtly service. If, as Louis Montrose rightly observes, "the otiose love-talk of the shepherd masks the busy negotiation of the courtier; [and] the shepherd is a courtly poet prosecuting his courtship in pastoral forms,"[5] what happens when the otiose love-talk is articulated not by a courtier, but by a king or a queen? What happens when the poem's speaker is no longer the person asking for favor, but the person dispensing it? When the speaker is no longer a "cunning princepleaser," in George Puttenham's trenchant phrase, but the prince? To state the obvious, the speaker in monarchic verse occupies a fundamentally different subject position than the speaker in courtier verse, and the poems reflect that fact.

Monarchic verse, however, does not function as a mirror for the monarch's undoubted authority. Monarchic verse is not simply, as Jonathan Goldberg describes it, "an instrument of royal power."[6] Rather, each monarch, albeit at different times and under different circumstances, used poetry as a vehicle for manipulating or appropriating the political imaginary of monarchy to enhance his or her position, and by "political imaginary," I mean, as Montrose defines it, "the collective repertoire of representational forms and figures—mythological, rhetorical, narrative, iconic—in which the beliefs and

---

3. Marotti, "'Love is not love,'" 398.
4. Distiller, *Desire and Gender*, 52.
5. Montrose, "'Eliza, Queen of Shepherds,'" 163.
6. Goldberg, *James I*, 55.

practices of Tudor [and Stuart] political culture were pervasively articulated."[7] Significantly, while their poetic practices differ considerably, Henry, Mary, Elizabeth, and James all turned to verse at moments when their positions were particularly insecure. While I have no doubt that these monarchs wrote poetry because they genuinely enjoyed doing so, nevertheless they did not write strictly for the pleasure it gave them. They picked up a quill when they perceived themselves assailed in some way, and they often used verse as an instrument for shoring up their authority through a manipulation of royal imagery, even when the verse they wrote was intended for their eyes alone. Henry VIII used verse at the start of his reign to establish his royal identity and to defend himself against his critics. Mary Stuart wrote poems following François II's death (which effectively destroyed her political position in France) and her disastrous marriage to the Earl of Bothwell (which led to the destruction of her political position in Scotland). Elizabeth wrote verse over the course of her entire life but usually did so either to assert her superiority (the response to Sir Walter Ralegh) or, like her cousin Mary, in the wake of a crisis, such as Mary's plotting against her, or the Armada. And James used verse in an attempt to ingratiate himself with Elizabeth or to project a pacific image of kingship. Certainly, these monarchs employed other strategies as well (portraits, for example), but verse was neither an insignificant nor an ineffective (at least for the most part) means of pursuing their goals. In short, monarchic verse does not represent the expression of absolute authority;

---

7. Montrose, "Spenser and the Elizabethan Political Imaginary," 907. Charles Taylor also provides a useful definition, although he substitutes "social" for "political": "the ways people imagine their social existence, how they fit together with others, how things go on between them and their fellows, the expectations that are normally met, and the deeper normative notions and images that underlie these expectations" (*Modern Social Imaginaries,* 22). The term itself has roots in left-wing French philosophy. The online dictionary *Le Trésor de la Langue Française Informatisé* cites both Sartre and Lacan in its definition of "imaginaire" as a noun (accessed 15 April 2009); see also Castoriadis, *Imaginary Institution of Society,* 127–32. Yet both Taylor and Montrose seem to be invoking the term without meaning to allude to its roots in French theory. The great advantage of this term is that unlike "ideology," with its inevitable connotations of force and of rulers using intellectual or abstract means to keep themselves in power (for example, Dollimore and Sinfield analyze the ideas of order comprising E. M. W. Tillyward's Elizabethan world picture as "an ideological legitimation of an existing social order," "Introduction," 8), "political imaginary" has a much more democratic purview. In short, everybody, from monarchs to the publishers of broadsides, can participate in the "political imaginary" through the images they conceive and propagate of monarchy in particular and politics in general. In short, I mean the term quite literally: "political imaginary" means "how politics gets imagined." For an interesting analysis of the connotations of "political imaginary" in Russian philosophy, see Buck-Morss, who points out that "the concept takes on a representational concreteness lacking in contemporary Western discussions" (*Dreamworld and Catastrophe,* 11). I am very grateful to Roger Kuin, Paul Anderson, and Raphael Falco for their help in tracking down the origins and precise definition of this term.

rather, these poems represent moments of authority asserting itself against considerable opposition. Monarchic verse, in other words, does not represent the workings of a static, all-encompassing power, but the intense dynamic of early modern authority.

Before proceeding, however, one first must ask why these monarchs turned to verse at all when there were so many other more traditional, and arguably more effective, means at their disposal, such as speeches to Parliament, diplomacy, progresses, audiences with subjects, direct commands, and so on. The answer, I suggest, lies in both the shift in poetry's cultural capital within humanist culture and the importation of Burgundian cultural forms to the court of Henry VII. Starting in the fourteenth century, poetry's humanist defenders (e.g., Petrarch, Boccaccio, and Mussatto) started defending it against the more general charge of encouraging immorality, and the more specific bias against Christians reading classical poets,[8] by arguing that classical poets are in fact theologians.[9] Writing in the late fourteenth century, Boccaccio, for example, asserted in the *De Genealogia* that poets "were the first to ponder theology."[10] While the Tudor-Stuart monarchic poets would make no such claims for their verse, this reevaluation of poetry led to its increased status within both the humanist educational curriculum and the social world of the court. A working knowledge of Homer or Virgil and an ability to compose a sonnet became distinguishing characteristics of the ideal courtier. According to Castiglione's Count Ludovico da Canossa, the ideal courtier is "versed in the poets, as well as in the orators and historians, and...practiced also in writing verse and prose."[11] Tudor-Stuart monarchs were all given humanist educations (Henry VIII's tutor was John Skelton), and so were taught, inter alia, both to value and to write verse. Consequently, poetry figured as a means by which these monarchs established their intellectual credentials and their positions among themselves (see Mary's and James's lyrics to Elizabeth), among the court (see Henry VIII's and Elizabeth's poems), among foreign diplomats and intellectuals (see Elizabeth's response to Paul Melissus), and among their subjects (see Elizabeth's Armada hymn and James's books of poems). By the end of the seventeenth century, monarchic verse had enough cultural capital that Royalists turned to verse as a strategy for transforming Charles I into the martyr king.

The genesis of monarchic verse in Tudor England can also be traced to Henry VII's decision to fashion his court along chivalric forms imported

---

8. Antipoetic sentiment, however, would continue as a "shaping presence" within early modern culture, including humanist culture. See Herman, *Squitter-wits and Muse-haters,* passim.

9. See Witt, "Coluccio Salutati," and Kallendorf, "From Virgil to Vida," generally on the tradition of poet as theologian.

10. Boccaccio, *Boccaccio on Poetry,* 122. See also Witt, "Coluccio Salutati," 544.

11. Castiglione, *Book of the Courtier,* 52.

from Burgundy. Certainly, Henry VII's appointment of Bernard André to the newly created office of the king's poet, and his employment of both André and John Skelton to educate both his sons, demonstrate the rise of poetry's status in the early Tudor court.[12] "For the first time," Gordon Kipling notes, "ignorance of letters brought shame in court."[13] Equally important, however, are the entertainments by William Cornish that brought together chivalric imagery, the language of courtly love, and contemporary politics. In, for example, the masque, or "disguising," performed for the Spanish ambassadors tasked with negotiating Katherine of Aragon's marriage to Arthur, Cornish

> allegorizes Prince Arthur's courtship in terms of the moralized *Roman de la Rose* imagery then popular at the court of Burgundy. In Cornish's entertainment, the prosaic, business-like ambassadors who had traveled ceaselessly between England and Spain to negotiate the marriage become emissaries of the Knights of Love, while the drawn-out political bargaining translates into the familiar allegorical episode from the *Roman* in which a group of amorous knights attacks a castle garrisoned by ladies. . . . When staged at French and Italian courts, similar entertainments had merely served as glorifications of courtly love. But in Cornish's hands, the harmony of dance resolves the strife of battle, and the disguising serves instead as a glorification of Tudor foreign policy, which resolves international conflicts through marriage.[14]

It is through Cornish's entertainments, in other words, that the confluence of chivalric language and politics enters English culture, not, as critics so often assume, with Wyatt's translations of Petrarch. Henry VIII continued to employ Cornish,[15] but unlike his father, he decided to actively participate in the disguisings, frequently taking on the guise of one allegorical figure or another. Given Henry VIII's humanist education and creative bent, it was a very short step from rehearsing someone else's lines to composing his own, and thus the tradition of monarchic verse begins in England.

And yet monarchic verse has received surprisingly little attention.[16] Despite all the enabling work that has been done regarding the intersections of poetry and politics in such "courtly makers" as Wyatt, Surrey, and Sir Philip

---

12. Kipling, *Triumph of Honour,* 11.

13. Ibid., 13.

14. Ibid., 102–3. See also Streitberger, *Court Revels,* 38–39.

15. See Roger Bowers's biography of Cornish in the *Oxford Dictionary of National Biography.*

16. Kevin Sharpe is perhaps the only person to consider monarchic verse as a separate genre ("King's Writ," 117–38); see also the essays collected in Fischlin and Fortier, eds., *Royal Subjects,* and in Herman, ed., *Reading Monarchs Writing.*

Sidney, among many others, the composition of verse by monarchs seems to have passed almost unnoticed. Almost nothing of substance has been written on Henry VIII's verse.[17] Although Mary Stuart remains a popular figure outside of academia, and her verse has been continuously available since the nineteenth century,[18] her poems have remained practically terra incognita.[19] And while Elizabeth's speeches have come under increasing scrutiny, her poetry remains nearly unexamined.[20] Granted, James's poetic works have received some attention (due, in no small part, to Ben Jonson's recognition of his monarch's poetic activities);[21] yet his verses remain the least studied and the least accessible of his works.[22]

The critical disinterest in monarchic verse is all the more surprising because in the aggregate, Tudor-Stuart monarchic verse covers nearly every genre available in the early modern period. Henry VIII may have restricted himself to courtly, chivalric lyrics (although, as we shall see, the lyrics he wrote early in his reign set the stage for the later poets Sir Thomas Wyatt and Henry Howard, the Earl of Surrey), but Mary, Queen of Scots produced occasional, encomiastic, erotic, and religious verse. Elizabeth also covered a wide range of genres (although perhaps not quite so wide as her contemporary reputation

17. With the exception of Herman and Siemens, "Henry VIII and the Poetry of Politics"; Siemens, "'Respect'"; and Siemens, "Thomas Wyatt, Anne Boleyn, and Henry VIII's Lyric."

18. See the editions by Sharman, Arbuthnot, and Bax as well as Henderson, *Casket Letters;* Lang, *Mystery of Mary Stuart;* and Armstrong, *Casket Letters.* A selection of Mary's poems, including the Casket Sonnets in their original form and a modern translation, can be found in Herman, *Reading Monarchs Writing,* 231–54. There is a desperate need for a reliable scholarly edition of Mary's letters, poems, and other writings.

19. Neglect of Mary Stuart in the major treatments of gender and of early modern women writers is abating. See Dunnigan, *Eros and Poetry;* Burke, "Queen, Lover, Poet"; Hopkins, "Writing to Control"; and Rigolot, "When Petrarchan Errors Become Political Crimes." I am grateful to François Rigolot for allowing me to read his fine essay in advance of publication.

20. Steven W. May, for example, cites only four items on Elizabeth's poetry in his "Recent Studies in Elizabeth I," 281–83. See also Ilona Bell, *Elizabethan Women;* Ilona Bell, "Elizabeth Tudor: Poet"; and Szönyi, "Cross-Dressing the Tongue."

21. In his fourth epigram, Jonson conflates his praise of James's verse and his kingship: "How, best of Kings, do'st thou a scepter beare! / How, best of *Poets,* do'st thou laurel weare" (*Ben Jonson,* ed. Herford and Simpson and Simpson, 8: 28)

22. Easily available, modern editions of James's political writings have proliferated, yet his poetry remains sequestered in the 1958 Scottish Text Society edition by James Craigie. I include a modernized selection in *Reading Monarchs Writing,* 281–323. As for James's verse, while Sharpe's assertion that it "has received no historical and little critical evaluation" remains largely true ("King's Writ," 127), there has been an upsurge of interest in James's work. See Goldberg, *James I,* 17–28; Sharpe, "Private Conscience," 117–38; Perry, *Making of Jacobean Culture,* 15–24; Sandra Bell, "Kingcraft and Poetry," 155–78; Appelbaum, "War and Peace in James VI/I's *Lepanto,*" 179–214; and the essays by Ives and Parkinson, Fleming, Dunnigan, Wortham, and Perry in Fischlin and Fortier, *Royal Subjects.* See also Fischlin, "'Like a Mercenary Poët'"; Dunnigan, "Marian and Jacobean Literature"; and Rickard, "From Scotland to England."

might suggest),[23] including epigrams, topical verse, poems that respond directly to other pieces of verse addressed to her, and a long, religious meditation in French; and James, who also penned love lyrics and translated the Psalms, added epic verse to the list of royal accomplishments.

Why has this rich body of work not received its due? While aesthetics surely plays some role in the marginalization of monarchic verse—the majority of these poems are competent but not masterpieces—that monarchs do not reach the same heights of poetic achievement as, say, William Shakespeare or John Donne, should not prevent our taking these texts seriously. Lack of poetic merit has not stopped critics from according serious and sustained attention to other less than wondrous poetic texts, such as the *Mirror for Magistrates* or Lucy Hutchinson's *Order and Disorder*, and many examples of monarchic verse are in fact quite good, a few truly excellent (in particular, Elizabeth's lyrics). Doubtless another factor that helps explain the neglect of monarchic verse is its availability. Only Elizabeth's verse is available in an accessible, reliable scholarly edition,[24] which raises the questions of canon and circulation.

James VI/I is unique in that he is the only monarch to authorize the print publication of his poetic works: *The Essayes of a Prentise, in the Divine Art of Poesie* (Edinburgh, 1584; second edition, 1585), *His Majesties Poeticall Exercises* (Edinburgh, 1591), and a separate printing of *His Majesties Lepanto* (London, 1603). James also contributed an elegy to Sir Philip Sidney in the Latin volume *Academiae Cantabrigiensis Lachrymae Tumulo Noblilissimi Equitis, D. Philippi Sidneii Sacratae* (Cambridge, 1587). Although some poems by Mary Stuart and Elizabeth appeared in print, they were published without the permission of either. (To my knowledge, none of Henry VIII's poems were published under his name over the course of the sixteenth and seventeenth centuries.) Instead, these monarchs preferred to restrict their audience to the court, a particular individual (a mode of transmission occasionally employed by James), or themselves. As we will see, several of Elizabeth's poems were intended for no one's eyes but her own. But even in the circulation of their

---

23. See the discussion in chapter 3.

24. Henry VIII's lyrics, both words and music, are recorded in two Henrician-era manuscripts, *Ritson's MS* (British Museum, Add. MS 5665) and *Henry VIII's MS* (BL, Add. MS 31.922). John Stevens printed the texts of Henry's songs (along with the other songs that appear alongside them) in the appendix to his *Music and Poetry in the Early Tudor Court*. A modernized, annotated version, edited by Ray Siemens, can be found in Herman, *Reading Monarchs Writing*, 217–29. Siemens's edition, *The Lyrics of the Henry VIII Manuscript*, is forthcoming from the Renaissance English Text Society. Elizabeth's poems are available in two reliable editions: *Elizabeth I: Collected Works*, ed. Marcus, Mueller, and Rose (hereafter cited as MMR); and *Queen Elizabeth I: Selected Works*, ed. May.

manuscripts, there were significant differences that had an impact on the interpretation of their verse.

Evidence suggests that Henry performed his lyrics before a courtly audience, who, we may presume, would immediately understand the political force of his verse. All of Henry's poems but one are recorded in a single manuscript, the *Henry VIII Manuscript.* The single variant, a version of "Pastime with good company," appears in *Ritson's Manuscript.* The one poem not included in the *Henry VIII Manuscript,* "The Eagle's Force," surfaces in a letter by Sir John Harington.[25] While this poem found its way into print, it did not do so under Henry VIII's name, but as part of Thomas Churchyard's contribution to *The Mirror for Magistrates.*[26] Other than that, none of Henry's poems were published during Elizabeth's lifetime. Even so, Henry's penchant for verse making quickly became public knowledge. The anonymous interlude *Youth* (c. 1514) employs Henry's lyrics, specifically those that present his persona of the youthful lover.[27] In a letter to Thomas Wolsey, Richard Pace noted that the royal almoner incorporated "Pastime" and another lyric, "I love unloved, such is mine adventure," into a sermon he delivered in the King's Hall in March 1521 (*LP,* 3.1, 447, item 1188), and Edward Hall records that during a progress in the second year of his reign, Henry exercised "hym self daily in shotyng, singing, daunsyng, wrastelyng, casting of the barre, plaiyng at the recorder, flute, virginals, and in setting of songes, [and] makyng of balettes."[28]

Mary Stuart and Elizabeth, on the other hand, present much more complex cases. As Elizabeth's editors Leah Marcus, Janel Mueller, and Mary Beth Rose reveal in their edition of Elizabeth's works, while some of Elizabeth's poems circulated widely (in particular, "The doubt of future foes"), the manuscript history of one of the most famous poems, "On Monsieur's Departure," is very uncertain, since the first evidence of the poem dates from the late seventeenth century,[29] and another, "When I was Fair and Young," circulated either anonymously or was attributed to a different author, depending upon the manuscript.[30] Even when we have an autograph manuscript of Elizabeth's, as is the case with her French Verses, uncertainties remain, as we do not know if these verses constitute an original poem (as Marcus, Mueller, and Rose believe) or a translation of a lost original (as Steven W. May and Anne Lake

---

25. There are no references to this poem in May and Ringler's *Elizabethan Poetry.*

26. See chapter 1, note 71.

27. *Two Tudor Interludes,* 54.

28. Hall, *Hall's Chronicles,* 515.

29. MMR, 302 n. 5.

30. MMR, 303 n. 1.

Prescott suggest).[31] In addition to the difficulties attending the provenance of many of her poems, we also have the problem of reconciling Elizabeth's reputation for writing in multiple genres with the rather small number of surviving poems. In *The Arte of English Poesie* (London, 1589), George Puttenham concludes his chapter on the canon of "the most commended writers in our English Poesie" with the queen, who, "last in recitall and first in degree," excels all others in the poetic arts: "[She]easily surmounteth all the rest that have written before her time, or since, for sence, sweetnesse and subtillitie, be it in Ode, Elegie, Epigram, or any other kinde of poeme Heroick or Lyricke, wherein it shall please her Majestie to employ her penne."[32] As Leah Marcus asks, "Where have all these supposed masterpieces disappeared to?"[33] Do we dismiss Puttenham's claims as mere flattery, or do we assume that the vast majority of Elizabeth's poems have disappeared without a trace?[34]

Like Elizabeth, Mary Stuart also developed a significant reputation for writing verse and wrote verse intended either for manuscript circulation (her elegy on François II, her diplomatic poems to Elizabeth) or for a single individual (the quatrain in her aunt's prayer book).[35] However, very much unlike the verse of both Elizabeth and Elizabeth's father, the most important of Mary's works—the sonnets to her lover and, for a short time, husband, James Hepburn, Earl of Bothwell—appeared in print shortly after their composition, albeit in a context that has led to enduring controversy over their authenticity. Many consider the Casket Letters generally, and the sonnets in particular, forgeries, as demonstrated by internal evidence, the disappearance of the originals, and their publication by Mary's archenemy, George Buchanan, as part of his general indictment of her.[36] Yet no one involved

---

31. MMR, 413 n. 1; May and Prescott, "French Verses of Elizabeth I," 97.

32. Puttenham, *Arte of English Poesie,* 73, 77.

33. Marcus, "Queen Elizabeth I as Public and Private Poet," 135.

34. Ibid., 136.

35. Pierre de Brantôme observes in his biography of Mary: "Above all, she loved poetry and poets, especially M. de Ronsard, M. du Bellay, and M. de Mainson-Fleur, who all made beautiful poems and elegies upon her. She was a poet herself and composed verses, of which I have seen some that were fine and well done.... [Her poems were] beautiful and dainty" (*Recueil des Dames,* 72–73; my translation).

36. In his introduction to the first edition of Mary's poems, Julian Sharman notes that the "sonnets to Bothwell have been, with many generations of history writers the subject of controversy" (*Poems of Mary Queen of Scots,* 8), and the controversy continues unabated. Many of the writers who argue against Mary's authorship base their views on a highly literal reading of the tropes Mary employs. Antonia Fraser, for example, writes: "There are references also to Bothwell's wealth, which were unthinkable for Mary to make. To her Bothwell was a comparatively poor man" (*Mary Queen of Scots,* 404). Fraser follows the equally literal commentary of M. H. Armstrong Davison, who avers that these poems were written by "the 'other woman,'." In his commentary on "Entre ses mains," for instance, Armstrong Davison states: "We can be quite certain that Mary never wrote these lines,

with their original discovery and dissemination considered them fakes, not even those who had a vested interest in declaring them forgeries, such as the French ambassador, La Mothe-Fénelon.[37] In addition, most historians and literary critics (with the notable exceptions of John Guy and Peter Davidson) do not contest Mary's authorship of these works.[38]

While we must accept that the precise canon of monarchic verse will, given the problems outlined above, always be shrouded in doubt, that does not justify shying away from analyzing this body of work as a distinct genre. Leah Marcus suggests that that there was nothing special about monarchic verse, observing that "even the poetry of a revered and powerful queen was not preserved with any particular meticulousness unless it happened to resonate powerfully with national priorities and crises," as was the case with "The doubt of future foes."[39] But the evidence suggests otherwise.

In 1609, for example, Sir John Harington responded to a request by Prince Henry for "suche scraps and fragments of witte and poesie as I mighte from my poore braine."[40] The first example that Harington provides comes from

---

for the statement that she put her son in Bothwell's full power was absolutely untrue" (*Casket Letters*, 211). Also contributing to this argument is A. E. MacRobert, who begins his consideration of the sonnets by asserting, "It is highly improbable that anyone deliberately forged all these Sonnets to incriminate Mary, but there may have been a little manipulation" (*Mary Queen of Scots*, 146), and ends by contradicting this nuanced assessment: "The overwhelming impression after reading the Sonnets is that it is easy to follow their content by assuming they were written by the unhappy French lady, but very difficult to accept that the Queen could ever possibly have written them" (148). MacRobert does not say who this "unhappy French Lady" might be. For a much more sophisticated treatment of the case against Mary's authorship, see Davidson, "New Evidence."

37. See the quote from La Mothe-Fénelon at the end of chapter 2. Pierre de Brantôme, who was briefly in Mary's service, asserted in his memoir that Mary could not have written the sonnets to Bothwell because they are "too coarse and too badly polished [trop grossiers et mal polis] to have come from her beautiful making"; and Ronsard thought so too: "M. de Ronsard was of my opinion as to this one day when we were reading and discussing them" (*Recueil des Dames*, 73). Brantôme, however, was writing hagiography, and admitting Mary's authorship would not help his idealizing purpose.

38. Guy, *True Life*, 386–88; Davidson, "New Evidence." On the other hand, Jenny Wormald defends the authenticity of the Casket Letters: "What it all amounts to is this. Outright forgery of the originals—as opposed to the odd interpolation in the copies—can only have been done by the Scots; and to suggest that her Scottish enemies forged something that they were then very unwilling to use, and managed in the process to fool Mary's own son and cousin, both of whom knew her handwriting, into believing that they were undoubtedly genuine, simply does not make sense" (*Mary Queen of Scots*, 177; see also 178). Guy asserts that "very few literary experts believe them [the Sonnets] to be genuine" (386), but that is in fact not the case. See Bax, "What the Reader Must Know," in *Letters and Poems by Mary Stuart, Queen of Scots*, 1–16; Travitsky, *Paradise of Women*, 88–89; Dunnigan, *Eros and Poetry*, 15–45; Hopkins, "Writing to Control," 45–46, 46 n. 22; Hopkins, *Writing Renaissance Queens*, 72–88; and Rigolot, "When Petrarchan Errors Become Political Crimes."

39. Marcus, "Queen Elizabeth I as Public and Private Poet," 151.

40. Harington, *Nugae Antiquae*, ed. Harington, 2: 246. Subsequent references to Harington's work will appear parenthetically in the text. For further analysis of this letter and the poem of Henry VIII it contains, see chapter 1. Sir John Harington's connection to Prince Henry was through his son, John Harington, 2nd Baron Harington of Exton, who was included in the intellectual circle

the pen of "that unfortunate, and yet in his godlinesse I wist most fortu-nate, King, Henrie the Sixthe" (2: 246), and the second example comes from Henry VIII. Significantly, Harington chooses these two authors because he believes that a royal request for examples of "witte and poesie" should be answered by royal examples of the same: "As I have thus given your High-nesse a short ensample of Royal poetrie, I will not in haste forsake the mat-ter, and descend from high to low; but will now venture to send to your readinge a special verse of King Henry the Eight" (248). After quoting the poem, Harington reiterates the point and adds that he would have included the verses of another "Royal poet" had time permitted: "Thus have I given your Highnesse another ensample of Royal poetrie; nor, if time did serve, or your patience would permit, should I omit some prettier verses of our late Princesse" (248). Of course, Harington also slipped in his "Ariosto, for your Highnesse entertainment" (249). But for Sir John Harington, "Royal poetrie" constituted a distinct subgenre of verse, and the royal position of the author informed the work itself. Concerning the poem he quotes from the pen of Henry VIII, Harington writes: "Had I no better reason than the rhyme, it were sufficient to think that no other than suche a King could write such a sonnet" (248). What exactly Harington means by this cryptic statement, I will consider in chapter 1. My immediate point, however, is that for Harington, monarchic verse, regardless of the particular genre, raises dif-ferent expectations than verse written by nonroyals, and it needs to be set apart and identified as "Royal poetrie" in order to be properly understood. Nor was Harington alone in these expectations.

The scribe who created the *Henry VIII Manuscript* carefully distinguished Henry's contributions from all the others. For everyone else, an attribution appears following the music and lyrics of each piece; but in Henry's case, the scribe writes "The kynge.h.viii." at the top of the leaf on which each piece begins. For example, "From my hart" appears as shown in figure 1. For Henry's song "Elas madam," we have not only the ascription "The kynge. H. viii," but the block "H" incorporates a small portrait of the king, as can be seen in figure 2.

Similarly, the manuscript of Mary's "Une seul penser" describes the con-tents as "Carmina Regina Scotiae,"[41] and George Buchanan, Mary's arch-nemesis, ascribes the Casket Sonnets to "the queen of Scottis."[42] Virtually all

---

created by King James for his son's companionship and intellectual development (Strong, *Henry Prince of Wales,* 42). Sadly, the younger Sir John Harington would not long outlive Prince Henry. He died in 1614.

41. BL, Cotton MSS, Caligula BV, fol. 323–24.

42. Buchanan, *Detectioun,* sig. Q.iiii.

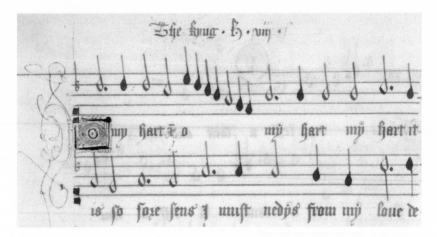

of the manuscripts of "The doubt of future foes" attribute the poem not just to a person, but to an institution. The version of the poem in Folger MSS V.b. 317, for example, ends with "Vivat Regina" (fol. 20), and the version in Bodleian Digby 138 begins with the ascription "*E. Reg*" (fol. 159r). As for James, while he modestly entitled his first book of poems *The Essayes of a Prentise, in the Divine Art of Poesie,* refraining from advertising his royal authorship, the commendatory sonnet by one "T. H." ensures that the reader knows the political status of the book's author, if not the author's name:

> If *Martiall* deeds, and practise of the pen
> Have wonne to auncient *Greece* worthie fame:
> If Battels bold, and Bookes of learned men
> Have magnified the mightie *Romain* name:
> Then place this Prince, who well deserves the same:
> Since he is one of *Mars* and *Pallas* race:
> For both the *Godds* in him have sett in frame
> Their vertewes both, which both, he doth embrace.
> O *Macedon,* adorned with heavenly grace,
> O *Romain* stout, decorde with learned skill,
> The *Monarks* all to the shall quite their place:
> Thy endless fame shall all the world fulfil.
>> And after thee, none worthier shalbe seene,
>> To sway the *Sword,* and gaine the *Laurell* greene.

(sig. ★ii)

FIGURE 2.   *Henry VIII MSS.*, fol. 32v (© British Library Board. All Rights Reserved, BL, Add. MS 31.922)

James's further publications proclaim his royal status much more brazenly. He not only entitles his next book of poems *His Majesties Poetical Exercises,* but the typography of the title page loudly privileges the author's status, as does the typography (perhaps accomplished by a more skilled typesetter) of the 1603 edition of *The Lepanto* (see the illustrations in chapter 4). Nonetheless, that there are generic expectations for monarchic verse does not mean that monarchs always obeyed them. Yet it is significant that the poems that depart from these protocols either were intended for private consumption (as I will argue is the case for Elizabeth's "Doubt of future foes," "When I was fair and young," and "On Monsieur's Departure") or contributed to Mary's disaster when made public (Mary Stuart's sonnets to Bothwell).

"Royal poetrie" thus illustrates the limitations of Michel Foucault's famous rhetorical question "What matter who's speaking?"[43] When it comes to this body of verse, it matters a great deal "who's speaking." The copyists and the printers of monarchic verse almost always carefully indicated the royal status of the author, and, as we shall see, the royal authors use their verse as a vehicle for monarchic self-fashioning. With all due respect to Foucault, in this case nothing matters more than who is speaking, for the speaker defines, to paraphrase Foucault, "the modes of existence of this discourse" and "where . . . it comes from; how it is circulated; [and] who controls it."[44] The meaning of the verse derives from the speaker's identity and thus requires, to adopt a phrase made famous by Clifford Geertz, "thick historicizing" in order to fully understand the intentions, accomplishments, and resonances of this rich body of verse.[45] That is the burden of this book.

---

43. Foucault, "What Is an Author?" 138.

44. Ibid.

45. Geertz's phrase is "Thick Description," invoked in "Thick Description: Toward an Interpretive Theory of Culture," in *Interpretation of Cultures,* 3–32.

CHAPTER 1

Henry VIII and the Political Imaginary of Early Tudor England

The standard narrative of Henry VIII's accession depicts the transition from Henry VII to his son in terms of day and night, youth and old age, virility and decrepitude. Edward Hall, for example, records that that while the late king's servants mourned wondrously, "the joy that was made for his death, by such as were troubled by rigor of his lawe," was equally, if not more, impressive. The mourners at Henry VII's funeral quickly dispelled their sadness by repairing to "the Palaice, where they had a greate and a sumptuous feast."[1] In contrast to the sour father, the son, records the Venetian ambassador, Andrea Badoer, is "magnificent" and "liberal" (*LP*, 1.1, 8, item 5). Contemporary historians have followed suit. Sidney Anglo, for example, writes: "The young, handsome, vigorous Henry VIII was now King, and England, it seemed, was emerging from the shadows into an era of sunshine."[2] J. J. Scarisbrick calls the newly crowned Henry VIII "a prodigy, a sun-king, a *stupor mundi*."[3] David Starkey observes that after Henry VIII came to the throne, the newly crowned monarch "stood his [father's] style of kingship on its head."[4]

---

1. Hall, *Hall's Chronicles*, 507 (hereafter cited parenthetically in the text).
2. Anglo, *Spectacle, Pageantry, and Early Tudor Policy,* 108.
3. Scarisbrick, *Henry VIII,* 20.
4. Starkey, "Intimacy and Innovation," 76.

While there is some truth to this narrative (no doubt, Henry VII was a crabby, dour man toward the end, and his son cut a much livelier figure), the details need to be nuanced in several ways. First, although Henry VIII's foreign and domestic policies differed radically from his father's, both monarchs well understood the ideological potential of spectacle to reinforce their policies and justify their regimes. The differences lay in the content of their spectacles, with Henry VII turning to British and Platonic mythology for legitimacy, and Henry VIII turning to chivalry. Second, it is mistake to assume that Henry VIII wielded uncontested power from the moment of his crowning. Nobody, to be sure, openly opposed his kingship, but there was resistance, significant and occasionally successful, to Henry VIII's personal behavior and policy initiatives, especially his desire to restart the Hundred Years War. While it is certainly true that Henry's return to chivalric imagery and display was aimed at impressing foreign diplomats,[5] Henry's taste in court entertainments also constituted a brilliantly strategic vehicle for projecting authority and establishing his dominance over the court, which, at the beginning of his reign, included many important holdovers from his father's administration (such as John Stiles, ambassador to the Spanish court; Richard Fox, bishop of Winchester; and his protégé, Thomas Wolsey).[6] Henry shifted the political imaginary toward chivalry because, in addition to its forming an essential part of the fabric of early modern kingship, chivalry's emphasis on the knight as warrior and the knight as lover also served the dual purpose of reflecting both his bellicose policies and his youthful position vis-à-vis the more senior members of the court. Paradoxically, Henry's adoption of the seemingly subordinate role of Youth, or of Coeur Loyal, the chivalric lover, had the effect of highlighting his monarchic position and thus his superiority to the elders who carped at the king's pastimes and, more substantively, argued against his desire for war. As we shall see, Henry's lyrics, mostly written between 1509 and 1513,[7] form an integral part of this intervention in the political imaginary. But to understand the magnitude of Henry's achievement, we must first return to the reign of his father, Henry VII.

---

5. Arthur B. Ferguson, *Chivalric Tradition in Renaissance England,* 51.

6. Gwyn, *King's Cardinal,* 2–3. On Wolsey's early career, see Cavendish, *Life and Death of Cardinal Wolsey,* 5–11.

7. *Ritson's MS,* which contains "Pastime with good company," dates from c. 1510, while the *Henry VIII MS*—so named because it contains most of Henry's lyrics—dates from 1515 (Stevens, *Music and Poetry in the Early Tudor Court,* 338, 386).

I

In a sense, Henry Tudor's military defeat of Richard III on Bosworth Field in August 1485 was the easy part. Now that he had the throne, Henry VII had to keep it, and the problem of security would occupy the new king for almost his entire reign.[8] Henry adopted a two-pronged approach to maintaining his hold on power. First, he decided from the outset to rule England as it had always been ruled—collaboratively with Parliament.[9] Consequently, in Polydore Vergil's words, Henry "summoned a parliament, as was the custom, in which he might receive the crown by popular consent," and then, "at the instigation of both nobles and people, he was made king at Westminster on 31 October and called Henry, seventh of that name."[10] Henry VII's decision to follow precedent in the manner of his coronation set the pattern for the rest of his reign: he allowed Parliament to function exactly as it had done before, with no innovations or alterations.[11] Henry's conservatism stemmed from something more than an aversion to change, let alone a disinterest in the details of government. Certainly, by declining to tinker with the machinery of government, Henry lent his new regime a sense of stability and continuity that it might otherwise have lacked, given that he came to the throne violently at the end of an extended period of civil strife. But his approach also arose from Henry's innovative decision to use history to justify his claim to the throne, in particular, his descent from the Welsh princes back to the primitive British kings.[12]

In the pageant at Worcester in 1486, for example, Henry was greeted with these verses:

Cadwaladers Bodde lynyally descending,
Longe hath bee towlde of such a Prince coming.
Wherfor Frendes, if that I shal not lye,
This same is the Fulfiller of the Profecye.[13]

---

8. Chrimes, *Henry VII,* 68.

9. On England as a mixed monarchy, see Fortescue, *On the Laws and Governance of England.* For example, Fortescue notes that the king of England cannot "change the laws without the assent of his subjects" (17).

10. Vergil, *Anglica Historia,* 5.

11. Chrimes, *Henry VII,* 144.

12. Anglo, *Spectacle, Pageantry, and Early Tudor Policy,* 35.

13. Ibid., 43.

Polydore Vergil reiterates this mythical connection with only the slightest hint of skepticism:

> Thus Henry acquired the kingdom, an event of which foreknowledge had been possible both many centuries earlier and also soon after his birth. For 797 years before, there came one night to Cadwallader, last king of the Britons…, some sort of an apparition with a heavenly appearance; this foretold how long afterwards it would come to pass that his descendants would recover the land. This prophecy, they say, came true in Henry, who traced his ancestry back to Cadwallader. The same prediction was made to Henry in his childhood by Henry VI.[14]

As Sidney Anglo has shown, Henry VII did everything he could to strengthen the association of the new regime with British history, and court culture responded. At his coronation banquet, for example, the King's Champion rode on a horse decorated with "Cadewaladras armes,"[15] and of course, Henry VII named his first son Arthur. Yet after the initial round of public ceremonies and celebrations, Henry chose to absent himself from the stage, preferring to rule without quite literally making himself a spectacle,[16] and his modest, yet grave approach to monarchy is reflected in his portraiture.

In a painting done in 1505 at the behest of Herman Rick, agent to Emperor Maximilian I, as part of the negotiations over Henry's possible marriage to the emperor's daughter,[17] Henry appears royal, but not overbearing (fig. 3). His robe is rich, as befits a king, but not overly so, and he wears only one piece of jewelry, the collar of the "toison d'or," or the Order of the Golden Fleece. The lack of ostentation in this portrait of Henry stands in distinct contrast to the portraits of his immediate predecessor, Richard III, who is depicted as a highly idealized knight, bedecked with rich clothing and wearing several rings.

The evidence, therefore, indicates that at the same time that Henry VII embarked on a deliberate campaign to anchor his reign, and soon his dynasty, as the prophetic conclusion of English history, thus tying together the roses of York and Lancaster as well as providentialism and historical myth, he also sought to project a distinctly unassuming style of monarchy. He eschewed chivalric imagery (perhaps because, as Larry D. Benson has suggested, chivalric literature echoed too closely England's chaotic political situation over

---

14. Vergil, *Anglica Historia,* 5.
15. Anglo, *Spectacle, Pageantry, and Early Tudor Policy,* 45.
16. Ibid., 51.
17. Strong, *Tudor and Jacobean Portraits,* 1: 149.

Figure 3. *Henry VII*, c. 1505 (© National Portrait Gallery)

the course of the fifteenth century[18]) and embraced a stolid, less exciting, if more reassuring to England's jangled nerves, model of kingship. All of this, of course, changed with the accession of Henry VIII, although, as we will see, the changes were neither seamless nor achieved without resistance.

II

Louis Montrose observes that "Henry VIII's kingly image had as one of its hallmarks the display of masculine prowess—martial, chivalric, and erotic,"[19] but this emphasis on "regal virility" (Montrose's phrase) applies to the middle and later parts of Henry's reign, as portrayed in Hans Holbein's 1537 wall painting (now lost) for the Privy Chamber at Whitehall. In this work, Holbein contrasts the magnificently regal Henry VIII, with his forward-thrusting feet, lustrous robes, physical bulk, and prominent codpiece, with the "self-contained demeanor" of his distinctly less impressive father (fig. 4).[20]

Yet at the very start of Henry's reign, there seems to have been a conscious attempt at iconographic continuity by someone other than the king. In what may be the first portrait of the newly crowned monarch (fig. 5), the artist echoes the pose used for Henry VII's portraits (see fig. 3). While the son wears more adornment than his father (a necklace), he is painted in an almost identical pose. Like his father, Henry VIII rests one hand on a ledge. In the other hand, he holds a red rose. Aside from their ages, the only truly substantial difference between the men in the two portraits is that Henry VII turns his eyes toward the spectator, whereas Henry VIII averts his eyes. In this painting, Henry seems to be portrayed as "Youth" (a figure we will return to below), but a youth whose likeness is almost identical to his late father's. The iconography emphasizes a transition without changes, not a significantly new direction.

The same principle applies to the monetary image of the king. Montrose observes that coins "bore what were the most widely disseminated of royal images,"[21] and so they are an excellent indicator of how monarchs desired to be viewed. Here again, the emphasis is on continuity. In a 1505 silver ryal, the king is shown in a lifelike profile (fig. 6). The first coins of the new king's reign are almost identical to those of his father's (fig. 7). They bear the same portrait, the only change being a shift in the inscription to "HENRIC VIII."[22]

---

18. Benson, Malory's "Morte Darthur," 198–99.
19. Montrose, Subject of Elizabeth, 21.
20. Ibid., 22.
21. Ibid., 95.
22. Challis, Tudor Coinage 72.

FIGURE 4. Holbein the Younger, *Henry VIII,* 1537 (© National Portrait Gallery)

FIGURE 5. *Henry VIII*, c. 1509 (Berger Collection at the Denver Art Museum. Photograph courtesy of the Denver Art Museum)

But if some in Henry's court wanted to illustrate the doctrine of "The King's Two Bodies" by maintaining visual continuity between the two monarchs,[23] Henry VIII clearly had other ideas, and they involved a radical change in England's political structure. In a little-known incident, Henry tried to alter the coronation oath to bring it into accord with his more expansive views of royal prerogative. The point of this oath, as many noted and would note repeatedly over the course of the English Revolution, is to remind the monarch that he or she is subject to the law, that he or she does not rule as an absolute monarch whose will is law.[24] The original oath begins as follows:

> This is the othe that the king shall swere at y[e] coronacion that he shall kepe and mayntene the right and the libertees of holie churche of old tyme graunted by the righteous Cristen kinges of Englond. And that he shall kepe all that londes honours and dignytes righteous and fre of the crowne of England in all maner whole w'out any maner of mynyshemnent, and the rightes of the Crowne hurte decayed or lost to his power shall again into the auncyent astate, And that he shall kepe the peax of the holie churche and of the clergie and of the people wt good accorde, And that he shall do in his iudgementes equytee and right justice wt discression and mercye.[25]

However, in a remarkable anticipation of the 1533 declaration of royal supremacy over the English church,[26] the not-yet crowned Henry tried to qualify the oath so as to emphasize the primacy of regal authority. For example, (in his own hand) Henry alters the opening of the oath as follows:

> The king shall then swere that he shall kepe and mayntene the lawfull right and the libertees of old tyme graunted by the righteous Cristen kinges of Englond to the holy chirche of ingland *nott preiudyciall to hys Jurysdiccion and dignite ryall* and that he shall kepe all the londes honours and dignytes righteous *nott preiudiciall to hys Jurysdiction and dygnite ryall and fredommes of the crowne* of Englond in all maner hole wtout any maner of mynyshment. . . . (my emphasis)[27]

23. On this doctrine, see Kantorowicz, *King's Two Bodies.*

24. According to Fortescue, the king "is bound by oath at his coronation to the observance of his law" (*On the Laws and Governance of England,* 48).

25. Quoted in Legg, ed., *English Coronation Records,* ed. Leopold G. Wickham, 240–41.

26. Guy, "'Imperial Crown,'" 67.

27. Legg, *English Coronation Records,* 240.

FIGURE 6.   Silver ryal, Henry VII (© The Trustees of the British Museum)

Yet Henry failed in this attempt to alter England's Ancient Constitution. There is no evidence that he took the revised version of the coronation oath,[28] and the oath used at Edward VI's coronation is the traditional one found in the *Liber Regalis.*[29] We do not know precisely who told Henry that he could not, of his own accord, change England's fundamental laws, but since at the start of his reign Henry's Privy Council consisted of his father's old counsellors,[30] most likely it was one of them, if not the entire council,

---

28. Ibid.

29. Ibid. The *Liber Regalis* is reprinted in Legg, 80–130. The coronation oath is reprinted on pp. 250–51.

30. Polydore Vergil writes that the newly crowned Henry VIII chose for his Privy Council intimates of his father ("parentis familiaribus"): William Warham, archbishop of Canterbury; the Chancellor, Richard, bishop of Winchester; Thomas Howard, Earl of Surrey; George Talbot; Charles Somerset; Thomas Lovell; Henry Wyatt; Thomas Rutall; Edward Poinings (*Anglica Historia,* 149).

FIGURE 7.   Silver ryal, Henry VIII (© The Trustees of the British Museum)

who put a stop to Henry's attempt to revise the oath and England's political structure.

Therefore, at the very start of Henry's reign, underneath the celebrations and the widespread praise, one senses an undercurrent of significant tension between continuity and change, between the old and the young. The iconographic evidence points toward a concerted effort to portray the new king in the same terms as the father. Yet Henry VIII had a very different view of the relationship between royal prerogative and Parliament's rights than that of his father, his father's counsellors, and, indeed, anyone else before him. He tried to put his views into practice by revising the coronation oath. Yet he was blocked in his first attempt to change the political landscape. It seems that whatever ideas Henry had about the extent of royal prerogative, he did not yet have the stature or the power to execute them. Someone, or some persons, opposed the king's will successfully. Henry's next attempt to alter the political imaginary through the reinvigoration of chivalric imagery and pas-times would yield (from his perspective) a better result, and his verse would form an integral part of this campaign.

Many contemporary historians and literary historians, such as J. J. Scaris-brick, Arthur B. Ferguson, and John Stevens, characterize the early Henrician court as obsessed by games, chivalric role-playing, and light allegory. Scaris-brick describes the early Henry VIII as a man who "lived in, and crowned, a world of lavish allegory, mythology and romance."[31] Henry's world was one in which, as John Stevens puts it, "people acted out their aspirations to a leisured and gracious life, where Lady Courtesy led the dance and Beauty, Simplesse, Swete-lokyng, Fraunchise, Mirth and Gladness danced with her."[32] Ferguson notes that the new king "delighted . . . to play the knight and en-couraged his courtiers to do likewise. . . . If Hall . . . can be said to speak for the taste of the court, these chivalric shows were valued more for their color than for their martial significance,"[33] and the one critic to address Henry's lyrics assumes that they reflect the putatively untroubled atmosphere of festivity and chivalry marking the first decade or so of Henry's reign. Thus Stevens dismisses Henry's lyrics as light, after-dinner entertainment, as another ele-ment of the "game" of courtly love.[34]

This rather naïve picture of the early Henrician court as an innocent, ongoing idyll has its roots, as the quote from Ferguson demonstrates, in a fundamental misreading of Hall's position toward Henry VIII, which is much more critical, much more sympathetic to dissent, than most critics allow.[35] Furthermore, Skiles Howard, Greg Walker, and Seth Lerer have shown how issues of power, prestige, and monarchic authority permeate the masques and disguisings of the early Henrician court.[36] Take, for example, the *Chateau Vert* spectacle produced on Shrovetide 1522 by Wolsey for the amusement and benefit of the king and, according to Hall, "certain noble men from the Emperor" (630). Recalling the passage in the *Roman de la Rose* in which the fortress containing the rose is under siege by the god of love and his fol-lowers (ll. 3267ff.),[37] according to Hall, the dignitaries were ushered into a

---

31. Scarisbrick, *Henry VIII*, 20.

32. John Stevens, *Music and Poetry in the Early Tudor Court*, 152.

33. Arthur B. Ferguson, *Indian Summer of English Chivalry*, 23.

34. Stevens, *Music and Poetry in the Early Tudor Court*, 152.

35. On Hall's initially implicit, but later very explicit criticism of Henry VIII, see Herman, "Henrician Historiography," 270–76.

36. See Howard, "'Ascending the Rich Mount,'" 16–39; Walker, *Plays of Persuasion*, 6–36; Lerer, *Courtly Letters*, 39–49.

37. Lorris and Meum, *Roman de la Rose*.

"great chamber" in which a castle had been constructed, and significantly this castle is a monument to female power: "And on every Tower was a banner, one banner was of iii. rent hartes, the other was a ladies hand gripyng a mans harte, the third banner was a ladies hand turnyng a mannes hart" (631). The women inhabiting this castle assumed the allegorical names of Beauty, Honor, Perseverance, Kindness, Constancy, Bounty, Mercy, and Pity (the feminine virtues, in other words) and are guarded by other ladies named Danger, Disdain, Jealousy, Unkindness, Scorne, Malebouche (Bad Mouth or Speech), and Strangeness. (Hall also records that these ladies "were tired [attired] to women of Inde" [631], which ensures that the feminine enemies of the king's will are identified absolutely with the Other.) Then the men entered with the allegorical names of Amorus, Noblenes, Youth, Attendaunce, Loyaltie, Pleasure, Gentlenes, and Libertie," and the king, "the chief of this compaignie," adopting the disguise of Ardent Desire. Hall describes the action thus:

> Ardent Desire . . . so moved the ladies to geve over the Castle, but Scorne and Disdain saied they would holde the place, then Desire saied the ladies should be wonne and came and encoraged the knightes, then the lordes ranne to the castle, (at whiche tyme out was shot a greate peale of gunnes) and the ladies defended the castle with Rose water and Comfittes, and the lordes threwe in Dates and Orenges, and other fruites made for pleasure, but at the last the place was wonne, but the Lady Scorne and her compaignie stubbernely defended them with boows and balles, til they were driven out of the place and fled. Then the lordes toke the ladies of honor as prisoners by the handes, and brought them doune, and daunced together very pleasauntly, which much pleased the straungers. (631)

Howard sees in this production a paradigm for how dance constitutes a rehearsal for gender roles,[38] yet we also need to remember that Wolsey produced the "assault on the Chateau Vert" for the benefit of the king and Charles V's ambassadors (the "straungers" in Hall's report). In other words, besides figuring gender, the evening of playacting also constituted a demonstration of Henry's political authority.[39] The king answers the challenge to his desires by asserting that "the ladies should be wonne" and encouraging his "knightes" to enact a "battle" that concludes with a mock rape. The reassertion of male dominance at the "battle's" conclusion emblematizes the reassertion of the

---

38. Howard, "'Ascending the Rich Mount,'" 17.

39. On how Jonson's masques refigured the authority of the Stuart court, see Orgel, *Illusion of Power.*

king's dominance over the (literally feminized) enemies who dared to defy him; the king's sexual potency, in other words, symbolizes his political potency, and vice versa. Doubtless, there was much laughter and good cheer at the actual event, but when Hall writes that the ladies were led "as prisoner by the handes," could anyone present at the entertainment not have understood that Wolsey also intended a lesson about masculine/royal authority for both the court and the emperor's representatives?

The underlying politics of this playacting exemplifies how the political imaginary functioned in the early Henrician court, how the symbols of chivalry could be harnessed for the purpose of establishing the monarch's political and masculine authority (one being a synonym for the other). Thus, in the "assault on the *Chateau Vert*," Henry displays both his personal and his professional virility. Like Henry's masques and disguisings, his lyrics also constitute vehicles for shaping the hierarchy of the court and for both defending and reinforcing the power of his monarchy.

III

Henry's lyrics can be grouped into two overlapping categories. In the first group of poems, in which Henry often emphasizes his faithfulness, the speaker adopts the role of the courtly lover. In the quatrain "Oh, my heart," for instance, the speaker mourns his imminent (and reasonless) departure from his lady:

> Oh, my heart and, oh, my heart,
> My heart it is so sore,
> Since I must from my love depart,
> And know no cause wherefore.[40]

Other poems in this group reiterate the speaker's ostensibly rock-solid devotion. In "Green grows the holly," Henry asserts:

> As the holly grows green
>   And never changes hue,
> So I am—ever have been—
>   unto my lady true.
>
> (*ll. 5–8*)

---

40. All references to Henry's lyrics, except when noted otherwise, will be to the selection edited by Ray Siemens in Herman, *Reading Monarchs Writing*, 217–29.

And in "Without discord," the speaker pleads for reconciliation:

> Without discord,
> And both accord,
>   Now let us be.
> Both hearts, alone,
> To set in one
>   Best seems me.
> For when one, sole,
> Is in the dole
>   Of love's pain,
> Then help must have
> Himself to save
>   And love to obtain.
>   (*ll. 1–12*)

The poems in the second group focus less on Henry's fidelity and more on defending the author's pastimes. "If love now reigned as it has been" asserts that, despite love's pains, "noble men then would surely ensearch / All ways whereby they might it reach" (ll. 2–3)—love being the obvious province of the noble, the aristocratic. Henry reiterates this point in "Though that men do call it dotage": "Love maintains all noble courage; / Who love disdains is all of the village" (ll. 13–14). The person who disdains love (and by implication the chivalric activities of the lover) has lost his place in the aristocracy; his disdain marks him as a peasant.

Such lyrics may seem like trifles, especially since, as Hall reports, their composition seems to have been part of Henry's overall absorption in neo-chivalric recreations:

> [The king exercised] hym self daily in shotyng, singing dau[n]syng, wrastelyng, casting of the barre, plaiying at the recorders, flute, virginal, and in setting of songes, makyng of balettes, & dyd set. ii. goodly masses, every of them fyve partes, whiche were songe oftentimes in hys chapel, and afterwardes in diverse other places. And whan he came to Okyng, there were kept both Justes and Turneys: the rest of thys progresse was spent in huntyng, hawkyng and shotyng. (515)

Yet we need to remember that unlike Wyatt's verse, or the poems arranged in the *Devonshire Manuscript*,[41] Henry's lyrics were never meant as private

---

41. See Remley, "Mary Shelton."

reflections, intended for at most a small coterie audience. Rather, they functioned as public performances—more specifically, monarchic performances—for the benefit of the court and whatever foreign ambassadors were in attendance, and there is strong evidence that Henry's lyrics were known outside the court as well.[42] To take one step further Lerer's insight that Henry's masques and disguisings "exemplify his understanding of the theatrical nature of both love and politics: his recognition that the court remains a world of masks,"[43] Henry's adoption of the persona of the Lover in his "balettes" constitutes an avenue for *doing* politics. Henry's love songs enact, in other words, precisely the conflation of "sexual and political potency, virility and kingship," that marks Holbein's much later portrait of Henry VIII, commemorating the birth of Edward, in which the king's phallus, his ability to conceive, is the central focus.[44]

The expressions of faithfulness, and the desire to dispel "discord" and achieve "accord," are, certainly, generic traits of the courtly lyric, but they take on further resonance when we remember that at the time Henry probably composed these lyrics, he was anything but faithful to Katherine of Aragon, his wife. In *The Interlude of Youth* (c. 1513–14), the author satirizes Henry VIII as a regular frequenter of brothels and associates him with Lady Lechery.[45] One sees in *Youth* a not very veiled criticism of the monarch's extramarital exploits, at least one of which resulted in a child. Hall records that in 1514, Henry, "in his freshe youth" fell into "the chaynes of love" with Elizabeth Blount (703).[46] Ironically, given Hall's descriptions of the king's pastimes, Blount's excellence in "syngynge, daunsyng, and in all goodly pastimes" (703) attracted Henry to her, and unlike his marriage with Katherine, this union bore masculine fruit: in 1519 "she bare a goodly manne child, of beutie like to the father and mother" (703)—Henry Fitzroy, later Duke of Richmond.[47]

In addition, as the correspondence of the Spanish ambassador, Luis Caroz, demonstrates, the private life and indiscretions of the king (as well as the state of the queen's reproductive organs) were not only public, but the subject of intense observation and speculation.[48] Despite the ambassador's report on

---

42. See below, note 45.

43. Lerer, *Courtly Letters,* 41.

44. Montrose, "Elizabethan Subject and the Spenserian Text," 315; Montrose, *Subject of Elizabeth,* 20–22.

45. Lancashire, *Two Tudor Interludes,* 54. Lancashire also notes that the author of *Youth* echoes Henry VIII's songs (54).

46. Scarisbrick, *Henry VIII,* 147.

47. Ibid. See also the entry on Henry Fitzroy in the *Oxford Dictionary of National Biography.*

48. *Supplement to Volume I and Volume II of Letters, Despatches and State Papers, Relating to the Negotiations between England and Spain,* ed. G. A. Bergenroth, 41–44. In a curious example of nineteenth

25 May 1510 that the king and Katherine "adore" each other, in his next letter, dated 29 May 1510, Caroz informs Ferdinand of the king's sexual adventuring:

> What lately has happened is that two sisters of the Duke of Bucking- ham, both married, lived in the palace. The one of them is the favorite of the Queen, and the other, it is said, is very much liked by the King, who went after her [y andava tras ella]. Another version is that the love intrigues were not of the King, but of a young man, his favourite, of the name of Conton [Sir William Compton],[49] who had been the late King's butler. This Conton carried on the love intrigue, as it is said, for the King, and that is the more credible version, for the King has shown great displeasure at which I am going to tell.[50]

Caroz's gossip concerns how the king got found out and his displeasure at having his infidelities revealed. Henry's bed hopping, of course, lends an ironic air to his pleadings for reconciliation and his assertions of eternal truth and fidelity. Yet in addition to the domestic comedy (with everyone in the court probably aware that even as the king swears eternal fealty, he is carrying on a "love intrigue"), there might be a more serious, diplomatic overtone to Henry's adoption of this persona before the court.

At the same time that Henry was either chasing other women or hav- ing his friends act for him, he was also assiduously attempting to enlist his father-in-law as an ally in his planned wars. Immediately upon his accession, he wrote to Ferdinand asking if he would be willing to attack France (Fer- dinand evidently told Henry to restrain himself), and he tried three times between 1510 and 1512 to carry out a military adventure of one type or another with him. In each case, however, Ferdinand pulled out without first bothering to tell Henry.[51] The likely connections to Henry's lyrics are twofold. Like the jousts and tourneys, Henry's songs are part of his attempt to construct his image as the ideal chivalric king who is both lover and

---

century prudery, the translator of Caroz's dispatch into English hides the anatomical details behind a veil of Latin, "la barriga de le Reyna" becoming "uterus reginae" (42).

49. According to the *Oxford Dictionary of National Biography,* Sir William Compton entered Henry's service in 1510 "as groom of the stool, and he served until 1526 as one of the king's most important and intimate personal servants, jousting with the king (nearly losing his life in 1510), keeping the king's linen, holding and disbursing large sums of money for the king's daily purchases" (Bernard, "Compton, Sir William").

50. *Supplement to Volume I and Volume II,* 39.

51. See Scarisbrick, *Henry VIII,* 24–34.

warrior, as we have seen. The songs, in other words, are directed at both the court *and* the foreign ambassadors, and they are part of Henry's project of symbolically demonstrating his masculinity. But if one is constantly trying to enlist one's father-in-law in a military venture, surely having one's infidelities known and broadcasted will not exactly help one's case, especially since the letters between Katherine and her father suggest the two had a warm relationship.[52] When, therefore, Henry swears, "So I am—ever have been—/ unto my lady true," it is at least possible that he also has his father-in-law—whose approval Henry clearly desired[53]—in mind as his audience. The love songs, therefore, are as much interventions in the political imaginary as Henry's portraits and the courtly masques. They constitute, in effect, a form of poetic diplomacy, contributing not only to Henry's image as a courtly lover, but also to the public illusion of marital bliss for the purpose of reassuring his father-in-law that he is indeed treating his daughter well and therefore should be trusted in other endeavors as well. In other words, Henry draws upon and manipulates the generic conventions of the courtly love lyric to provide an acceptable face for marital relations, which themselves are suggestive of national political strength, stability, and Henry's ability to deal with political accord.

In addition to their diplomatic overtones, Henry's songs also demonstrate their monarchic perspective through the handling of power within the poems themselves. From the Provençal poets onward, power is conventionally delegated to the female object of desire. The male (at least superficially)[54] continually begs the woman for grace in language that could just as easily describe the desire for the monarch's or the lord's patronage or favor. It is the same parallel between political and erotic experience that Wyatt, his contemporaries, and his followers found so productive.[55]

Henry's "Alac! Alac! What shall I do?" ("Alac! Alac! What shall I do? / For care is cast in to my heart / And true love locked thereto") and its companion, "Hey Nonny Nonny, Nonny Nonny No!" exemplify this paradigm. The two lyrics, taken together, provide one of the rare instances of a male

---

52. See, for example, Ferdinand's letters to Katherine, *LP,* 1.1, 25, item 9, and 89, item 67; and Katherine's letter to Ferdinand, *LP,* 1.1, 60, item 127.

53. Given Henry VIII's evident desire to separate himself politically (and likely, personally) from the late Henry VII, it is interesting that John Stile, ambassador to the Spanish court for both Henry VII and Henry VIII, consistently refers to Ferdinand as "yowr noble good fader" (*LP,* 158–60, item 345).

54. See Vickers, "Diana Described"; Quilligan, "Sidney and His Queen."

55. See, for example, Greenblatt's chapter "Power, Sexuality, and Inwardness in Wyatt's Poetry," in *Renaissance Self-Fashioning.*

poet writing in a female voice.[56] In "Hey Nonny," the speaker hears a maid "right piteously complain" and then rehearses what he hears:

> She said, alas,
>> Without trespass,
>> Her dear heart was untrue.
> In every place,
>> I know he has
>> Forsaken me for a new.
>> *(ll. 9–14)*

I will return below to the inversion of the conventional assumption of male fidelity and female lability. Right now, however, I want to note that the lyric also inverts the language conventionally used to describe the power relations between the desirer and the desired. The female voice complains:

> And now I may,
>> In no manner away,
>> Obtain that I do sue.
> So ever and aye
>> Without denay [deny]
>> My own sweet heart, adieu.
>> *(ll. 21–26)*

To state the obvious, Henry as king is the object of everyone's desire. He is the person sued, not the person suing, for favor. Nowhere is this more evident than in "If Love Now Reigned as it Has Been," where Henry offers a riddle to his audience: "To lovers I put now sure this case: / Which of their loves does get them grace?" One must remember that the original audience would have heard this question as emanating from their monarch, and just as the lady must "sue" the male, so now the elder disdainers must sue the youthful, regal lover for political and amorous "grace," the two being conflated. If, in the court of love, the choice lady offers the best grace to her suitor, in the court itself it is the king who offers grace. Thus this lyric combines Henry's literary personae and his actual position.

While Henry's lyrics may seem to rehearse the same suing for grace expected of courtiers,[57] there is a crucial difference. Because the speaker is not

---

56. See Harvey, *Ventriloquized Voices.*

57. Consider Henry's lyrics "Though that men docCall it dotage" (l. 17), "Who So That Wyll for Grace Sue" (l. 1), "Without discord" (ll. 19–20), and "Lusty youth should us ensue" (in which "disdainers...sue to get them grace," ll. 14–15).

a courtier, expressing the woes of a courtier in erotic terms, but a monarch, Henry adjusts the erotic story accordingly. The lady, not the male lover, is now the one complaining that she cannot "in no manner away, / Obtain that I do sue" (ll. 22–23). It would have been impossible for Henry to constitute himself as a desiring subject for the simple reason that in his own estimation he is *not* a subject (even to the pope, as the Reformation will later make clear).[58] Consequently, Henry alters the conventions of erotic verse so that they not only accord with his own position at the top of the hierarchy— indeed, not just as a monarch, but as an absolute monarch—but also remind everyone, through the fact of public performance, that he is indeed the king, and kings "in no manner" sue, even in matters of the heart.

Yet the story also ends happily. After overhearing the lady complain, the royal speaker suddenly, almost miraculously, appears, and makes everything better, though of course without apologizing for his previous indiscretions:

> She had not said
>> But, at abraid, [suddenly]
>> Her dear heart was full near
> And said good maid,
>> Be not dismayed,
>> My love, my darling dear.
>> *(ll. 45–50)*

Without meaning to push the interpretation too far, it is important to note that the song also rehearses the culture of surveillance that is beginning to develop in Henry's court: one has a sense that the royal speaker can observe his desiring subject(s) without revealing his presence, and then, through an act of will, of power, suddenly make things better. The underlying implication, one that will be developed in "Pastime with good company" and "Though some say that youth rules me," is that this power can be used for other, less benign, purposes as well.

This note of threat, so strangely foreign to conventional lyric verse, is amplified by the oddly discordant note at the end:

> In arms he hent [held]
>> That lady gent
>> In voiding care and moan.

---

58. For what happens when a monarch transgresses these expectations, see the analysis of Mary Stuart's verse in the next chapter.

The day they spent
        To their intent
    In wilderness, alone.
            (*ll. 51–56*)

This seems like a traditionally comedic conclusion, with the lovers in each other's arms. Yet two points are worthy of attention. First, the song allows the pair only one day of "voiding care and moan," thus implying that there will be more "care and moan" in the future. Second, Henry reinforces this implication by situating the ending "in wilderness." Stevens glosses this word as "the country" (398), but the *Oxford English Dictionary* records no such use before 1644, and virtually all previous usages are some variation on "a tract of solitude and savageness" (*OED* 1.b). Assuming that neither Henry nor his audience would have had any trouble associating Henry's lyrics at some level with the court, this moment anticipates Wyatt's and Surrey's much later court satires; only then it is Wyatt's Caesar and Surrey's Sardanapalus registering, however briefly and allusively, the dangers of courtly life.

The use of "wilderness" also conveys a sense of sexuality's dangers, and perhaps also Henry's or his culture's distrust of women. The two themes come together again in "Whereto should I express," which begins with the royal speaker bemoaning his departure from his lady:

Whereto should I express
        My inward heaviness?
    No mirth can make me fain,
        Till that we meet again.
            (*ll. 1–4*)

This seemingly conventional lyric strays toward the unconventional near the end. At first, the speaker reverses conventional gender expectations and asserts (perhaps anticipating Donne's "A Valediction Forbidding Mourning") "You are not variable," ascribing to the woman the fixedness more usually associated with masculinity. The next stanza, however, makes clear that the beloved's invariability is not due to any unusual merit on her part but results instead from the royal speaker's act of will. "*I* make you fast and sure," the speaker sings. Even when the speaker admits a degree of powerlessness (he must leave, even though he doesn't want to), the poem very firmly reminds the audience that the speaker, however much in the throes of love melancholy, remains very much in charge.

The speaker's monarchic position also manifests itself in several of the lyrics in which Henry defends himself. The first three lines of "Pastime with good company," for example, sound like a mere declaration of high spirits:

> Pastime with good company,
> I love and shall until I die.
> Grudge who likes, but none deny[.]
>
> (*ll. 1–3*)

In this text, Henry implicitly adopts the persona of Youth addressing the aged disdainers opposing his actions. According to convention, though, in the relationship of Youth and Old Age, it is Youth who is (putatively) subservient. However, when Henry invokes this convention, he in effect redefines it to endow Youth with the authority of his kingship. The fourth line—"So God be pleased, thus live will I," with manuscript variants also urging an equivalently valid reading of "So God be pleased, *this life* will I" (my emphasis)—transforms the song into a vehicle by which Henry establishes his independence, "thus live [or "this life"] will I" serving to remind one and all that these desires are the desires of the king. The line functions as an assertion of power, of independence. It is not simply a declaration of high spirits. And no matter how frivolous the circumstances of performance, it would be hard for any courtier or lady mindful of the very few practical limitations on royal power to miss the overtone of threat vibrating in the last line of the burden:

> For my pastance:
> Hunt, sing, and dance.
> My heart is set!
> All goodly sport
> For my comfort.
> Who shall me *let*?
>
> (*ll. 5–10; my emphasis*)

Who among you will let [prevent] me, the king, from pursuing my heart's desires? the king warbles to the assembled. Similarly, in "Lusty Youth should us ensue [imitate]," Henry uses a song that superficially appears to be an apologia for sowing wild oats to assert his royal independence:

> For they would have him his liberty refrain,
> And all merry company for to disdain.
> But I will not do whatsoever they say,
> But follow his mind in all that we may.
>
> (*ll. 5–8*)

Yet Henry's assertions of authority in these texts also testify to the presence of genuine insecurity. Defenses respond to attacks; they do not exist by themselves, and Henry's asserting his right to live as he would strongly suggests the presence of an unignorable "they" who wanted to restrain the king's liberty. Even though Henry's accession was widely (and wildly) celebrated, Henry's policies and pastimes very quickly instigated significant opposition from some members of the nobility and from humanists. Although Henry ultimately got his way, at the time he could not have known that he would, and we need to situate his lyrics within the context of the real, if ultimately overcome, resistance to his policies and preferred modes of recreation.

Hall records that while many applauded the king's pastimes, such as his taking part in tournaments, the older members of the court disapproved because of the dangers posed to the king and therefore the country:

> The ancient fathers much doubted [the prudence of Henry's hobby], considering the tender youth of the king, and divers chances of horses and armour: in so much that it was openly spoken, that steel was not so strong, but it might be broken, nor no horse could be so sure of foot, but he may fall. (520)

In addition, many members of the old guard were particularly unhappy with the young king's desire to reverse his father's pacific policies and go to war for the sake of chivalric honor. Henry's reign may have begun with a grand sense of sweeping out the old and celebrating the new, but we need to keep in mind that Henry's first Privy Council consisted of people who had served under Henry VII, and Henry continued to employ Henry VII's diplomats, such as Sir John Stile, and some clearly balked at Henry's desire to involve England in a costly foreign venture.[59] Nor was resistance restricted to either the court or the old guard. Polydore Vergil reports that Henry's initial proposal to join Ferdinand in his campaign against the French in Italy met at first with considerable skepticism:

> King Henry then summoned to London a council of his nobles. When they were assembled there the good king, full of devotion to the church, publicly explained how he had been requested by both Pope Julius and King Ferdinand his father-in-law to take up arms in defence of the church. For this reason he had summoned his nobles,

---

59. See Baker-Smith, "'Inglorious glory,'" passim.

so that when asked they might speak their minds, whereby he could decide this weighty business from the general views of all. And to enable them to give their opinions, he questioned each separately. *After a long debate, many came to the conclusion on several grounds that there was no need to take up arms then;* because in the war against the French the pope had as allies King Ferdinand and the Venetians, whose support of the papal arms ought to be the more eager since it closely concerned their own interests; also because England was far distant from Italy, and her assistance could only with difficulty be sent there; finally because, if they entered the war, being so far removed from Italy and Spain, it might perhaps happen that, the French having been evicted from Italy, the whole burden of the war would fall on this country, which would thus be involved in war while its allies were enjoying peace. *This view seemed correct to many,* but nevertheless the king scarcely agreed with it, for, owing to his confidence in his own resolution, he considered it to be dishonourable to him if so great a war waged against the Roman church should come to an end before some efforts of his own had been employed to end it. Wherefore the religious and most valiant prince, not unmindful that it was his duty to seek fame by military skill, preferred so justifiable a war rather than peace.[60]

Thomas Wolsey also initially tried to halt the king's warmongering, mainly because of the expense. In a report to Bishop Fox, Wolsey groused about the malign influence of Sir Edward Howard, the Lord Admiral, "by whose wanton means his Grace spendeth much money, and is more disposed to war than peace" (*LP,* 1.1, 462–63, item 880). Yet even Howard started to look askance at Henry's project, not because he objected to war in principle, but because the king's forces were so ill-supplied. Writing from Plymouth, where Henry's fleet had gathered, Howard told Wolsey that "was never army so falselie vitailled," and that if he does not send enough money to keep the troops fed, "we shalbe driven to come again in to the Downes and let the Frenchmen take ther pleasure."[61] Once in France, he wrote again to Wolsey wishing that "the King had never trusted the King of Aragon more than they do," since Ferdinand did not meet his promise to supply troops and food (*LP,* 1.1, 590, item 286). Shortly thereafter, Wolsey received a report from William Knight detailing how the army, far from a chivalric juggernaut, is "unlearned," ignores orders, and despite pacifying one mutiny, "many bands

60. Vergil, *Anglica Historia,* 161; my emphasis.
61. *Original Letters Illustrative of English History,* ed. Ellis, 1: 147, 148.

now declare they will go home at Michaelmas, if they should die for it" (*LP,* 1.1, 618–19, item 1327).

In 1512, Henry's youthful disregard for danger also ran into considerable resistance from his counsellors. Henry announced that since "his English subjects were of such high spirits that they tended to fight less willingly and less successfully under any commander other than their king," the obvious course was for him to lead the troops personally.[62] Significantly, Henry had to browbeat his nobles into agreeing with him:[63]

> Wherefore he again summoned a council of nobles and there was a general discussion concerning the newly proposed expedition. *Many considered it too perilous that the king in the first flush of his youthful maturity in arms should expose himself to the danger of so great a war.* They accordingly thought that a commander of the army should be appointed who would conduct the war according to the king's wishes. *This view was thoroughly approved by many but not by the king, who held to his original opinion* and argued that it behooved him to enter upon his first military experience in so important and difficult a war in order that he might, by a signal start to his martial knowledge, create such a fine opinion about his valour among all men that they would clearly understand that his ambition was not merely to equal but indeed to exceed the glorious deeds of his ancestors. . . . He persistently asserted that he wished with the approval of all to take charge of the matter himself; if this were conceded he was sure that at no point would he be deprived of divine assistance in undertaking so meritorious a war. When the nobles saw that the king, on account of the confidence he had in his own great valour, maintained his opinion with such loftiness of mind and prudence, *they were unable not to agree with him.*[64]

Vergil indirectly implies his distance from Henry's glorious, yet politically irresponsible, desires through careful diction and irony. It is Henry's "confidence"—overconfidence?—that leads to their agreement, but their agreement is hedged by the double negative: "*non* potuere *non* in eius tandem sentientiam ire."[65] Henry eventually got his war, but only after King

---

62. Vergil, *Anglica Historia,* 197.

63. Ibid., 199; my emphasis. See also David Starkey's rather fanciful recreation of this incident in *Reign of Henry VIII,* 49.

64. Ibid., 199; my emphasis. See also David Starkey's rather fanciful recreation of this incident in *The Reign of Henry VIII: Personalities and Politics,* 49.

65. Vergil, *Anglica Historia,* 198; my emphasis.

Louis refused peace, saying via Henry's ambassador that he "would not by any means agree to making peace on the terms which the pope demanded."[66] And even then Henry received permission for only a limited intervention as Ferdinand's ally.

Even as Henry worked to revive chivalry, he also made known his desire to patronize humanists. William Blount, Lord Mountjoy, for example, reported to Erasmus in a letter dated 27 May 1509 that the king wished "he had more learning." Mountjoy responded that the king was not expected to be more learned, and that he always had the option of subsidizing scholars. Henry replied: "Certainly; we could hardly live without them" (*LP,* 1.1, 27, item 51). But the humanists without whom Henry could not live were quite open about their disapproval of war and chivalry, as demonstrated by such popular works as Thomas More's *Utopia* and Erasmus's adage deconstructing the eagle as a noble creature, *Scarabeus aquilam querit* ["The Beetle Searches for the Eagle"]. Erasmus also openly condemned Henry's ventures. In a letter to Adolphus, Prince of Veere, Erasmus expresses his distress that Lord Mountjoy, his patron, "favors the Prince in these tumults of war," and that he "cannot express how he grieves that such tumults should arise, *nemine obsistente*" (*LP,* 1.1, 713, item 1546). Given the prominence of the humanists, it seems highly unlikely that Henry remained ignorant of their views on war or indifferent to their disapproval. The king might metaphorically twist John Colet's arm after his impolitic sermon denouncing war, but Erasmus and others were less immediately pliable.[67]

Then there is the matter of Thomas Wolsey. Vergil (like Hall and so many others) may have hated the cardinal, but they were not alone in their dislike of him, and Vergil records how Henry's indifference to advice made Wolsey's rise possible:

> Wolsey [conducted] all business at his own pleasure, since no one at all was of more value to the king. It was certainly as a result of this that several leading counselors, when they saw so much power coming into the hands of one man, withdrew gradually from the court. Canterbury and Winchester were among the first to leave, going into their dioceses. But before they left, *like truly responsible statesmen,* they earnestly urged the king not to suffer any servant to be greater than his master: they borrowed this saying from Christ, who, in the gospel according to St. John, says to his disciples, "Verily, verily, I say unto you,

---

66. Ibid., 163. See also Starkey, *Reign of Henry VIII,* 49.
67. Baker-Smith, "'Inglorious glory,'" 138–40.

the servant is not greater than his lord." Aware at all events that these remarks were directed at Wolsey, Henry replied to them that he would make it his first business diligently to ensure that any servant of his was obedient and not autocratic. Then Thomas duke of Norfolk retired to his estates; and afterwards even Charles [Brandon] duke of Suffolk followed the others.[68]

The implication of the last sentence is that despite Henry's assurances, Wolsey continued on his autocratic path. Furthermore, if Canterbury and Winchester act as "truly responsible statesmen" by warning Henry, then Henry by implication acts irresponsibly by not heeding their advice.

Consequently, the curious defensiveness radiating from a number of Henry's lyrics becomes more understandable. It would have been clear to Henry that not only his elders, but also the humanists whose favor he courted, and a certain amount of public opinion, disapproved of his chivalric role-playing and his warmongering. Henry thus adopts the persona of Youth to preempt or answer criticism of how he chooses to conduct his life, but he goes against the generic expectations of Youth by asserting his royal right to do exactly as he pleases. Unlike the conclusion of *The Interlude of Youth,*[69] there is no repentance in Henry's poems, no acknowledgment of wrongful behavior or repudiation of Riot, Pride, and Lady Lechery. To be sure, Henry concludes "Pastime" by assuring his audience: "The best ensue. / The worst eschew. / My mind shall be. / Virtue to use. / Vice to refuse. / Thus shall I use me!" (ll. 25–30). But Henry redefines "Virtue" to include precisely the behaviors that so alarmed his elders. In "The time of youth is to be spent," Henry explicitly takes on his critics and defends his chivalric games as encouraging virtue:

> The time of youth is to be spent,
> But vice in it should be forfent [forbidden].
> Pastimes there be I note truly
> Which one may use and vice deny.
> And they be pleasant to God and man:
> Those should we covet [desire] when we can.
> As feats of arms, and such other
> Whereby activeness one may utter.

---

68. Vergil, *Anglica Historia,* 231–33; my emphasis.

69. At the conclusion of *Youth,* the title character embraces Christianity and rejects his previous behaviors: "Here all sin I forsake / And to God I me betake" (ll. 738–39).

Comparisons in them may lawfully be set,
For, thereby, courage is surely out fet [gained].
Virtue it is, then, youth for to spend
In good disports which it does fend.

In "Lusty Youth should us ensue," Henry once again defends himself, this time against all "disdainers":

Lusty Youth should us ensue.
His merry heart shall sure all [i.e., disdainers] rue.
For whatsoever they do him tell
It is not for him, we know it well.

For they would have him his liberty refrain,
And all merry company for to disdain.
But I will not do whatsoever they say,
But follow his mind in all that we may.

(*ll. 1–8; my emphasis*)

The next two stanzas constitute a defense of not just Youth's "pastance," but Henry's "merry company":

How should youth himself best use
But all disdainers for to refuse?
Youth has as chief assurance
Honest mirth with virtue's pastance.

For in them consists great honour,
Though that disdainers would therein put error.
For they do sue to get them grace,
All only riches to purchase.

(*ll. 9–16*)

And yet Henry, perhaps bowing to the inevitable, grants that the disdainers have a point, and that he will work toward balance:

With good order, counsel, and equity,
Good Lord grant us our mansion to be.
For without their good guidance
Youth should fall in great mischance.

For Youth is frail and prompt to do
As well vices as virtues to ensue.
Wherefore by these he must be guided,
And virtue's pastance must therein be used.

Now unto God this prayer we make,
That this rude play may well betake
And that we may our faults amend
And bliss obtain at our last end. Amen.

(ll. 17–28)

Whether or not one finds the final turn to religion convincing, this lyric enacts a masterful diplomatic performance. In all likelihood, Henry must have been humiliated, or at least frustrated, by the disapproval of his elders, and this lyric demonstrates his attempt to turn these affronts to his authority to his advantage by essentially arguing both sides of the issue. That is to say, Henry initially rebuts critics by calling them "disdainers" and by asserting once more his royal will ("I will not..."). Yet Henry then turns and admits that youth is indeed frail and in need of guidance. Hence the final turn to religion. The lyric concludes, in other words, with Henry turning an erosion of royal authority into a strengthening of it.

"Though some say that youth rules me," however, provides the most interesting, because the most overt, example of Henry using verse to challenge and reassure his elders simultaneously. The song begins in a seemingly defensive, if not apologetic, mood:

Though some say that youth rules me,
    I trust in age to tarry.
God and my right, and my duty,
      From them shall I never vary,
      Though some say that youth rules me.

(ll. 1–5)

Yet Henry's incorporation of his royal motto, *Dieu et mon droit,* in the third line both reassures his audience that the king is mindful of his royal position and reminds them of the power invested in the crown (power that, as we know, Henry wanted to expand). In the next stanza, Henry furthers his offensive by asking his critics how they acted in their youth: "I pray you all that aged be / How well did you *your* youth carry?" (ll. 6–7; my emphasis).

Henry ends this lyric with a strategically placed revelation of the author's name and, most importantly, his title:

> Then soon discuss that hence we must
> > Pray we to God and Saint Mary
> That all amend, and here an end.
> > Thus says the King, the eighth Harry,
> > Though some say that youth rules me.
> > > > (*ll. 16–20*)

More than "Pastime with good company," this song deserves the title "The King's Ballad" because it would be inconceivable for anyone other than Henry VIII to perform it. And, for this reason, this lyric is the most deeply political of Henry's efforts. What begins as a somewhat sheepish defense hearkening back to the conventional youth-age debates of medieval poetry becomes an overt assertion of royal power and royal prerogative. It is the king, and the eighth of that name to sit on England's throne (a position that gives him the collective authority of the previous seven, not the least being Henry V), who issues this defense of his life; and by including this self-referential allusion to his position and his name's history, Henry VIII forcefully reminds his listeners that if youth rules the king, it is the king who rules everyone else.

IV

"Though some say that youth rules me" nonetheless admits that the king's authority has been challenged. No such doubts are evinced in what appears to be Henry's final poem,[70] written approximately fifteen years after the lyrics included in *Ritson's Manuscript* and the *Henry VIII Manuscript*. The poem in question is included in a letter written in 1609 by Sir John Harington in response to a request from King James's son, Prince Henry, for "suche scraps and fragments of witte and poesie."[71] As noted in the introduction, Harington decided that only verses by royal authors could appropriately answer a prince's request for verse. While Harington's first example comes from the pen of Henry VI, the second example that he recommends is "a special verse

---

70. In "'Respect,'" Siemens examines the possibility that a short poem inscribed in a book of prayers belonging to Katherine Parr may have been composed and inscribed by Henry. However, as Siemens points out, the handwriting is "quite different" from extant examples of Henry's (189), and it seems quite unlikely that the aging monarch would reassure his queen after Stephen Gardiner's attacks by suggesting that she "set doughts asyed and to some / sporting fall" (186).

71. Harington, *Nugae Antiquae*, ed. Harington, 2: 246–49.

of King Henry the Eight, when he conceived love for Anna Bulleign." Harington comments further:

> And hereof I entertain no doubt of the Author, for, if I had no better reason than the rhyme, it were sufficient to think that no other than suche a King could write suche a sonnet; but of this my father oft gave me good assurance, who was in his household. This sonnet was sunge to the Lady Anne at his commaundment, and here followeth:

> THE eagle's force subdues eache byrd that flyes;
>   What metal can resyst the flaminge fyre?
> Dothe not the sunne dazzle the cleareste eyes,
>   And melt the ice, and make the froste retyre?
> The hardest stones are peircede thro wyth tools;
>   The wysest are, with Princes, made but fools.

While there is some controversy over attribution, I will proceed on the assumption that Henry VIII penned this lyric toward the start of his infatuation with Anne Boleyn,[72] that is to say, during the summer or autumn of 1526.[73]

---

72. This lyric was first noted by Walter Thornbury in his short 1874 *Notes & Queries* article, "Henry VIII as a Poet"; Thornbury remarked on the "despotic self-consciousness of the last line" (403). The attribution is in question because these lines also appear as part of Thomas Churchyard's "Shore's Wife's Lament" (which appears under its original title, "How Shore's Wife, King Edward the fowerth's Concubine, Was by King Richard despoiled of all her goodes, and forced to doe open penaunce," in *The Last parte of the Mirour for Magistrates* [London, 1575], sig. X.iiiv). In their *Elizabethan Poetry,* May and Ringler do not attribute the poem to Henry VIII but cite instead the 1563 edition of the *Mirror for Magistrates* (STC 13445). However, I attribute the poem to Henry VIII for a number of reasons. First, there is the specificity of Harington's letter, his knowledge of the circumstances surrounding the lyric's composition and performance, and what Harington knew from his father. Second, the poem's ascription to Henry VIII thus predates Churchyard's poem, and its priority lends greater weight to Henry as author. Third, May and Ringler confirm Harington's attribution of the couplet to Henry VI, citing a 1586 manuscript compiled by William Briton of Kelston (2:921, 1: 172). As this anthology is the only place where the couplet appears, it seems that Harington's father had access to royal verse that did not circulate widely, if at all, lending further support to the claim for Henry VIII's authorship. As for the poem appearing in someone else's poem, as Leah Marcus has argued, it was not unheard of for royal verse (Elizabeth's, in particular) to appear in print "erroneously ascribed to other poets" ("Queen Elizabeth I as Public and Private Poet," 136). Finally, as my analysis indicates, I disagree with Ray Siemens's judgment that this poem seems "quite unlike that which might result from the budding love of a monarch and noblewoman" ("'Respect,'" 188). It is quite the opposite: the poem fits perfectly with Henry's conception of himself and his power. While absolute certainty is not possible, I would argue that the preponderance of evidence supports Henry VIII as author of this poem, not Thomas Churchyard.

73. For a chronology of Henry's relationship with Anne Boleyn, see Eric Ives, *Life and Death of Anne Boleyn,* 90; and Warnicke, *Rise and Fall of Anne Boleyn,* 56–60.

FIGURE 8. *Henry VIII,* 1520 (© National Portrait Gallery)

The apex of Henry's chivalric politics, the Field of the Cloth of Gold, oc-curred in 1520, and in 1524 the king participated for the last time in a tour-nament.[74] But while chivalric forms continued to be symbolically potent

---

74. On the Field of the Cloth of Gold, see Anglo, *Spectacle, Pageantry, and Early Tudor Policy,* 124–59; on Henry's last tournament, 115–16.

(and would remain so throughout the early modern period),[75] the political imaginary surrounding Henry VIII had started shifting toward illustrating the monarch's individuality and power. In the 1520 portrait shown in figure 8, for example, the monarch is considerably more adorned than in his earlier portraits (cf. figs. 4 and 5). Anticipating the later portraits by Holbein, the emphasis in this work is not on dynastic continuity (note the absence of the Tudor rose), but on the king's personal magnificence. The significant increase in adornment is matched by the significant increase in the king's bulk, but the effect is to emphasize Henry's physical power (the frame seems too small to contain him), an effect magnified by his stern expression and beard.

One sees another view of the same development in a 1526 miniature by Lucas Horenbout (fig. 9). Once again, Henry is no longer portrayed as either Youth or an exponent of the Tudor dynasty. Instead, the image is of a king whose grave face seems to express impatience with anything other than serious matters. Both portraits suggest a man who has come into his own, has left childish things behind, and would brook no opposition. Like Kent looking into King Lear's countenance, the viewer sees authority in these portraits.

This shift in iconography toward emphasizing the monarch's personal magnetism and power is of a piece with other developments, such as the reorganization of the court in 1519. When Henry first came to power, he brought with him a cohort of friends, "young gentlemen," as Hall calls them (581)—occasionally referred to in the state papers as Henry's "henxmen"[76]— who acted in a manner that the King's counsellors found utterly inimical to the dignity of their position and the king's person. In what must have seemed like a classic example of Old Age restraining Youth, the council met secretly to put a stop to this state of affairs. Hall reports:

> The kynges counsaill secretly communed together of the kynges gentlenes & liberalitee to all persones: by the whiche they perceived that certain young men in his privie chamber not regardyng his estate nor degree, were so familier and homely with hym, and plaied such light touches with hym that they forgat thmeselfes: . . . yet the kynges counsail thought it not mete to be suffred for the kynges honor, & therfor thei altogether came to the king, beseching him al these enormities and lightnes to redres. To whom the kyng answered, that he had chosen them of his counsaill, both for the maintenaunce of his honor, & for

---

75. See, for example, McCoy, *Rites of Knighthood*.
76. For example, *LP,* 1.1, 468, item 768; and 412, item 897.

FIGURE 9.   Miniature of Henry VIII by Lucas Horenbout, 1526 (Fitzwilliam Museum, Cambridge)

the defence of all thyng that might blemishe thesame: wherefore if they sawe any about hym misuse theimselfes, he committed it to their reformacion. (598)

The result was that "the kynges minions" were banished and "foure sad and auncient knightes, put into the kynges privie chamber" (598).[77] Although by 1521 the king's "minions" had returned,[78] the sense that the king had

---

77. Lerer, *Courtly Letters,* 42–43; Starkey, "Intimacy and Innovation," 80–81.
78. Scarisbrick, *Henry VIII,* 119.

come into his own and bid adieu to the attractions of youth nonetheless continued. The year 1521, for example, "saw Henry write a book [the *Assertio Septem Sacramentorum*], acquire a title [Defender of the Faith], destroy a duke [Buckingham] and secure the throne."[79] Also, while Henry restarted his French war in 1523, this time his model was not the chivalric hero Henry V, but the more politically pragmatic Henry VII: he hoped that Francis would "make a way for him as King Richard did for his father."[80] Even so, in what must have been a highly resonant move, in 1526 Henry VIII finally started issuing coins featuring his own image, not his father's.[81] Henry VIII's personal behavior also suggests maturation and the replacement of lust with an awareness of dynastic needs. By 1524, Henry had ceased to sleep with Katherine, while the need for a male heir grew along with the realization that Katherine could not supply that need. Eric Ives observes: "With the final recognition that he would have no son by Katherine, Henry's position changed. Occasional illicit pleasure was no longer enough."[82] Enter Anne Boleyn.

Yet, as Harington's letter attests, Henry VIII pursued Anne Boleyn in very different terms than he had Katherine. Fittingly, given the political developments over the preceding few years and the shifts in Henry's iconography, he no longer invokes chivalric figures or adopts a subservient position toward his beloved. Those images are no longer part of the Henrician political imaginary,[83] having been replaced by images that unconditionally project the monarch's authority.[84] The Harington lyric both reflects these changes and suggests how Henry contributed to them. Rather than invoking the conventional image of the Petrarchan or chivalric lover rendered prostrate

---

79. Ibid., 123.

80. Quoted in Scarisbrick, *Henry VIII*, 128.

81. Challis, *Tudor Coinage*, 72.

82. Eric Ives, *Life and Death of Anne Boleyn*, 83.

83. In his introduction to *The Great Tournament Role of Westminster,* Sidney Anglo also notes the decline in chivalric imagery toward the middle of the 1520s as the king started to become more absorbed by domestic politics (73).

84. Henry VIII's private letters to Anne Boleyn reveal a very different side to the king's wooing. Far from insisting on his authority, Henry adopts the more traditional persona of the lover seeking favor from his mistress. The first letter, for example, begins "My mistress and friend, I and my heart put ourselves in your hands, begging you to recommend them to your favor, and not to let absence lessen your affection to us" (35). I am grateful to Kevin Sharpe for this insight. The letters also evince a previously unsuspected linguistic playfulness. At the end of the fifth letter, Henry incorporated a message into his signature—"H seeks AB No Other Rex"—and he drew a little heart around "AB" (43). One finds the same, including the heart, at the end of the eleventh letter (55), and the twelfth concludes with a heart surrounding "AB" in between "H" and "R", but no message (57). Only an arrow is missing. If one did not know that their relationship would end with Anne's beheading, the effect would be charming (a term not often associated with Henry VIII).

by his rejecting beloved, Henry emphasizes the speaker's power. Fittingly, for a monarch, he describes himself as an "eagle" that "subdues each byrd that flyes," a fire that no metal can resist, a sun dazzling "the cleareste eyes." In accordance with the changes in the political imaginary, throughout this short lyric Henry assumes his domination of one and all. The "disdainers" of the earlier lyrics no longer need be acknowledged. Rather, the poem revels in the speaker's innate, supreme authority, an authority that is both political and phallic ("The hardest stones are peircede thro wyth tools"). Despite the clever turn at the end, suggesting that love transforms the monarchic speaker into a fool, there is no mistaking the superior position of this wooer, which is reinforced by the conditions of the lyric's performance. According to Harington's account, Henry did not perform the lyric himself, as he probably did "Pastime with good company" and "Though some say that youth rules me." Instead, "the sonnet was sunge to the Lady Ann at [the king's] commaundment." Truly, only "a King could write suche a sonnet."

To conclude, Henry's lyrics are not just the remnants of an early Tudor parlor game. Rather, they are as much a part of the political imaginary of the early Henrician court as Henry's tournaments and portraits, and they both reflect and instantiate the shifts in the figures of politics during this period. Most of the lyrics were written at the start of Henry's reign, and they directly and publicly respond to the anxieties caused by the crowning of a new king whose policies and personality differ radically from the previous monarch's. Faced with elders who disapproved of his actions, Henry used lyric verse as a medium for actively asserting royal authority and royal diplomacy. Henry's lyrics assert his power as much as Henry's successes in the tiltyard. The defensiveness of these lyrics, however, also demonstrates that Henry's domination of the court and of English policy was not yet complete. The ghost of Henry VII still hovered in the form of an iconographic style that did not yet distinguish the son from the father, and the counsellors retained from the father's regime. But as the 1520s progressed, Henry succeeded in exorcizing this ghost. The portraits now emphasized the king's regality and magnificence, and the coinage now bore Henry VIII's image, not one borrowed from his father. Henry VIII was now firmly in command, and the one lyric from this period reflects this. In this short piece of verse, Henry does not sue for grace; rather, he commands. Henry's final lyric thus reflects his political maturity and unquestioned dominance over the court. Finally, as much as we need to recognize the place of Henry's lyrics within the political forms and figures of his court, they also demonstrate how we need to alter the literary history of early modern England. Conventionally, discussions of Henrician verse begin (and end) with Wyatt and Surrey,[85] who are often credited not only with importing Italian forms into English verse, but also with using erotic terms to talk politics. The latter distinction more properly belongs, however, first to William Cornish, and then to Henry VIII—the first early modern "courtly makers" to "glaunce at greater matters" (as Puttenham put it) in lyric verse.[86]

---

85. See, for example, Sessions, "Literature and the Court," 229–31. Henry's lyrics are not included in the index of the *Cambridge History of Early Modern Literature,* in which Sessions's article appears, and Sessions repeats the canard about Henry's lyrics resounding "with the bluff jollity of a far less anxious court" (238).

86. Puttenham, *Arte of English Poesie,* 74, 53.

CHAPTER 2

Mary, Queen of Scots and the Poetics of Monarchy

Like Henry VIII, Mary Stuart wrote verses that combined the public and the private, and, again like Henry, Mary's verse almost always draws on her status as a monarch, but there the similarities end. As we saw in chapter 1, Henry VIII's verse harmonized with the political imaginary of early Tudor England, even as Henry shaped the imaginary to his own ends, and Mary's early verse, written during her brief reign as queen of France, harmonized with French ideas. But there was no such harmony once Mary returned to Scotland; indeed, her assumptions about religion and politics were fundamentally at odds with those dominant in Scotland. Most obviously, Mary was Catholic, and Scotland Protestant. Yet differences in religion, partly because Mary knew enough not to impose her religion on her subjects, were subordinated to differences over the proper role of the monarch and of women generally. Mary had absorbed French ideas of monarchy, namely, absolutism, just as she had absorbed the poetic models provided by the Pléiade. The two are not as distinct as they may seem, as Mary would also have absorbed the French tradition of monarchic verse, as practiced by François I (perhaps the most prolific of royal poets) and his sister, Marguerite de Navarre.[1] As for gender,

---

1. There are only two editions of François's poems: *Poésies et Correspondance du Roi François Ier,* ed. Champollion-Figeac; and *François Ier: Oeuvres Poétiques,* ed. Kane. On the politics of François's verse, see Middlebrook, "'Tout mon Office,'" 1132–34.

while one can find strong evidence of misogyny in French political thinking, Mary also had before her examples of exceedingly powerful, exceedingly intelligent women, in particular, her mother-in-law, Catherine de Medici, and Henri II's mistress, Diane de Poitiers. Unfortunately, Mary brought these concepts into a land that considered them inimical. Scotland's monarchy was far from absolute, and, as John Knox demonstrates, hardly open to notions of female independence. Yet the matter is even more complicated, as Mary initially governed Scotland in rough accordance with Scots norms: she subordinated herself to her male advisors and (initially) her husband, even while retaining her identity as queen. Nor did she impose Catholicism upon her subjects, or persecute anybody for their religion. However, once Bothwell arrived on the scene, Mary's actions so departed from Scots convention that they ultimately led to her political demise. The sonnets to Bothwell, as we shall see, reflect in small scale the sexual and political tensions that would justify her deposition.

I

Mary's early life in France shaped her future thinking and behavior in several significant ways. First, she acquired a powerful sense of herself as a monarch. Mary's position in the French court was so exalted that her future father-in-law, Henri II, decided that Mary should precede his own children on official occasions. As Jane Dunn observes, "Mary had been brought up to believe she was a precocious prodigy, irresistible as a beauty and beyond gainsaying as a queen."[2] John Guy, a much more skeptical biographer, also avers that Mary "accepted, even relished, her royal status."[3]

Second, in addition to showing that she read such authors as Plutarch, Plato, and Cicero, Mary's Latin themes (written when she was eleven and twelve) demonstrate particular attention to the accomplishments of women. Mary's tutor (we do not know his name) designated that fifteen of these sixty-four short compositions be devoted to the achievements of learned women. Mary doubtless had some exposure to the misogyny rippling through early modern culture, yet her teachers clearly wanted her to understand that women could be educated and powerful. The young Mary clearly absorbed the lesson: when she was not yet thirteen, Mary delivered an oration to the French court defending the education of women.[4]

---

2. Dunn, *Elizabeth and Mary,* 97.

3. Guy, *True Life,* 79.

4. Ibid., 71; and Fraser, *Mary Queen of Scots,* 49–50. Guy notes that nearly all of Mary's references come from a single source, a letter by Angelo Ambrogini of Montepulciano (*True Life,* 72), just as

Finally, Mary developed a love for French poetry, which she studied under Pierre de Ronsard, the chief poet of the Pléiade. As her contemporary and biographer, Pierre de Brantôme, writes, "Above all, she loved poetry and poets, especially M. de Ronsard, M. du Bellay, and M. de Mainson-Fleur, who all made beautiful poems and elegies upon her."[5] Furthermore, Brantôme continues, Mary "was a poet herself and composed verses, of which I have seen some that were fine and well done.... [Her poems were] beautiful and dainty."[6] In addition to its aesthetic virtues, Mary Stuart's early verse demonstrates that she absorbed the models provided by both the Pléiade and François I. Her poems assume her position as queen (although the contingency of her position also shapes the contours of her verse, in particular, the elegy on François II). Mary's first surviving poem, written in 1559, during her brief reign as queen of France, is, according to the headnote, a "quatrain écrit dans le livre de Messe de sa tante Anne de Lorraine, La duchesse d'Aerschot" (quatrain written in the Mass book of her aunt, Anne of Lorraine, the Duchess of Aerschot):

Si ce lieu est pour écrire ordonné
Ce qu'il vous plaît avoir en souvenance,
Je vous requiers que lieu me soit donné
Et que nul temps m'en ôte l'ordonnance.
Reine de France Marie

[If this place is ordained for writing
Because you are pleased by this souvenir,
I require that you give me this place,
And that Time never remove this edict.
Queen of France, Mary][7]

The poem begins with a subtle assertion of power, an act that shifts the initiative from her aunt back to Mary. If (Si) her aunt has "ordained" (ordonné) this space in the Mass book for writing, then Mary in turn "requires" that she reserve this space in perpetuity for herself. Rather than complying with someone else's commands, Mary has her aunt comply with her own as a

---

Montaiglon notes that a letter by Politianus contains nearly all the names of learned women in Mary's themes (xii). The question, however, is not whether Mary was widely read, but whether she imbibed a sense that a virtuous woman could also be learned and powerful, and the answer is clearly yes.

5. *Recueil des Dames* 72–73 (my translation).

6. Ibid, 73.

7. My text for this poem is from Robin Bell's collection *Bittersweet within My Heart,* 14. While the translation is my own, I have consulted Lisa Hopkins's rendering of the poem in "Writing to Control," 73.

condition for obeying the first one. Furthermore, Mary equally "requires" Time never to remove "this edict" (l'ordonnance), which may refer to the one issued by her aunt, but more likely to the one just issued by Mary. Furthermore, the use of "ordonné / ordonnance" not only anticipates, as Robin Bell suggests,[8] Mary's playing on "sujets / assujettie" in "Entre ses mains" (see below), but gives the poem a distinctly legislative air, as these terms describe the acts of monarchs or ruling bodies. In *An Alveary or Triple Dictionary, in English, Latin, and French* (1574), John Baret, for example, defines *ordonner* as "to establish: to ordeyne."[9] In his *Dictionarie of the French and English Tongues* (1611), Randle Cotgrave defines *ordonner* as "to ordaine, enact, order, decree," and *ordonnance* as "an ordinance; edict, order, decree, statute ...; A precept, appointment, commandment."[10] Jean Nicot's *Thresor de la Langue Française* (1606) is even more specific, giving as an example the following sentence: "*le Roy ordonna* de faire accoustrer une longue salle en laquelle le lendemain se trouva grand nombre de Seigneurs et Dames" [the king commanded that a large room be decorated in which the next day one would find a large number of lords and ladies].[11] Consequently, in the space of four short lines, Mary transforms herself from the person complying with another's orders into the person issuing orders. She moves from a subordinate to a superior position. As Lisa Hopkins notes, "Mary herself is *never* the subject of a command,"[12] which is proper for the woman who, as the final line underscores, is the queen of France (reine de France), and it is suggestive that Mary puts her position first and name second, implying a subtle privileging of the former.[13]

Mary's sense of herself as monarch in this poem echoes her image in the iconography, which emphasizes her regality and never subordinates her or Scotland. In the medal struck for the marriage of François and Mary, the two are portrayed facing each other and sharing a crown that combines the fleur-de-lis of France with the crosses of Scotland. The central position of the fleur-de-lis is balanced by the inscription, which privileges François and Mary's status as monarchs of Scotland over their position as next in line for the French crown: "FRAN ET MA GRR FRANCO SCOTOR DELPHIN

---

8. Bell, *Bittersweet within My Heart,* 14.

9. Baret, *An Alveary or Triple Dictionary, in English, Latin, and French,* http://leme.library.utoronto.ca/search/results.cfm (accessed 14 May 2007).

10. Cotgrave, *A Dictionarie of the French and English Tongues,* sig. LLLiiir.

11. In *Dictionnaires d'Autrefois: French Dictionaries of the 17th, 18th, 19th, and 20th Centuries,* http://colet.uchicago.edu/cgi-bin/dico1look.pl?strippedhw=ordonner (accessed 20 February 2007); my emphasis.

12. Hopkins, "Writing to Control," 75.

13. Ibid.

VIEN" (Francis and Mary, by the Grace of God, King and Queen of Scots, Dauphin [and Dauphinesse] of Vienne).[14] Similarly, a bust attributed to Ponce Jacquino and dating to c. 1559/60 portrays Mary with a closed, imperial crown made of linked fleurs-de-lis.[15]

In 1560, however, Mary's position suddenly and irrevocably changed with the death of her husband, François II.[16] The loss transcended the personal, because her position as France's monarch as well as the dynastic ambitions of the Guise family died along with her spouse. Mary could no longer style herself "reine de France," and she had to confront the fact that her erstwhile mother-in-law, Catherine de Medici, obviously had no love for her, a fact driven home when Catherine demanded the return of the crown jewels only one day after her son's demise, and then ordered a full inventory.[17] Mary found herself in a nightmarish situation, having lost three members of her immediate family (her mother, her father-in-law, Henri II, and her husband) in short order along with her place in the world, and her elegy on François II seems to reflect her desolation:

> En mon triste et doux chant,
> D'un ton fort lamantable,
> Je jette un deuil tranchant,
> De perte incomparable,
> Et en souspirs cuysans
> Passe mes meilleurs ans.

> [In my sweet and sad song,
> Of most lamenting tone,
> I look deeply
> At my incomparable loss,
> And in bitter sighs,
> I pass my best years.][18]

> (*ll. 1–6*)

---

14. Smailes and Thomson, *Queen's Image,* 25.

15. Ibid., 29.

16. In his report to Cecil, Throckmorton reminded Elizabeth's counsellor that diplomatic correspondence should now reflect Mary's new status: "The superscription of the Queen's letter to her ought to be to the Queen of Scotland and Dowager of France" (*CSPF,* 3, 424, item 774).

17. Fraser, *Mary Queen of Scots,* 109. Guy, on the other hand, posits that Mary voluntarily surrendered the jewels and left the royal apartments (*True Life,* 115–16).

18. Brantôme, *Recueil des Dames,* 75–77. Robin Bell includes this poem along with a translation in his collection (*Bittersweet within My Heart,* 16–20), but the Pléiade edition is more reliable. I have taken the translation from Jane Stevenson and Peter Davidson, eds., *Early Modern Women*

The poem reflects Mary's transformation from queen of France to queen dowager through the reversal of the language of command in the Mass book poem. Whereas in the earlier work, Mary takes control by "requiring" her aunt and time to obey her wishes (Je vous requires), now she forgoes requiring anything of anybody: "Et n'est rien si exquis / Qui de moy soit requis" (And there is no fine thing / Which I desire now, ll. 15–16). Her only subject now is the image of François embedded in her heart:

> Je ne vois autre objet,
> Pour beau qui se presente,
> A qui que soit subject
> Oncques mon coeur consente
>
> [I see no other thing
> As beautiful as he is not in it
> To no other matter
> Will my heart ever agree.]
> <div align="center">(<i>ll. 55–58</i>)</div>

At the same time this poem participates in a different sort of monarchic self-fashioning, as Mary refers, rather self-reflexively, to the paintings and drawing of herself "en deuil":

> J'ay au coeur et à l'oeil
> Un portraict et image
> Qui figure mon deuil
> En mon pasle visage,
> De viollettes taint,
> Qui est l'amoureux tainct.
>
> [In my heart and eyes
> I have a portrait and image
> Which represents my mourning
> And pale cheeks
> Of smothered roses
> Which were once the complexion of love.]
> <div align="center">(<i>ll. 25–30</i>)</div>

Poets: An Anthology, ed. Jane Stevenson and Peter Davidson (Oxford: Oxford University Press, 2001), 67–68.

The "portrait et image" that Mary refers to in this poem are likely the images of Mary "en deuil blanc" that were first created after the death of her mother, Mary of Guise, for the explicit purpose of diplomatic advantage.

According to the reports by Sir Nicholas Throckmorton, Elizabeth's ambassador to the French court, even though news of the death of the "Queen Dowager," Mary of Guise, reached France on 21 June, Mary was not told until a week later, 28 June, "whereupon the King and she have taken again their mourning weeds" (*CSPF,* 3, 254, item 233). Mary's grief, however, did not prevent her from participating in diplomacy, in particular, in an initiative to establish her own relations with Elizabeth. On 22 August, Throckmorton reported that Mary's uncle, the cardinal, said that "the French Queen was minded for a beginning to declare her good affection towards Elizabeth, to send her her picture, and to have the like of her" (*CSPF* 3, 248–49, item 446). As Louis Montrose notes, the exchange of portraits was an essential element "in the maintenance of cordial relations with the rulers of other states,"[19] and so, the chosen image was of more than casual significance. Significantly, Throckmorton and Mary discussed what sort of image would best accomplish her desire to cement relations with her cousin, and the ambassador suggested that a picture of Mary in mourning would have the greatest effect:

> "M.l'Ambassadeur," quoth she, "I perceive you like me better when I look sadly than when I look merrily, for it is told me that you desired to have me pictured when I wore the deuil." "No madam, not for that cause only," quoth Throckmorton, "but specially because your Majesty spoke more graciously and courteously to me in that apparel than you did at any time before, whensoever I have had to say with you." (*CSPF* 3, 251–53, item 446)

Consequently, Elizabeth received a portrait of Mary "en deuil," likely the original of the portrait now residing in the Royal Collection (fig. 10).[20]

The painting eschews the sort of iconography one consistently finds in Elizabeth's portraiture, such as the image painted around 1560 of an androgynous Elizabeth, "neither distinctly male nor distinctly female," which she sent to her suitor King Eric of Sweden.[21] Sarah Dunnigan observes that

---

19. Montrose, *Subject of Elizabeth,* 5. See also Strong, *Gloriana,* 22.

20. See Strong, *Tudor and Jacobean Portraits,* 1: 219–20. According to Lionel Cust, three versions of the "deuil blanc" portraits circulated in England, and two similar portraits entered the Royal Collection during the reign of Charles I (*Notes on the Authentic Portraits,* 53–55).

21. Frye, *Elizabeth I,* 36–37.

FIGURE 10.   François Clouet, Mary "en deuil" (The Royal Collection © 2009 Her Majesty Queen Elizabeth II)

"Mary was apotheosized into *la reine blanche,* pictorially and rhetorically."[22] Mary, however, participated in that process. She understood that her image "en deuil" was in itself a source of authority, that appearing "en deuil"

---

22. Dunnigan, *Eros and Poetry,* 23.

enhanced her cultural and diplomatic capital as much as, say, Elizabeth appearing festooned with pearls or as an androgyne. Mary sends Elizabeth the portrait Throckmorton wants less because she wants to memorialize her mother's loss or to publicize her grief than because it would be more politically efficacious in establishing an equal relationship with the English queen (*CSPF,* 3, 501, item 889). That Mary wanted to be known as the mourning queen is also supported by several drawings by François Clouet of Mary "in white mourning" (en deuil blanc) that likely date from after the death of her husband (see fig. 11).[23]

Mary's strategy clearly worked, according to at least two sources. In his "Elegie," Mary's old tutor, Pierre de Ronsard, attests that a portrait of Mary "en deuil" hung at Fountainbleau, where it became an object of his adoration and, possibly, others': "The thing I hold most rare—the ornament of my studies and my books—is that portrait which hallows the place like a sacred image enshrined in the temple of a great god."[24] Ronsard interprets the absence of any adornment, let alone the sort of elaborate iconography present in Elizabeth's portraiture, as enhancing Mary's natural beauty and her inherent authority: "Your lovely hands boast no ornament save their natural whiteness, your slender fingers, like saplings of unequal growth, bear no precious rings and your fair throat wears no finery but its natural pallor for a jewel."[25] Mary's first biographer, Brantôme, shares this view and notes that Mary "en deuil" became a work of art: "The whiteness of her face rivaled the whiteness of her veils, and in this contest artifice was the loser, the veils paling before the snows of her skin. And so a courtly poem was written, where the queen was pictured wearing the deuil."[26]

The elegy on François II participates in this construction of Mary's image in two ways. First, the poem continues in words the construction of Mary "en deuil" in the portraits, and for the same purpose—to increase Mary's prestige and authority by portraying her as, in Brantôme's words, "la triste

---

23. Guy believes that both the painting and the Clouet drawings were executed after the death of Mary's mother, but before the death of her husband (*True Life,* 109). Smailes and Duncan, however, date these works to the period immediately following Mary's loss of three members of her immediate family: Mary of Guise (her mother), Henri II (her father-in-law), and François II (her husband) (*Queen's Image,* 31).

24. "J'ay toutefois pour la chose plus rare / (Dont mon estude et mes livres je pare) / Vostre semblant qui fait honneur au lieu, / Comme on portrait fait honneur à son Dieu" ("À Elle-Mesme," ll. 5–8); Ronsard, *Oeuvres Complètes,* 2: 661. I have used the prose translation by Helen Smailes, in Smailes and Duncan, *Queen's Image,* 33.

25. Et vostre main de plus belles la belle / N'a rien sinon sa blancheur naturelle, / Et vos longs doights cinq rameaux inegaux / Ne sont pompeux de bagues ny d'anneaux, / Et la beauté de vostre gorge vive / N'a pour carquan se blancheur naïve / (ll. 13–18; trans. Smailes, *Queen's Image,* 33).

26. Quoted in Smailes and Duncan, *Queen's Image,* 33.

FIGURE 11.   François Clouet, Mary "en deuil blanc" (Bibliothèque Nationale de France; Bridgeman Art Library International)

Reyne" (a strategy that continued after her return to Scotland).[27] However, just as Mary's depiction "en deuil" in Clouet's drawings needs to seen in the context of Throckmorton's interview with her, the drawings and the poem

---

27. Brantôme, *Recueil des Dames,* 78. On 30 May 1562, Mary wrote to the "Laird of Ormiston" to inform him that either he or his son was to accompany the queen for her meeting with Elizabeth (which never happened). Her instructions included how to dress: "As all her train will be in 'dule,' he is to address such as be in his company after that sort" (*CSPF,* 5, 61, item 117).

should be seen as part of Mary's assertion of control over her marital affairs. While it may seem a little heartless, scheming and rumors of a second marriage started almost immediately after her husband's death. On 6 December, Throckmorton reported that "the house of Guise [want] to find the means to marry their niece to the said new King," and on 31 December he wrote to the Privy Council: "Now that death hath thus disposed of the late French King, whereby the Scottish Queen is left a widow, one of the special things your Lordships have to consider, and to have an eye to, is the marriage of that Queen" (*CSPF,* 3, 423, item 773; 472, item 883). In a note to Cecil the same day, Throckmorton asserts that "the Duke of Austria shall marry the Queen of Scotland" (*CSPF,* 3, 75, item 834), although ten days later he notes that "the Guises continue in their purpose for the Queen of Scotland's marriage with the Prince of Spain, and that the King of Navarre and the Constable are as earnest for the Earl of Arran" (*CSPF,* 3, 492, item 871). Other candidates for Mary's hand included the king of Denmark, the king of Sweden, the dukes of Ferrara and Bavaria, and the Holy Roman Emperor, Francis I.[28]

Mary, however, was not interested in marrying anybody, as a letter from the Lords of Scotland to the Privy Council makes clear: "That the Queen is not yet towards a marriage, what grief it is to her subjects and danger to the state" (*CSPF,* 3, 434, item 784). What is more, Mary decided that she ought to have the right to decide when and whom she would marry, if so minded. In mid-January 1561, Throckmorton reported to Elizabeth that Mary had sent four gentlemen into Scotland: "Their commission is to labour the Estates of Scotland that she may be at liberty to marry where and whom she lists, notwithstanding the clause in the late covenant of marriage, in which it is said that she, over-living the late French King, shall marry with the consent of the Estates of Scotland" (*CSPF,* 3, 501, item 889). A few days later, Throckmorton recorded that Mary had once agreed to abide by the original marriage contract but has now changed her mind: "The Queen of Scotland has changed her determination in treating with her subjects concerning her marriage" (*CSPF,* 3, 512, item 915).

Mary's assertion of sexual independence might have caused something of a crisis, given the French resistance to women in official positions of power. In a fascinating observation, Throckmorton noted that misogyny, not family hierarchy, would likely govern who would probably become the next monarch of France: "The government by all opinions will light upon the King

---

28. Guy, *True Life,* 117.

of Navarre, for they cannot like that the Queen Mother, being a woman, should have the pre-eminence in matters of state" (*CSPF,* 3, 470–71, item 832). Mary, however, balanced her assertions of sexual independence by fostering an image of piety and dutiful mourning; hence the declarations in her elegy of single-minded devotion to François's memory, and her sense of his spiritual presence:

> Sans cesse mon coeur sent
> Le regret d'un absent.

> [Ceaselessly my heart feels
> Sorrow for the one who is absent.]
> (*ll. 41–42*)

> Si je suis en repos,
> Sommeillant sur ma couche,
> J'oy qu'il me tient propos,
> Je le sens qu'il me touche[.]

> [If I am resting
> Sleeping on my couch,
> I hear him speaking to me,
> I feel him touch me[.]
> (*ll. 49–52*)

These lines implicitly signal to the Estates of Scotland, her Guise uncles, and everyone else that Mary has no interest in marrying, as she is still devoted to her late husband, even as she defies their desire to control "where and whom" she should marry. Fulfilling gender expectations in one direction thus allowed Mary to break them in another. Concerning Marguerite de Navarre and Louise de Savoie, Leah Middlebrook remarks that "it was essential that women who sought power in sixteenth-century Europe cultivate images of themselves as paragons of chastity and moral prudence,"[29] and I suggest that Mary's construction of herself as a paragon of grief in both word and image had the effect of defusing the threat to masculine authority posed by her assertion of independence.

---

29. Middlebrook, "'Tout mon Office,'" 1112.

II

When Mary arrived in Scotland in 1562 to begin her personal rule, she faced three seemingly insurmountable obstacles: her politics, her religion, and her gender. First, in theory, if not always in practice, the French monarchy was absolute, meaning that the monarch made the law, not the reverse. As Jean Bodin expresses it in *Six Livres de la République,* "The power of the law lies in him who has the sovereignty and who gives force to the law through the words, 'we have said and have ordained, we do say and ordain, etc.'"[30] While Bodin would not publish these ideas until 1576, it is clear that Mary believed that she was the absolute monarch of Scotland: as such, she not only had the right to marry "where and whom she lists," but could distribute the benefices of her realm without having to consult anybody else (*CSPF,* 3, 501, item 889). In 1566, Mary would assert in an essay defending the divine right of kings that "God has chosen kings and commanded the people to obey them," and while "princes and nobles" assist the monarch, they do not "dictate to them."[31] Mary's adherence to absolutism also entailed a positive revulsion against what she perceived as its opposite: republicanism. After the Chaseabout Raid (an uprising by the Earl of Moray sparked by Mary's marriage to Henry Stewart, Lord Darnley and so called because the rebels and the queen's forces never fought), Mary told the French ambassador, Michel de Castelnau, that Moray and his allies "were outright 'republicans'. . . set on destroying the 'ancient monarchy,' [setting in its place] a 'republic' in which sovereignty was vested in the nobles."[32]

The problem of politics overlapped almost perfectly with the second problem—religion—because, to state the obvious, Mary was Catholic, and Scotland officially Protestant. Mary also had good reason to view Protestants as inimical to the interests of monarchy generally, as in 1559 the Protestant lords suspended the regency of Mary's mother, the Catholic Mary of Guise, then called the Reformation Parliament in 1560, officially broke with Rome,

---

30. Bodin, *On Sovereignty,* 55. See also Figgis, *Divine Right of Kings,* 107–36.

31. "Essay on the Science of Government," *Queen Mary's Book,* ed. Arbuthnot, 133. Arbuthnot notes that the original is in the handwriting of Mary's secretary, Charles Nau, and was "very probably the outcome of an argument between himself and his royal mistress" (132 n. 1). At her trial, Mary would reassert her understanding of herself as "an absolute Queen," not accountable to anyone other than God: "She answered, That she was no subject, and rather would she die a thousand deaths than acknowledge herself a subject. . . . She protested, that she was no subject of the queen's, but had been and was a free and absolute queen, and not to be constrained to appear before Commissioners, or any other Judge whatsoever, for any cause whatsoever, save before God alone the highest Judge" (quoted in Lewis, *Trial of Mary Queen of Scots,* 96, 100).

32. Guy, *True Life,* 224.

and established Presbyterianism as the state religion. Furthermore, in 1562, the Scots Parliament issued "a new proclamation against the sayers or hearers of mass, to the great regret of the miserable Papists," Randolph told Cecil, since "the pain is death" (*CSPS,* 1, 630, item 1111). Mary was the only person in Scotland who could hear Mass legally.[33] (Ironically, this provision was couched in terms of rights theory, as the proclamation specifically exempted the queen: "reserving all wayes her owne libertie within her howse" [*CSPS,* 1, 630, item 1111].)

Finally, there was Mary's gender. While the "Querelle des Femmes" had been simmering since the fourteenth century, the ascension of the Catholic Mary Tudor instigated a series of contributions to the debate over women that specifically called into question the legitimacy of female rule. In 1558, Christopher Goodman, for example, rejected the legality of women's rule:

> For God is not contrarie to him self, which at the begynninge appointed the woman to be in subjection to her housbande, and the man to be the head of the woman (as saithe the Apostle) who wil not permitte so muche to the woman, as to speake in the Assumblie of men, muchelesse to be Ruler of a Realme or nation. Yf women be not permitted by Civile policies to rule in inferior offices, to be Counsellours, Pears of a realme, Justices, Shireffs, Bay lives [bailiffs] and such like: I make your selves judges, whither it be mete for them to governe whole Realmes and nations?[34]

And John Knox would publish his infamous *The First Blast of the Trumpet against the Monstrous Regiment of Women* that year. The prospects, in short, of a female, Catholic absolutist monarch in Scotland were not good.

And yet, against all odds, and against all expectation, Mary successfully negotiated these difficulties during the first years of her reign. Pace Jenny Wormald's argument that the Scots queen showed a criminal disregard for the responsibilities of monarchy,[35] Mary evinced a subtle understanding of diplomacy, the importance of symbolic gestures, and the limits on how far she could push fundamental beliefs without reaching the breaking point. For example, François II's untimely death threw into turmoil the moves toward

---

33. See also Burns, *True Law of Kingship,* 153–84.

34. Goodman, *How Superior Powers Oght to be Obeyd,* sig. d.iii.v. The marginal note reads: "The gouernment of women is against nature, and Gods ordinance."

35. "[Mary] had a very high sense of what was due to her as queen. What was apparently lacking was the recognition that there was something fundamental due from her" (Wormald, *Mary Queen of Scots,* 105).

ratifying the Treaty of Edinburgh, which provided for the removal of French troops from Scotland, pledged both England and France not to interfere in Scottish affairs, and declared that Mary and François (later, obviously, Mary alone) would abstain from using "the arms and style of the Queen of England," meaning that the French would abandon their claim to the English throne (*CSPF,* 3, 173, item 281).[36] In a particularly humiliating move, the treaty also specified that Mary (originally, Mary and François) would be held responsible for the implementation of the provisions (there is no equivalent clause for Elizabeth).[37] The Treaty of Edinburgh, it should be remembered, was negotiated by Mary's Guise uncles without the permission or even knowledge of the royal couple. Nonetheless, when Throckmorton asked the "Queen Mother," Catherine de Medici, where matters stood with the treaty, she disclaimed (with what sounds like unseemly schadenfreude) all responsibility for Scots affairs: "Since the King was dead," Catherine said, "it now was in the Queen of Scotland [i.e., Mary] to make answers for the matters of Scotland" (*CSPF,* 3, 468, item 832). The Constable of France, Anne de Montmorency, repeated Catherine's disavowal of responsibility for Scots affairs: "As for the matters of Scotland, it was in the Scottish Queen to answer" (*CSPF,* 3, 468, item 832).

Mary took in stride this sudden foisting of Scotland's problems upon her, and she skillfully parried Throckmorton's and the Earl of Bedford's entreaties for immediate ratification, even though, as Throckmorton reported, before her husband's demise "there was no great account made of her" (*CSPF,* 3, 472, item 833). Pressed by the two ambassadors to ratify the treaty immediately, Mary responded by demurring "that she was without counsel, the Cardinal of Lorraine [her uncle] being absent; and that the Queen advised her to take counsel of the wise men of her realm, none of whom were here" (*CSPF,* 3, 573, item 1030). When the Earl of Bedford offered that ratifying the treaty would demonstrate "her intent to embrace the Queen's amity," Mary added her youth to the reasons why she needed to delay: "She replied that she had no counsel, and that the matter was great for one of her years" (*CSPF,* 3, 573, item 1030). Throckmorton then astutely observed that Mary did indeed have counsel, in particular, her other uncle, the Duke of Guise, was in the next room, along with "others"; Mary responded that the treaty was concluded before her ascension to throne, and therefore, "she was not to be charged with anything that was done in her late husband's time, and

---

36. See also *CSPS,* 3, 442–44, items 851–55.

37. "In the said treaty the French King and Queen are by a special clause bound to the Queen of England to perform and keep the said covenants with the Scots" (*CSPF,* 3, 178, item 311).

that now she would be loath to do anything unadvisedly" (*CSPF,* 3, 573–74, item 1030).

Given the ideological, political, and religious barriers Mary faced, overt defiance of male diplomats at this juncture would not have been a wise move, even though, as we have seen, Mary asserted her independence in other areas. The difference is that while the question of marriage was, for the moment, abstract, the treaty was very concrete; bluntly declining its ratification would have antagonized England and, perhaps more importantly, likely further inflamed those who did not think any queen's authority legitimate. The scholarship on Elizabeth has repeatedly emphasized how she often turned gender expectations to her advantage,[38] and we can see Mary doing the same in this episode. Rather than confronting Elizabeth's ambassadors, rather than employing masculine aggression, Mary used the assumption that women are inferior, that they ought to be ruled by their male superiors (who are superior because they are male), to her advantage. Thus she puts off the very insistent Bedford and Throckmorton with the ruse that she must seek counsel first, as not only a ruler, but as a female ruler should. By appearing appropriately subservient to her male advisors, Mary not only mollifies those actively opposed to her rule but does so in a manner that gains her political and diplomatic advantage. (Ironically, the treaty would be ratified in 1587, the year of Mary's execution.)

Mary's awareness of gender politics also applied to her relations with Elizabeth. As Guy notes, Mary's campaign to arrange a meeting with Elizabeth to break the deadlock over the Treaty of Edinburgh constituted the primary objective of her diplomacy once she returned to Scotland.[39] Mary's advisor Lord James and her ambassador to England, William Maitland, had embarked on a concerted effort to break the impasse, with the former writing to Elizabeth and the latter addressing William Cecil. James proposed that Mary would relinquish her immediate claim to the English throne in return for recognition as Elizabeth's heir. Initially, Elizabeth agreed to appoint commissioners to renegotiate the treaty, but suddenly (doubtless to Cecil's relief, since he always considered Mary a threat to his queen's safety) Elizabeth reversed herself, because, as she told Maitland, naming an heir, any heir, would create trouble: "Princes cannot like their own children. Think you that I could love my own winding sheet?"[40] Consequently, Mary proposed a

---

38. See, for example, Frye, *Elizabeth I;* Montrose, *Subject of Elizabeth;* McLaren, *Political Culture;* Levin, *"Heart and Stomach of a King";* and Crane, "'Video and Taceo.'"

39. Guy, *True Life,* 152.

40. Ibid., 139–40, 151.

summit between the two monarchs, and initially Elizabeth agreed. By June 1562, preparations for a meeting between the two queens were proceeding apace, and Mary received a letter from Elizabeth that she found especially encouraging. Thomas Randolph, the English ambassador, describes her response: "[She] said above anything she desired to see her good sister; and next, that they might live like good sisters together, and that she purposed to send La Croc with a ring, with a diamond fashioned like a heart; that her meaning should be expressed in a few verses which the writer should see" (*CSPF,* 4, 101, item 201). While the French original of these verses has been lost, Thomas Chaloner printed a Latin version (which may be Mary's own translation) in his *De Republica Anglorum* (1579) under the title "Adamas Loquitur" (The Diamond Speaks):

> Non quia duritie superem ferrumque focumque,
> > Sculpta nec artificis glorior ipsa manu,
> Nec quia gemma nitens operoso cingar ab auro
> > Pura quidem, & Phoebi sydere candidior:
> Sed potius cordi similis mea forma, quod ipsum
> > Cor Dominæ, excepta duritie, exhibeat.
> Nam quod ab oppositis non vincitur, & sine *nævis*
> > Candida quod tota est, his ego, & illa, pareis
> Credere quis possit? Postquam me emiserat illa
> > Mi Dominam rursus posse placere *novam?*
> Sed placet: hoc faustæ fælix en debeo sorti,
> > Me Regina iterum, nec minor ista, tenet.
> O utinam ambarum bene possem adamantina vincla,
> > (Ore favete omnes) cordibus *injicere.*
> Que neque liuor edax, neque falsis acta susurris
> > Suspicio, aut caries temporis ulla, terant.
> Tunc ego ab Eois dicar celeberrima gazis,
> > Hic etiam gemmas vincere præcipuas.
> Tunc ego perstringam tremulo fulgore coruscans,
> > Adstantum immissis lumina seu *radiis.*
> Tunc ego seu pretio, seu quae me provocet arte,
> > Gemma, adamas firmo robore prima ferar.

> [Neither because I surpass both iron and flame in strength,
> > And fashioned by the hand of a craftsman, am I proud,
> nor, because I, a shining gem, surrounded with wrought gold,
> > am I spotless, indeed, and brighter than Phoebus' star:

but rather my form is like a heart, because it
> portrays—its hardness excluded—the very heart of my Lady.
For, because [she] is not conquered by her challengers, and because
> she is wholly brilliant without blemish, in these ways I and she
>> are equal.
Who could believe it? That, after that one [Mary] had sent me away,
> it is possible that a new Lady could please me?
But she does: happy, I surely owe this to lucky fortune,
> a queen again, and one no less than that one, holds me.
O would that I could bind the hearts of these two
> (All you look favorably on!) with adamantine bonds,
which neither destructive envy nor suspicion, roused by false
> whispers, or any decay over time, may weaken.
Then I will be called the most famous of Eastern riches,
> here even [be said] to surpass outstanding gems.
Then I, gleaming with tremulous flash, will dazzle the
> eyes of those standing by with my emitted rays.
Then I, whether because of my value or the skill that called me forth,
> shall I be considered a gem, the diamond best in firm strength.][41]

Assuming that the Latin translation is accurate, the poem is remarkable
for a number of reasons. First, "Adamas Loquitur" represents an innovation
in the tradition of monarchic verse. While Henry VIII and François I wrote
poems that did political work, so far as we can tell they intended their efforts
for more local audiences. Mary, on the other hand, decided to use verse as
other monarchs used portraits and other gifts. "Adamas Loquitur" thus represents the first time a monarch, certainly the first time a Tudor or a Stuart
monarch, used verse as an instrument of international diplomacy.

---

41. Sig.Z1r. I owe the translation of this poem to my colleague, Brad L. Cook, and I am
grateful for his invaluable help with this text. A translation by George Conn appeared in *Vita
Mariae Stuartae Scotiae Reginae* (Rome, 1624). The textual situation is further complicated by the
existence of a very similar Latin poem by Buchanan, which he says he wrote for Mary to accompany the gift of a diamond heart (*Queen Mary's Book,* ed. Arbuthnot, 174). It is impossible at this
distance to know whether Mary composed one poem and Buchanan another, or whether Buchanan is the original author. Chaloner's assertion in the headnote to this poem that he presents
a translation of the original French only adds another aspect to the mystery, as it is not clear
whether he presents his translation or Mary's: "TRANSLATIO QUORUNDAM CARminum
quae Gallico primum sermone conscripta, à [s]erenissma Scotiae Regina in mutuae amicitiae pig-
nus, unà cum excellentis operis ANNULO, in quo insignis adamas prominebat, ad Sereniss, Anglie
Reginam Elizabetham missa suerant" (A translation of certain verses first written in French, sent
by the most serene Scots Queen, along with a ring of most excellent workmanship, in which a
remarkable diamond was prominent, to the most serene Queen Elizabeth of England).

Even so, Mary is evidently aware of the conventions surrounding the conflation of erotic and political languages. Like such English courtier poets as Sir Thomas Wyatt and (later) Sir Philip Sidney, Mary uses the language of courtly love as a way of talking about diplomatic relations. Thus Mary's desire for the union of two hearts—"O utinam ambarum bene possem adamantina vincla, / (Ore favete omnes) cordibus injicere" (O would that I could bind the hearts of these two [All you look favorably on!] with adamantine bonds)—figures the desired alliance between England and Scotland. But there are two crucial differences. First, unlike Wyatt and Sidney, Mary is not addressing a coterie audience. She undoubtedly knew that her poem would be widely distributed among the diplomats of the English court, as was indeed the case. On 12 July 1562, the new English ambassador to Scotland, Sir Henry Killigrew, sent a letter to Robert Dudley that included a copy of the French verses (he refers to "these feaw versis in frenche which were sent our quyne"), suggesting that Dudley would do well to "make these speake Inglysche," and promising to send the Latin a bit later ("by the next I wyll send the Latin verses").[42] Second, Mary does not speak from a position of subservience. Thus the diamond will pass, not from person to person, or from lover to beloved, or even from lady to lady (domina-dominam), but from queen to queen: "Me Regina iterum, nec minor ista, tenet" (A queen again, and one no less than that one, holds me).

The poem also continues Mary's playing with gender roles and expectations when the "speaker"—the heart-shaped diamond—compares itself to Elizabeth's heart but immediately qualifies the comparison, which extends only to shape, not to content: "Sed potius cordi similis mea forma, quod ipsum / Cor Dominae, excepta duritie, exhibeat." The recipient is not, in other words, hard-hearted, like the traditional, rejecting beloved. She is not Dante's "domina petrosa" or Petrarch's "domina Laura." Presumably, her soft, or at least softer, heart suggests a greater amenability to the speaker's suit. However, if Elizabeth is the female object of desire in this poem, then Mary, by implication, occupies the position of the masculine lover, using verse to prosecute "his" suit and gain "his" lady's favor. The poem thus echoes Mary's penchant for exploring the limits of gender roles for both entertainment and politics. John Guy reports that Mary apparently enjoyed cross-dressing; she "liked to roam incognito with her Maries [the four ladies-in-waiting who were all named Marie] through the streets of Edinburgh

---

42. State Papers 12/23/53 (*CSPD,* 1, 202, item 53). See also *Queen Mary's Book,* ed. Arbuthnot, 174. I am extremely grateful to Mary Robertson of the Huntington Library for help in tracking down the microfilm of this letter and for her transcription of the contents.

wearing men's clothes."[43] Mary also imported this practice into her court entertainments, much to the surprise of the audience: "At a masque after a banquet in honor of the French ambassador, they appeared dressed as men again, causing shock and consternation."[44] Mary evidently conceived of her diplomacy with Elizabeth in these terms. When anybody broached the topic of marriage, Mary would respond, only partly in jest, "that she would have no else but Elizabeth."[45] Mary's implicit androgyny in this poem, however, also has distinctly monarchic resonances as well. François I was painted as a hermaphrodite, combining the attributes of five male and female deities,[46] and Elizabeth, c. 1560, sent King Eric of Sweden an androgynous portrait of herself, as noted above.[47] By simultaneously occupying the positions of female ruler and male suitor, Mary thus aligns herself with the Platonic idealization of androgyny as well as Elizabeth's representation of herself as combining both genders as a strategy for preempting the opposition to her challenges of traditional gender roles.

However, there is yet another aspect to this poem's manipulation of gender conventions. Throughout this text, Mary emphasizes the equality of the two monarchs. The jewel will pass, Mary writes, from queen to queen, from "Lady" to "Lady," and if the two hearts of the queens are joined "with adamantine bonds" (adamantina vincla), then they will form one jewel that "will dazzle the / eyes of those standing by with my emitted rays" (Tunc ego perstringam tremulo fulgore coruscans, / Adstantum immissis lumina seu radiis). Mary's emphasis on similitude echoes her consistent emphasis on the close relationship between herself and Elizabeth, which was undoubtedly intended to further Mary's claim as Elizabeth's heir. At the same time, it seems to have had two additional purposes.

First, while we know that the fates of these two queens would be spectacularly different, and that Mary's reputation would fall in almost inverse proportion to the rise of Elizabeth's, the matter would have appeared very differently in 1560. At that point, Mary had a great deal of cultural capital (partly enhanced, as we have seen, by her manipulation of the image of herself "en deuil"). She had a reputation, as Antonia Fraser notes, for being "modest, intelligent and anxious to do her best as a ruler by taking wise advice."[48]

43. Guy, *True* Life, 147.

44. Ibid.; Bingham, *Darnley*, 104.

45. Guy, 152.

46. On this portrait, see Wind, *Pagan Mysteries in the Renaissance*, 213–14; and Meyer, "Marguerite de Navarre."

47. See Frye, *Elizabeth I*, 36–37.

48. Fraser, *Mary Queen of Scots*, 113.

Elizabeth, on the other hand, enjoyed no such favor. One contemporary fumed: "Nothing is treated earnestly, and though all things go wrong they jest, and he who invents most ways of wasting time is regarded as one worthy of honour."[49] Throckmorton complained (with reference to the scandal surrounding the conveniently accidental death of Robert Dudley's wife) to the Marquis of Northampton about Elizabeth's parlous reputation in France: "One laugheth at us, another threateneth, another revileth the Queen. Some let not to say, What religion is this that a subject shall kill his wife, and the Prince not only bear withal but marry with him?" (*CSPF*, 3, 348, item 623). Mary's harping on the equivalence between the two monarchs, in both her diplomacy and her verse, seems intended to put Elizabeth in debt by implicitly transferring some of Mary's capital to Elizabeth.

Yet if in one sense the two queens enjoyed very different reputations, on another level, they faced the same problems and the same enemies, and Mary's poem continues her campaign to create a mutual bond with Elizabeth based upon gender. In his report to Elizabeth dated 22 August 1560, Throckmorton reports that Mary did something very unusual. Normally, Mary would speak to the English ambassador only in the presence of Catherine de Medici, and both would stand, signifying the formality of the interview. However, after Throckmorton talked with the various leaders in French politics, he was brought to Mary's chamber, where she received him without Catherine's presence, and instead of standing, "she was now set in a chair under her cloth of state, and would needs have him sit upon a low stool right before her" (*CSPF*, 3, 250, item 446). Mary evidently wanted to speak with Throckmorton alone, and in a more intimate setting. Throckmorton then repeated to Mary "that which he said to the King and Cardinal, touching the ratification" of the Treaty of Edinburgh (*CSPF*, 3, 250, item 446). Mary's response is especially interesting. At first, Mary acts the dutiful wife, subsuming her identity and will into her husband's: "She answered... that what the King, her husband, resolved in that matter, she would conform herself to"; yet Mary then asserted her own identity, her own agency. First, she did not answer, as one would expect, in French, but in "Scottish" (*CSPF*, 3, 250, item 446). Mary then embarked on what can only be called an independent diplomatic initiative to forge a relationship with Elizabeth that would run parallel to, yet independent of, Elizabeth's relationship with the other rulers of France (i.e., the Guise uncles and Catherine de Medici). Immediately

---

49. Quoted in Read, *Mr. Secretary Cecil and Queen Elizabeth*, 285.

after telling Throckmorton that "his will [i.e., her husband's], is mine," she proceeds to demonstrate that she very much has a will of her own:

> And, M. l'Ambassadeur, I have as much cause to esteem her [Elizabeth's] amity as any other, for I am the nearest kinswoman she hath, being both of us of one house and stock, the Queen, my good sister, coming of the brother and I of the sister, so as being issued out of the same race I have the same heart she hath.... And write unto her from me that as I am her nearest kinswoman, so I will for my part in all my doings make it good, looking for the like at her hands, and that we may strive which of us shall show most kindness to the other.... And though I be her sister, because I am a Queen as she is, which name worketh kindness between sisters, yet tell her that there is more betwixt her and me, for we be both of one blood, of one country, and in one island.... For my part I say nothing, M. l'Ambassadeur, (quoth she,) but I will perform it. (*CSPF,* 3, 250–51, item 446)

While Mary's emphasis on family, on "both of us of one house and stock," undoubtedly reflects her desire to be named Elizabeth's heir, Mary also seeks in her diplomacy to establish an independent relationship with Elizabeth based upon the mutuality of rank and gender—"I am a Queen as she is, which name worketh kindness between sisters." In subsequent correspondence, Mary continues to emphasize the equivalence between Elizabeth and herself. Answering Elizabeth's letter of condolence after François's death, Mary tells the ambassadors that "the Queen now shows the part of a good sister, whereof she has great need, she will endeavour to be even with her in goodwill" (*CSPF,* 3, 566, item 1030). Later that day, Mary summoned Bedford and Throckmorton for another exclusive audience, where she repeated that "there were more reasons to more perfect amity between them [Mary and Elizabeth] than any two Princes in Christendom, for they were both in one isle, of one language, the nearest kinswomen that each other had, and both Queens" (*CSPF,* 3, 573, item 1030). Mary's poem "Adamas Loquitur" renders exactly these sentiments into Latin elegiac meter, suggesting that the point of the exercise, as well as the point of their meeting, in Mary's mind, was not simply dynastic politics (although that obviously plays a significant role), but to forge a closer bond between the two monarchs on the basis of their mutual position as queens, that is, female rulers in a male world.

Nor was Mary alone in understanding that Elizabeth and she had a common bond in their gender. In 1565 the Dutch lawyer Peter Frarinus published *An Oration against the Unlawfull Insurrections of the Protestants* (translated into

FIGURE 12. Woodcut from Peter Frarinus, *An Oration against the Unlawfull Insurrections of the Protestants* (1566), sig. K7r. (By permission of the Folger Shakespeare Library)

English in 1566), which included, at the book's end, a woodcut illustrating Knox and Goodman's attacks on queenship (fig. 12). Significantly, while the woodcut nominally distinguishes between Knox and Goodman (they look alike, but the viewer is told which is which), there is no distinction between Mary and Elizabeth.[50] While Frarinus's larger point is to condemn Knox and Goodman as examples of the dangers Protestants pose to legitimate authority, the illustration also suggests how the misogynists do not distinguish between the two queens on the basis of religion. Rather, all that matters to them is gender. "Adamas Loquitur" suggests that the two queens take the lack of distinction between them on the part of their mutual antagonists and turn it into a strength.

At first, the poem and the gift appeared to have succeeded in their purpose. Despite Cecil's reservations, Elizabeth agreed to a meeting. Events in

---

50. See Walton's discussion of this image in *Catholic Queen, Protestant Patriarchy,* 42.

France, however, put an end to Mary's plans. After news arrived of the massacre of Protestants in the village of Vassey at the hands of the Duke of Guise, Elizabeth delayed the meeting until the following year, and once the Wars of Religion started in earnest three months later, as Guy writes, plans for a summit between the two queens were permanently shelved.[51] Mary then set about finding herself a proper husband, who turned out to be Lord Henry Darnley, the worst possible choice.

III

Mary's sonnets to Bothwell need to be seen in the context of her long march toward deposition in 1567, as they symbolize exactly how Mary finally overstepped the bounds of what the Scots political imaginary would allow. In the first years of her reign (1561–63), Mary was so reticent about exerting her authority that Frarinus considered it a scandal: "It were to long to rehearse, how the noble Queene of Scotland that now raigneth, was driven a great while to live like a poore privat women in her own Realme, to obey her own subjectes, and to doe no more then they gave her leave."[52] While Frarinus exaggerates the degree of Mary's subservience, it is true that she carefully avoided any confrontations with Knox or the Lords of the Congregation.[53] Faced with a resolutely Protestant culture that emphatically rejected absolutism, Mary decided against confrontation in either religion or politics. That policy, however, started to shift in 1563, when Mary started to assert herself as an independent monarch. While the immediate cause for this change was Mary's insistence on her right to choose her husband, the question of gender became inextricably bound up with the question of politics.

In the spring of 1565, John Knox inveighed against Mary's plans to marry Henry Darnley, because of his Catholicism, calling him "ane infidel (and all Papistis are infidellis)" and warning that allowing a Catholic to become "your Soverane" will "bring Goddis vengeance upoun the countrey, a plague upoun your self, and perchance ye shall do small conforte to your Soverane."[54] Mary then summoned Knox to appear before her for this sermon (which he admits offended both "Papistis and Protestantis"[55]), and the ensuing argument encapsulates the contrary assumptions of both parties. Mary assumed

---

51. Guy, *True Life*, 153–55.

52. Frarinus, *Oration*, sig. E6r (I have silently adopted the modern usage of i/j and u/v).

53. Walton, *Catholic Queen, Protestant Patriarchy*, 95. See also Donaldson, *All the Queen's Men*, 54–56.

54. Knox, *History of the Reformation*, 2: 385–86.

55. Ibid., 386.

that Knox had no right to advise the queen on this issue: "What have ye to do...with my marriage? Or what are ye within this Commonwealth?"[56] Knox replied (echoing his sermon):

> A subject borne within the same...Madam. And albeit I neather be Erle, Lord, nor Barroun within it, yitt hes God Maid me, (how abject that ever I be in your eyes,) a profitable member within the same....Whenoever that the Nobilitie of this Realme shall consent that ye be subject to ane unfaythfull husband [i.e., a husband belonging to the wrong faith, not adulterous], thei do as muche as in thame lyeth to rununce Christ, to banishe his treuth from thame, to betray the fredome of this Realme, and perchance shall in the end do small confort to your self.[57]

As Kristen Walton points out, Knox conceived of Mary's challenge to traditional gender roles in terms of Scotland's political structure as a commonwealth, "and as he was a subject of that commonwealth, the privilege of being concerned with the politics of the state was his due and therefore a right."[58] George Buchanan, despite his impassioned animus against Mary, nonetheless allows that the matter was more controversial, and in doing so, he reveals that while some people did not regard Mary's desire to marry who she would as problematic, others recognized that the stakes for a monarch's marriage are far higher than for the marriage of a commoner or even an aristocrat:

> The question now being widely discussed, whether a Queen, on the death of her husband, could marry any other she might choose, at her own discretion. Some thought a widowed Queen ought not to be denied the freedom allowed to the common people. Others, on the other hand, asserted that the case was different for an heiress to a kingdom, who by the same act took a husband to herself and King to the people. Many were of the opinion that it was more equitable that the people should choose a husband for a girl, then that a girl should choose a King for a whole people.[59]

---

56. Ibid., 387. See also Walton, *Catholic Queen, Protestant Patriarchy,* 107.
57. Knox, *History of the Reformation,* 387.
58. Walton, *Catholic Queen, Protestant Patriarchy,* 107–8.
59. Buchanan, *The Tyrannous Reign of Mary Stewart,* 85.

Mary, on the other hand, approached the matter from the opposite perspective. The Scots queen considered herself an absolute monarch, accountable only to God and not obligated to consult with anyone. Thus she decides,
as noted above, that contrary to her marriage contract, she remains "at liberty
to marry where and whom she lists," and that she will not negotiate "with
her subjects concerning her marriage" (*CSPF,* 3, 434, item 784; 501, item
889). Furthermore, Mary conflated her prerogatives as a monarch with her
prerogatives as a woman: after Elizabeth wrote to her opposing the marriage,
Mary replied that "it was in the power of women to choose themselves hus-
bands. That she had chosen the said Earl, and that she could not now set her
heart on another."[60] Mary was equally adamant with Elizabeth's ambassador,
John Thomworth, whom the English queen sent to Scotland to convince her
cousin not to marry Darnley. Mary tartly responded that she did not "en-
quire what order of government her good sister observed within her realm."
Even further, Elizabeth's meddling contravened Mary's status as an absolute
monarch: princes, she said, were "subject immediately to God, and to owe
account or reckoning of their doings to none other."[61]

In sum, Mary believed that as an absolute monarch and as a woman, she
had the right to choose a husband / king as she saw fit, regardless of what
anybody in Scotland or England thought of the matter. Knox and Buchanan,
on the other hand, regarded Mary as obligated to consult others, because
Scotland, as Buchanan would write, was ruled "according to written law and
the consent of the nobility," not by "the whims of one person,"[62] and equally
importantly, because women should be ruled by men.[63]

Faced with this seemingly irresolvable conflict, Mary retained her political acumen. She recognized that she could not completely defy Scotland's
political and gender norms, and so, as if to balance her inversion of gender
expectations in choosing a husband, she promoted Darnley as the dominant
partner in their marriage. She issued a proclamation ordering that Darnley
"be namit and sttylit King of this our Kingdome, and that all oure letters to
be direct eftir oure said marriage, swa to be completit, be in the names of
the said illuster Prince, our future husband, and us as King and Quene of
Scotland conjunctlie."[64] As the diction of this proclamation suggests ("King

---

60. "Father Edmund Hay to Father Polanco," in *Papal Negotiations,* 198; Walton, *Catholic Queen,
Protestant Patriarchy,* 125.

61. Quoted in Guy, *True Life,* 209.

62. Buchanan, *Tyrannous Reign,* 99.

63. Thus we face the paradoxical situation of absolutism, usually associated with tyranny, being
more open to women's rights than the constitutionalist position.

64. Quoted in Walton, *Catholic Queen, Protestant Patriarchy,* 126.

Figure 13.   Silver ryal, 1565 (© The Trustees of the British Museum / Art Resource, NY)

and Quene of Scotland"), Mary placed Darnley's name before hers on every document. Furthermore, Mary recognized the importance of promulgating images that would reassure her subjects of the conventionality of their monarch's marriage. Consequently, she "had coins minted with the faces of king and queen, listing *Henricus Rex* before *Maria Regina*" (fig. 13).[65] The only portrait of Mary and Darnley as king and queen of Scotland (at the time residing at Hardwick Hall) shows Mary slightly in the background with her hand resting on her husband's arm. Darnley, as if to emphasize his masculine authority, rests his hand on his sword.[66]

---

65. Ibid., 128.
66. Bingham, *Darnley,* 110.

FIGURE 14.   Silver medal, 1565 (© The Trustees of the British Museum)

Alas, the relationship soured even before they took their vows, partly because of Darnley's desire to be officially recognized as king of Scotland (the
Crown Matrimonial) and his insistence on acting as Mary's equal in state affairs.[67] Mary asserted her authority both political and symbolically. Randolph
reported to Cecil the inversion of traditional gender roles: "He [Darnley]
was wont in all writings to be first named, but now he is placed second."[68]
Mary even recalled the earlier coinage that placed her husband's name first,

---

67. According to the memoirs of Lord Herries, "The King had done some things and signed
papers without knowledge of the Queen...which she took not well. She though although she had
made her husband partner in the Government, she had not given the power absolutely into his
hands....She thought nothing should be done by him, in relation to affairs of state, without her
concurrence and knowledge" (quoted in Bingham, *Darnley,* 120).

68. Bingham, *Darnley,* 131.

replacing it with new coins that placed her name before the erstwhile king's, as exemplified by the medal shown in figure 14, which was also struck in 1565.[69] As Walton points out, "The Scottish queen was no longer content to play the role of a wife subordinate to her husband or of a queen on equal footing with her king. . . . [Instead] Mary took the role of the stronger, patriarchal figure ruling both kingdom and home, while she dismissed Darnley from his role in the Scottish government."[70] Whereas in the past Mary had played at cross-dressing,[71] and had hinted at adopting the male position in "Adamas Loquitur," now Mary had literally become "the king" by iconographically changing places with Darnley, and refusing to allow him any genuine authority. Rather than aligning with the dominant political imaginary, her imagery now challenged it.

Had the situation stopped here, Mary probably could have survived this crisis; especially since Darnley's politically reckless and personally odious behavior had made him thoroughly hated.[72] Her queenship could even have survived Darnley's murder, had she quickly found and prosecuted those responsible, since his absence made things easier for all concerned.[73] The final straw, however, was Mary's inexplicable, politically disastrous decision to favor and then marry James Hepburn, Lord of Bothwell;[74] these acts finally put Mary beyond the limits of what Scots culture would tolerate. While Knox may have "harangued" Mary about Darnley, and while many bridled at Mary's insistence on acting without consultation, the Scots political establishment accepted Mary's pursuit of him because Darnley had English royal blood in his veins, and so helped Mary's bid to be recognized as Elizabeth's heir. Darnley, notwithstanding his religion, remained within Scotland's national interest. But Bothwell was a different story, since he brought nothing to the table. His elevation irrevocably upset the delicate balance among the Scots nobles, leading to Mary's deposition. While the Casket Sonnets alone did not bring Mary down, they brought into sharp focus the confluence of gender and constitutional issues that would determine Mary's political fate; one observer, in fact, considered the sonnets the most damning piece of evidence, as we shall see below.

---

69. Ibid.; also 116–17. The recall was so successful that only two examples of the "Henricus et Maria" coin survived (116).

70. Walton, *Catholic Queen, Protestant Patriarchy*, 132–33.

71. See above.

72. On Darnley's bad behavior, see Guy, *True Life*, 200–207, 226–32; and Bingham, *Darnley*, 120–21.

73. Wormald, *Court, Kirk, and Community*, 143–44.

74. Guy, *True Life*, 302; Wormald, *Court, Kirk, and Community*, 143.

IV

The Casket Sonnets continue Mary's assertiveness, her adoption of the supposedly male prerogatives, in her erotic life. To state the obvious, Mary's gender precedes her political position,[75] and many critics have pointed out the inherent difficulties of a woman writing Petrarchan poetry. The early modern love lyric is a genre, according to Gary Waller, "entirely structured by male categories" and necessitating "the fixing of the female as a body which is the subject of power, requiring her passivity as the object of anguish or manipulation."[76] Or, as Anne Rosalind Jones puts it, "The amorous discourses available to [women] had been constructed by male writers, who represented women as the silent objects of love rather than its active, articulate pursuers."[77] Petrarchan verse is, arguably, a genre largely predicated upon the suppression of feminine voice and agency. But, as we have seen, Mary was anything but a silent object. Rather, for both Darnley and Bothwell, she was most certainly an active, articulate pursuer, and she continues this inversion of expectations in her love lyrics. Rather than portraying herself as either the passive recipient of male attentions or the passive mourner of an unconstant male (as, say, Mary Wroth does), Mary often adopts the masculine position of the active, desiring agent. As the anonymous translator of Mary's "French Sonnettes" remarks, "She here prefereth hir self in deserving to be beloved of Bothwell."[78]

First, Mary inverts the conventional understanding of constancy. As Jones points out, constancy was usually figured as a feminine trait associated with the *refusal* of sexual favors; constancy is supposed "to be admired or overcome by men's uses of rhetoric."[79] Mary, however, turns this convention on its head in a number of ways. As perhaps one would expect, Mary regularly constructs herself as a rock, unmoved and unmoveable in her love. The first sonnet, "O Dieux," begins by asking divine assistance in proving that her love does not seem "vain" to Bothwell but firm (ne luy semble vain / De mon amour & ferme affection),[80] and concludes with Mary asking, "What is

---

75. Sarah Dunnigan also notes that the subject of the Casket Sonnets is "female erotic desire," and that "their discovery arguably constitutes the most significant articulation of eros and poetry in sixteenth-century Scotland for it seemed that the moment eros was feminised, and rendered explicitly monarchical, Scotland entered political turmoil" (*Eros and Poetry,* 15).

76. Waller, "Struggling into Discourse," 248.

77. Jones, *Currency of Eros,* 1.

78. *Detectioun,* sig. Q.iii.

79. See Jones, "City Women and Their Audiences," 304.

80. All references to Mary's sonnets are to Buchanan's *Detectioune.* The translations are my own. I have enclosed in square brackets corrections to obvious printer errors.

left to prove my constancy?" (Que reste il plus pour prouver ma constance?). In "Entre ses mains," Mary asserts that her love will never change, no matter what "tempeste ou bonnace"—storm or fair weather—they face, and she concludes "Mon amour croist" by promising that she will soon prove to him "ma constance," and that Bothwell will find her (like Elizabeth) without change, *semper eadem:* "et sans changer me trouvera tout une."[81] In the third sonnet, "Elle pour son honneur," she accuses Lady Bothwell of misusing her "constancy" for her own "profit,"[82] and in "Vous la croyez," she once again accuses Bothwell of doubting her "ferme constance." The difference, however, is that Mary is not asserting her "constance" in chastity, but in erotic pursuit. Her purpose, as she says in "De vous je dis," is "to win you [Bothwell] in spite of all envy" (De vous gaigner maugré toute l'envie). Analogously to Louise Labé's addresses to a lover she thinks has abandoned her, Mary maneuvers "both inside and outside ideologies of the feminine" in order to win her lover back,[83] which brings us to Mary's second inversion of expectations.

Not only does Mary adopt the traditionally masculine position of the desiring lover, but she explicitly asserts that she will use masculine rather than feminine strategies to prove her "constance." Mary concludes "Entre ses mains," for instance, by saying that "he will know my constancy" (il cognoistra...ma constance) not by "my tears or feigned obedience" (Non par mes pleurs ou fainte obeyssance)—that is, through stereotypically feminine trickery or passivity—but by "various deeds" (Divers espreuve[s])—namely, through masculine action and straightforwardness. Mary repeats this desire to assert her masculine constancy in "Mon amour croist," when she again combines the assertion of constancy with assuming the male duty of seeking honor: "For him I wish to search for honor / And will do so much that he will truly know" (Pour luy je veux recercher la grandeur, / Et feray tant qu'en vray cognoistra) that Mary loves him. The emphasis, again, is on doing, on action, rather than passively hoping that Bothwell will leave his wife and return to her, and most of the poems include some reference to some action that Mary took on behalf of her love.[84] For Bothwell, she *leaves* her family, allies, and friends, she *risks* her

---

81. Given the strained relations between Elizabeth and Mary, one wonders if Mary intended to appropriate rhetoric of constancy for her own purposes.

82. The Anglo-Scots reads: "Sche useth constancy for hyr awin profit" (sig. R.iii).

83. Jones, "City Women and Their Audiences," 305.

84. Andrew Lang noted: "The queen throughout is much more the pursuer than the pursued. Bothwell is cold, careless, breaks promises, is contemptuously negligent, does not write, is suspicious, prefers his wedded wife to his mistress....The passion, in the Letters, is all on the side of Mary" (*Mystery of Mary Stuart,* 350–51).

name and conscience, and she *writes* about the differences between herself and her rival.[85]

The corollary of Mary's adoption of an active, masculine position is her explicit distancing of herself from traditionally feminine traits and methods. In "Vous la croyez," Mary accuses Bothwell of thinking of her as a "typical" woman:

> Vous la croyez, las trop je l'appercoy
> Et vous doutes de ma ferme constance,
> O mon seul bien & mon seul esperance,
> Et ne vous puis asseurer de ma foy
> Vous m'estimez legier qui le voy,
> Et si n'avez en moy nul asseurance
> Et soupconnez mon coeur sans apparence,
> Vous deffiant à trop grand tort de moy.
> Vous ignorez l'amour que je vous porte,
> Vous soupconnez qu'autre amour me transporte,
> Vous estimez mes parolles du vent,
> Vous depeignez de cire mon las coeur,
> Vous me pensez femme sans jugement.
> Et tout cela augmente mon ardeur.

> [You believe her, alas, too well I see you do
> And you doubt my firm constancy,
> O my sole wealth and my sole hope.
> And I cannot make you sure of my faith.
> I see that you judge me light,
> And so you do not have any confidence in me
> And you distrust my heart without any evidence,
> Your distrust does me great wrong
> You do not realize the love I bear for you.
> You suspect that some other love transports me.
> You consider my words mere wind.
> You think my heart malleable as wax.
> You think me a woman without judgment.
> And all this increases my passion.]

---

85. "Pour luy tous mes parentz j'ay quité, & amis," ("Pour luy aussie"); "J'ay hazardé pour luy & nom & conscience" ("O dieux"); "J'ay mis la main au papier pour escrire" ("Ne vous voyant").

Bothwell, in other words, assumes that Mary is fickle, that she is faithless, and, most interestingly, that she is not very smart, but the poem itself implies that Mary does not conform to these gender stereotypes, arguing that she is constant, that her heart is as solid as a rock, and that she is "une femme *avec* jugement."

However, if Mary consistently adopts the male role of the constant, ardent lover (while relegating Lady Jean Gordon to the realm of the feminine and the fictive), she assigns Bothwell the role of the *in*constant lover. In a complete reversal of the endless recitations of female inconstancy and male dependability, now Bothwell is the fickle one, whose loyalty and faith Mary is consistently uncertain of.[86] In "Et maintenant elle commence à voir," Mary asserts that Bothwell is now returning to his wife:

> Ses pleurs, ses plaincts remplis de fictions,
> Et ses hautz cris & lamentations,
> Ont tant gaigné qui par vous sont gardez
> Ses lettres escriptes ausquelz vous donnez foy
> Et si l'aymez & croyez plus que moy.

> [Her tears, her plaints filled with fictions,
> And her great cries and laments,
> Have so won you that you keep
> Her letters and believe them.
> And so you love and believe her more than me.]

And "Vous la croyez" plays on Mary turning the charge of inconstancy back at Bothwell: "You believe her, alas, too well I see you do/ And you doubt my firm constancy" (Vous la croyez, las trop je l'appercoy / Et vous doutez de ma ferme constance). The final, unfinished sonnet begins with Mary writing because Bothwell has not shown up, even though he promised he would: "Not seeing you, as you had promised, / I have put my hand to paper to write" (Ne vous voyant selon qu'avez promis / J'ay mis la main au papier pour escrire).

Along the same lines, the inversion of masculine and feminine positions also replicates the homosocial triangles illuminated by Eve Kosofsky Sedgwick.[87] Rather than exemplifying the male traffic in women, exemplified for Sedgwick by the first eighteen of Shakespeare's sonnets, Mary's minisequence

---

86. Dunnigan also notes that Mary's sonnets "boldly subvert the conventionally gendered, hierarchical relation in the European love lyric between the abject male lover and aloof, socially or politically, superior *donna*" (*Eros and Poetry*, 28).

87. Sedgwick, *Between Men*, 28–48.

exemplifies female traffic in men! The drama of the sequence lies both in Mary's expressions of explicitly physical desire for Bothwell and in her competition for Bothwell's affections with Lady Jean Gordon, the man's wife:

> [E]lle pour son honneur vous doibt obeyssance
> Moy vous obeyssant j'en puis recevoir blasme,
> N'estant, à mon regret, comme [e]lle vostre femme.

> [She, for her honor, owes you obedience
> I in obeying you can receive blame,
> Not being, to my regret, like her, your wife.]

As much as Mary clearly despises her rival, she still allows her the same agency that she grants herself. In "Et maintenant elle commence" (a poem we will return to below), rather than constructing her rival as a passive, suffering figure to whom Bothwell returns, Mary describes Lady Jean actively wooing her husband back:

> Et voudroit bien mon amy decevoir,
> Par les escriptz tout fardez de scavoir
> Qui pourtant n'est on son esprit croissant
> Ains emprunté de quelque autheur eluissant

> [And she would now deceive my beloved
> Through writings all painted with learning,
> Which could not have come from her mind
> But cribbed from some dazzling author]

Furthermore, offering another example of male inconstancy, the sonnet records that the "feigned" letters accomplish their task:

> Et ses hautz cris & lamentations,
> Ont tant gaigné qui par vous sont gardez
> Ses lettres escriptes ausquelz vous donnez foy
> Et si l'aymez & croyez plus que moy.

> [And her great cries and laments,
> Have so won you that you keep
> Her letters and believe them.
> And so you love and believe her more than me.]

Significantly, Bothwell responds in these sonnets, he does not initiate, and what's more, he responds to the traditional means used to "woo" women, namely, feigning. Ironically, he has done what Sidney's Astrophil so ardently wishes Stella would do: he has read, and she has obtained his pity and his grace.[88] Finally, it is worth noting that Bothwell, like Petrarch's Laura, and to a lesser extent, like Sidney's Stella, is silent. "The basic configuration" of Shakespeare's sequence, Sedgwick writes, "includes a stylized female who functions as a subject of action but not of thought," and Mary reverses this role.[89] In Mary's poetry, however, women act and men respond.[90] If Mary prefers herself as deserving of Bothwell's love, Bothwell is not the one doing the preferring. To invert Nancy Vickers's formulation, Mary's speech—really, Mary and Lady Gordon's speech—seems to require his silence.[91]

Finally, Mary contradicts the traditional roles assigned to women by including and privileging physical desire. It is significant that Mary refers to Bothwell as her "ami," calls herself "votre amie," and uses the verb "aimer" to describe her emotions; both the noun and the verb had erotic overtones. In 1611, Randle Cotgrave, for instance, would define "ami" thus: "A friend; a lover, a paramour; a loving mate, a deere companion."[92] And Mary uses the verb "aimer" specifically to describe sex. In addition to the already remarkable spectacle of an early modern woman writing explicitly erotic, as opposed to Neoplatonic, poetry, Mary also appropriates the standard Petrarchan trope of freezing/burning in "Quant vous l'aimiez" and deploys it toward a very different end:

> Quant vous l'aimiez elle usoit de froideur.
> Sy vous souffriez pour s'amour passion
> Qui vient d'aymer de trop d'affection,

---

88. "Pleasure might cause her read, reading might make her know, / Knowledge might pity win, and pity grace obtain" (*Sir Philip Sidney,* ed. Herman, 128).

89. Sedgwick, *Between Men,* 33.

90. Compare the role of passivity in Marguerite de Navarre's verse, which is linked to her faith in God (see Cottrell, *Grammar of Silence*). Even though everyone at the time, including her brother, François, recognized Marguerite's diplomatic abilities and importance, I am not aware of any studies of how Marguerite's position as queen shapes her verse. One possible reason for the concentration upon religion to the exclusion of politics might be, as Susan Snyder suggests, that the title Queen of Navarre "carried with it a fairly limited sovereignty, such power as there was residing with her husband Henri de Navarre, with the kingdom itself being largely under Spanish rule" (Snyder, "Guilty Sisters," 443). See also Gary Ferguson, *Mirroring Belief;* Prescott, "Pearl of the Valois," 61–76. I am grateful to François Rigolot for alerting me to this connection and bringing Cottrell's and Ferguson's books to my attention.

91. Vickers, "Diana Described," 108–9.

92. Cotgrave, *Dictionarie,* sig. Dv1r.

Son doig monstroit, la tristesse de coeur
N'ayant plaisir ne vostre grand ardeur

[When you made love to her, she lay frigid
So that you suffered a passionate love for her
That comes from loving with too much emotion,
Her finger showed her heart's discontent,
Taking no pleasure in your great ardor.]

The metaphor no longer describes the lover's divided internal state, nor does coldness signal the purity of the beloved's soul. Instead, Mary appropriates this trope to denounce Lady Gordon's frigidity (froideur), approve of Bothwell's performance in bed (his "grand ardeur"), imply her own sexual responsiveness, and conclude with some rather mean comments about Lady Jean Gordon's taste in clothes:

En ses habitz monstroit sans fiction
Qu'elle n'avoit paour qu'imperfection
Peust l'effacer hors de ce loyal coeur.

[In her clothes, she showed without fiction
That she never feared that poor taste
Would erase love from a loyal heart.]

And yet, as much as Mary challenges traditional gender roles, she also confirms them in the abuse she heaps upon Bothwell's wife. As we have seen, Mary asserts that Lady Jean Gordon uses "tears" (pleurs) and "feigned obedience" (fainte obeyssance) in order to manipulate Bothwell. Ironically, given that she is writing verse, Mary associates the feminine with falsity, and this assumption underlies one of the most remarkable poems in the sequence (although I have cited lines of this poem previously, because of its importance I quote the poem here in its entirety):

Et maintenant elle commence à voir
Qu'elle estoit bien de mauvais jugement
De n'estimer l'amour d'un tel amant
Et voudroit bien mon amy decevoir,
Par les escriptz tout fardez de sçavoir
Qui pourtant n'est on son esprit croissant
Ains emprunté de quelque autheur eluissant,

A faint tresbien un envoy sans l'avoir
Et toutefois ses parolles fardez,
Ses pleurs, ses plaincts remplis de fictions,
Et ses hautz cris & lamentations
Ont tant gaigné qui par vous sont gardez
Ses lettres escriptes ausquelz vous donnez foy
Et si l'aymez & croyez plus que moy.

[And now she starts to see
That she had very bad judgment
Not to value the love of such a lover;
And she would now deceive my beloved
Through writings all painted with learning,
Which could not have come from her mind
But cribbed from some dazzling author.
She crafted well a letter without having the brains.
And yet her filched words,
Her tears, her plaints filled with fictions,
And her great cries and laments
Have so won you that you keep
Her letters and believe them.]

Imitation in early modern culture is, of course, a massive and complicated topic. Even so, it is neither an exaggeration nor a simplification to assert that early modern poetics was primarily concerned with investigating the relationship between *imitatio* and originality, with the emphasis at the start on *imitatio.* According to Joel Spingarn, "The imitations of the classics became, in a word, the basis of literary creation [and] a dogma of literary criticism in the Cinquecento."[93] Mary, as noted above, certainly knew the poetry produced by the Pléiade, and Ronsard was her tutor. As one might expect, questions regarding the imitation of nature and classical writers, and the relationship between originality and imitation, figured significantly in the Pléiade's poetics. While Joachim du Bellay, for instance, argued for the importance of the vernacular and for the necessity of achieving a literature that would equal the accomplishments of the past, this had to be achieved through imitation, not through pure originality. The only way, he asserts in his *Défence et Illustration de la Langue Française,* that French can create its own achievement is through

---

93. Spingarn, *History of Literary Criticism,* 131; see also Kinney, *Continental Humanist Poetics,* 19 and passim.

imitation of the classical past: "Sans l'immitation des Grecz & Romains nous ne pouvons donner à nostre Langue l'excellence & lumiere des autres plus fameuses"; "le moyen de l'enrichir & illustrer... est l'imitation des Grecz & Romains."[94] Given the presence of Ronsard's works in Mary's library and his personal relationship with her, it is particularly significant that he, too, emphasized the importance of classical imitation for both young poets and himself. In the preface to the 1550 volume of his *Odes,* Ronsard proclaimed himself "imitateur des poetes Grecs" in that he "redit souvent memes mots, memes sentences, & memes trais de vers" [will frequently repeat the same words, the same sentences, and the same verse forms],[95] and in the *Hylas,* he compared himself to a bee, selecting the finest passages from different "flowers" and then fashioning his work from them.[96]

And yet, despite the conventional, if complex, valorization of imitation, Mary's sonnet condemns imitation as the refuge of an inferior mind. In so doing, Mary implicitly proposes a radically new relationship between imitation, originality, and composition that anticipates by about thirty years the Muse's injunction in *Astrophil and Stella,* sonnet 1, to "look in thy heart and write."[97] In direct contrast to the theories put forward by du Bellay and others, Mary represents drawing on other writers as pure theft and a sign of her rival's insincerity and lack of intelligence. In order to deceive her lover (Bothwell), Lady Gordon must resort to the literary products of someone who is really talented (an "autheur eluissant"). For Mary, imitation, the picking and choosing of the best passages, is relying on "stolen words" (parolles fardez), or, as the anonymous Anglo-Scots translator puts it, on "paintit learning."[98] According to Mary's sense of poetics, there has to be a correspondence between the writer's sentiments, the writer's abilities, and the words on the page. Consequently, she condemns Lady Gordon's use of words and phrases that could not have come from her mind, because, according to Mary, Lady Gordon does not have the brains (sans l'avoir) for such writing.

Interestingly, Mary accompanies her privileging of originality over imitation with a condemnation of fiction, which she associates with duplicity.[99] Just as Lady Gordon's words are stolen, her tears and sighs are "remplis de

---

94. Quoted in Castor, *Pléiade Poetics,* 67. On the complexities of du Bellay's views on imitation, see Margaret W. Ferguson, *Trials of Desires,* 23–28; and Cave, *Cornucopian Text,* 60–77.

95. Quoted in Castor, *Pléiade Poetics,* 71.

96. See *Hylas,* in *Oeuvres complètes,* ed. Laumonier, 15: 252).

97. Sonnet 1, *Astrophil and Stella,* ed. Herman.

98. Buchanan, *Detectioune,* sig. R.iiii. See also Dunnigan, *Eros and Poetry,* 21.

99. On Renaissance distrust of fiction, see Nelson, *Fact or Fiction;* and Herman, *Squitter-wits and Muse-haters.*

fictions," "full of dissimulation" in the Anglo-Scots,[100] and one finds the same dichotomy in other poems. In "De vous je dis," Mary asserts that her love for Bothwell is "no fiction" (nulle fiction); in "Quant vous l'aimiez," Lady Gordon's clothes show "without fiction" (sens fiction) her bad taste; and in "Entre ses mains," Mary asserts that Bothwell will know her constancy through concrete evidence, "not by a feigned obedience" (Non par... fainte obeyssance). Mary figures herself by contrast as the epitome of truth, whose words are original to her, not "stolen" or "cribbed" from someone else. From the perspective of feminist thought, Mary's constitution of herself as a desiring subject who privileges originality over copying sounds like an entirely positive challenge to the patriarchal construction of women as passive, intellectually deficient, generally inferior creatures. And yet, at the same time, Mary's "subjectification" of herself is highly problematic, even dangerous.

V

In "Wit and its Relation to the Unconscious," Sigmund Freud repeats an anecdote that nicely illustrates the complicated relationship between monarchy and subjectivity Louis XV commanded a cavalier to concoct a joke at his [the king's] expense. The king wanted to be the "subject" of the witticism. The courtier answered him with the clever bon mot "Le roi n'est pas sujet"— "The king is not a subject."[101] As we have seen, Mary never thought of herself as anything other than a woman, a queen, who had agency and desire, just as men do. In this sense, the courtier in Louis XV's court was wrong: le roi ou la reine est un suject; the queen most certainly is a subject. However, the problem is that subjectification can also entail exactly the opposite. The word itself, *sub-ject,* means "that which is *thrown under,*"[102] and the transformation into a "subject" can also mean the stripping away of agency, of personhood. The courtier meant that the French king is subject to, inferior to, nobody, that subjecthood is inimical to the very nature of monarchy, because the monarch is obeyed rather than obeys. Certainly, that is how Mary thought of herself. In Mary's sonnets, however, these two incompatible meanings collide. Mary's belief in her absolute monarchy grants her the language and the ability to equal masculine subjectivity. But, ironically, she uses this empowering subjectivity to *dis*-empower herself. That is to say, while Mary's political

---

100. Buchanan, *Detectioune,* sig. R.iiii.
101. Freud, 650. I found this anecdote in Kastan, *Shakespeare after Theory,* 109–10.
102. De Grazia, Quilligan, and Stallybrass, *Subject and Object,* 5.

subjectivity enabled her to assert her sexual subjectivity, her sexual subjectivity leads Mary to subjectify herself in the literal sense, to throw herself under someone else's will, with disastrous results. In the end, the monarch is not, *cannot* be, a subject.

While, as we have seen, Mary often refuses the passive role usually assigned to women, all of her actions are *for* Bothwell, never for herself, a fact that she emphasizes by reiterating the phrase "pour luy"—"for him"—in successive lines. In "O Dieux," the first sonnet, she repeats the phrase four times in the closing five lines:

> Pour luy tous mes amis j'estime moins que rien
> J'ay hazardé pour luy & nom & conscience:
> Je veux pour luy au monde renoncer:
> Je veux mourir pour luy avancer.
> Que reste il plus pour prouver ma constance?

> [For him I value all my friends as less than nothing
> And of my enemies I hope well.
> I have risked for him fame and conscience:
> I would for him renounce the world:
> I would die to advance him.
> What is left to prove my constancy?]

In "Mon amour croist," Mary begins three of the four lines of the concluding quatrain with the phrase:

> Pour luy jattendz toute bonne fortune.
> Pour luy je ve[u]x garder santé & vie.
> Pour luy tout vertu de suyvre j'ay envie,
> Et sans changer me trouvera tout une.

> [For him I await good fortune.
> For him I wish to keep good health and long life.
> For him I wish to follow each virtue,
> And he will find me always without change.]

To be sure, Mary's self-subjection, her consistent action "pour luy," constitutes another expression of her desire for Bothwell, and so an element of empowerment hovers over these lines. But the politics of Mary's self-subjection turn her acting "pour luy" into something completely different.

The problematic is also intimated by Mary's equally consistent use of the formal "vous" rather than the intimate "tu" to refer to Bothwell. While the rules for usage were not formalized until the seventeenth century, and while in medieval and some early modern French the two pronouns were used interchangeably, by the middle of the sixteenth century "vous" was increasingly associated with the court and used to signal a hierarchical relationship. One conventionally used "vous" to address a superior, not the opposite. For instance, Mary always used "vous" when addressing Elizabeth, in particular when submitting (or at least claiming that she is submitting) to Elizabeth's will.[103] Furthermore, the convention in love poetry seems to have been to use "tu" to signal intimacy. Pernette du Guillet, for instance, author of the very popular *Rymes* (1545), consistently addresses the object of her desire as "tu" in her epigrams.[104] And yet Mary without exception addresses Bothwell as "vous" rather than "tu." For example, she begins "Elle pour son honneur" as follows (my emphasis):

Elle pour son honneur *vous* doibt obeyssance
Moy *vous* obeyssant j'en puis recevoir blasme,
N'estát, à mon regret, comme elle *vostre* femme.

[She, for her honor, owes you obedience
I in obeying you can receive blame,
not being, to my regret, like her, your wife.]

She also uses and repeats "vous" and related forms in "Par vous mon coeur" (again, my emphasis):

Par *vous* mon coeur & par *vostre* alliance
Elle à remis sa maison en honneur
Elle à jouy par *vous* la grandeur
Dont tous les siens n'ayent nul asseurance

---

103. "Je me sousmetay à vos commandemants"; "Vous aurés fayt une profitable conqueste de moy" (quoted in Lang, *Mystery of Mary Stuart,* 352).

104. E.g., Epigram IV: "Ton eloquence, avecques ta faconde, / Et hault sçavoir, auquel tu es appris, / Demonstre assez le bien en toy compris" (Your eloquence and your eloquent speech / And the high learning you devote yourself to / Show forth love's height, summed up in you); Pernette du Guillet, *Rymes,* ed. Graham, 11; translation by Jones, "Lyonnais Neoplatonist," 224. François Rigolot informs me that Labé's personae also use "tu," although she "sometimes shifts from 'tu' to 'vous' when she wants to distance herself from her unfaithful lover" (personal communication). Pernette du Guillet will also occasionally use "vous," as in Chanson IX (Je suis le Journée / Vous, Amy, le Jour; I am the Daytime / You, my love, the day; in *Rymes,* 82; translated by Jones, "Lyonnais Neoplatonist," 226), but she mostly employs the less formal "tu."

De *vous* mon bien elle à eu la constance,
Et à gaigné pour un temps *vostre* coeur.
Par *vous* elle à eu plaisir en bon heur,
Et pour *vous* à receu honneur & reverence,
Et n'a perdu sinon la jouyssance
D'un fascheux sot qu'elle aymoit cherement

[Through you, my love, and through your marriage,
She restored honor to her house.
She enjoyed through you such greatness
Of which her family never had assurance.
From you, my love, she has had constancy
And for a while won your heart.
From you she had pleasure and good fortune,
And from you she received honor and reverence;
And she lost nothing but the pleasures
Of a tiresome fool she once loved dearly.]

Certainly, Mary's use of "vous" rather than "tu," along with her repeated declarations that she does everything "pour luy," for her man, could be construed as an almost classic example of the "subversion-containment" paradigm explored in Stephen J. Greenblatt's earlier work.[105] By using "vous," which implies respect, distance, and the authority of the addressee, Mary contains her subversions of gender roles and gender relations by reconfirming masculine superiority, exactly as she blunted the challenges to masculine authority in her pursuit of Darnley by literally reinscribing him as her superior. Bothwell may be the (silenced) object of her expressed sexual desire, but she still refers to him as a superior. Even so, the connotations are, I think, more politically explosive than simply illustrating Mary's manipulation of early modern gender codes.

At several points in her sequence Mary invokes a cliché of Petrarchan discourse: the avowal of service and obedience to the beloved. The formula is especially clear in "De vous je dis":

De vous je dis seul soustien de ma vie
Tant seulement je cerche m'asseurer,
Et si ose de moy tant presumer

---

105. The "subversion-containment" model received its fullest articulation in Greenblatt's influential essay "Invisible Bullets," 21–65.

De vous gaigner magré toute l'envie.
Car c'est le seul desir de vostre chere amie,
De vous servir & loyaument aymer,
Et tous malheurs moins que riens estimer,
Et vostre volunté de la mien [suivre].
Vous cognoistrez avecques obeyssance
De mon loyal devoir n'omettant lascience
Aquoy je [estudiray] pour toujiurs vous complaire,
Sans aymer rien que vous, soubz la subjection,
De qui je veux sans nulle fiction
Vivre & mourir & à ce je obtempere

[Of you, I say, the sole support of my life,
I only seek an assured commitment,
And yet I dare presume so much of myself
To win you in spite of all envy.
Because the sole desire of your dear lover
Is to serve and loyally love you
And to consider all misfortunes less than nothing.
And for my will to follow yours.
By this, you will know the obedience
In my loyal devotion, never forgetting
Always to study how best to please you,
Loving nothing but you, under the subjection
Of the one whom I, with no fiction,
Live and die for, and obey.]

Mary once more puts herself in the active position by daring "To win you in
spite of all envy" (De vous gaigner magré toute l'envie). But having constituted herself as a subject in terms of agency, she reverses herself by declaring
herself Bothwell's "subject." Furthermore, she asserts in this sonnet that her
sole desire is to "serve" (De vous servir) and "obey" Bothwell. In "Elle pour
son honneur," Mary does the same: "Moy vous obeyssant."[106]

Mary's language here would be perfectly unexceptional if she occupied
the conventional subject position of the sonneteer. As Marotti points out
in "'Love is not love,'" "Rivalry with peers for status, money and power

---

106. Mary draws a contrast with Bothwell's wife, who *owes* Bothwell the deference of a wife/
servant to a husband/lord (Elle pour son honneur vous doibt obeisance).

could be fictionalized as the wooing of a woman of superior station."[107]
And it is not only a woman, as Wyatt's love letter to Henry VIII, "Tagus,
Farewell," demonstrates. This language, in other words, conventionally reflects the speaker's subservient status, be it erotically, politically, or both. Thus
Mary is doing considerably more than reinscribing masculine superiority
and feminine inferiority. Her adoption of what for anybody else (anybody,
that is to say, who is not a monarch) would have been a purely conventional
position implicitly entails Mary's abandonment of the superior position of
monarch, to which Mary draws attention by concluding her poem with the
verb "obtempère," which Cotgrave defines as to "obey" and "to be at the
commaund of."[108] Needless to say, absolute monarchs were not supposed to
"be at the commaund of" anybody (except God). As Mary told Throckmorton in 1561, "God commandeth subjects to be obedient to their princes,
and commandeth princes to read His law and govern themselves thereby, and
the people committed to their charges."[109] Subjects obey, princes govern, not
vice versa.

But if these lines gain their power from Mary's privileging of her erotic
subjectivity over her political identity, at other times in the sequence, Mary
employs the opposite strategy of explicitly using her monarchic power in
order to entice her lover. Mary ends "Pour luy aussi" by stating that she has
"gambled rank and conscience" (j'ay hazardè grandeur & conscience) for
Bothwell for one end alone: "l'alliance." The translation of this term is tricky,
as it can refer to marriage or friendship. Mary herself uses the word in the
former sense in "Par vous mon coeur" when she disparagingly says that Lady
Jean Gordon received everything from her marriage to Bothwell: "Through
you, my love, and through your marriage / She restored honor to her house"
(Par vous mon coeur & par vostre alliance / Elle à remis sa maison en honneur). Using this sense, the final line of "Pour luy aussi," "Brief de vous seul
je cerche [cherche] l'alliance," could be construed as meaning "In short,
I have sought to marry you alone." But "alliance" could also mean political alliance, and that may have been its primary meaning during the Renaissance.
Cotgrave, for instance, gives the following definition: "Alliance; confedera-
tion, fellowship, combination; agreement, consent; a league of friendship."[110]
Edmond Huguet's *Dictionnaire de la Langue Française du Seizième Siècle* gives

---

107. Marotti, "'Love is not love,'" 398.
108. Cotgrave, *Dictionarie*, sig. Kkk iiiiv.
109. Throckmorton to Elizabeth, 23 June 1561 (quoted in *Queen Mary's Book*, ed. Arbuthnot,
137); see also *CSPF*, 4, 151, item 265.
110. Cotgrave, *A Dictionarie*, sig. D iiiir.

Rabelais as an example of this meaning's currency: "Comment Pantagruel arriva en l'isle Ennaisin et des etranges alliances du pays." Moreover, the Anglo-Scots translation of this line is "I seke the aliance of you onely,"[111] which suggests that for the anonymous translator, Mary is seeking something more along the lines of a political alignment than something more private. For Mary to "cerche l'alliance" with Bothwell alone, therefore, casts the personal into the arena of state, which makes perfect sense, as a monarch's marriage *is* a matter of state, and her desire to marry Bothwell is a political matter that will have serious political consequences. Mary signals her awareness of this in "O Dieux" when she asserts: "I would die to advance him" (Je veux mourir pour luy avancer). Given the fact that the author of these lines was the queen, however embattled, of Scotland, one must assume that "avancer" means political advancement, such as honors at court, peerages, money, political influence, and so on not only for Bothwell, but for his family and followers. Mary's language, in sum, demonstrates her awareness (at some level) that her personal desires are in fact an intervention into the complicated morass of Scottish factional politics, and this is certainly how her nobles interpreted her seeking an "alliance" with James Hepburn, Earl of Bothwell.

Without diminishing in any way the man's culpability in the murder of Darnley, Mary's husband, the objection among the aristocracy to Bothwell's marrying the queen arose less from horror at the blood on his hands and more from his having destroyed the delicate balance of power among Scotland's constantly feuding nobles. Although Bothwell's family had a history of trying to rise by wooing widowed queens,[112] it had not counted on the problems resulting from success. With Bothwell's marriage and his promotion to Duke of Orkney came of course the rise of his friends and family;[113] yet the Scots nobility were more concerned with Bothwell's sudden increase of power over them than with avenging Darnley's untimely demise. Notwithstanding their earlier support of Bothwell's marriage to the queen,

> the forces of aristocratic reaction were coalescing against his meteoric rise. Furious at the realization that Bothwell—one of their own number—had made himself a virtual dictator, on 1 May a party of dissidents gathered at Stirling. They vowed in yet another communal

---

111. Buchanan, *Detectioune,* sig. Siv.

112. Wormald, *Mary Queen of Scots,* 45.

113. "At his investiture, four of his followers were, as was customary, knighted. His cousin, James Cockburn of Langton; the Captain of Dunbar, Patrick Hay of Whitelaw; the nominee for Edinburgh Castle, Patrick Hepburn of Beaston; and James Ormiston of the ilk, better known as the Black Laird, were chosen for the accolade" (Gore-Browne, *Lord Bothwell and Mary Queen of Scots,* 355).

bond to strive by all means in their power to set their queen at liberty, and defend her son Prince James.... The pattern of Scottish politics was forming once more into the same shapes of family alliances and feuds, in which the power of one noble could not be allowed to grow unchecked.[114]

Doubtless, there is considerable truth to Bothwell's challenge to the confederate lords who were about to separate him from Mary: "What harm have I done them? I never wished to displease any, but have sought to gratify them all. Their words proceed from envy of my favour. But Fortune is free to any who can win her. There is not a man of them but wishes himself in my place!"[115]

When, therefore, Mary writes the following quatrain, she is not only explicitly invoking her position as queen; she uses her authority to promise exactly what her nobility feared most:

> Entre ses mains & en son plein pouvoir
> Je metz mon filz, mon honneur, & ma vie,
> Mon païs, mes subjectz, mon ame assubjectie
> Est tout à luy.

> [Into his hands and his absolute power
> I place my son, my honor and my life,
> My country, my subjects, my subjected soul
> Are all for him.[116]]

What seems to be extreme rhetoric also has extreme political consequences. First, this sonnet assumes that Mary's country and her subjects are indeed hers to give, thus replaying on a small scale the conflict between Mary's absolutism and the constitutionalism that flared when Mary married Darnley. As Buchanan writes, many objected to her taking Darnley as husband because she did so by her own authority: "They had put a herald in the place of the council, and made a proclamation instead of consulting the council."[117] Rather than being governed by law and precedent, Mary was "a ruler whose

114. Fraser, *Mary Queen of Scots,* 320.

115. Quoted in Gore-Browne, *Lord Bothwell and Mary Queen of Scots,* 375–76.

116. Dunnigan notes how this passage "conceives the transference of 'powre' in literal and metaphorical terms: erotic submission enfolds within it the political" (*Eros and Poetry,* 39).

117. Buchanan, *Tyrannous Reign,* 87.

own will was to be the law," and the kingdom "was not accustomed to be ruled by the whims of one person, but according to the written law and the consent of the nobility."[118] We also need to remember that "mon filz" refers to the future James VI, and the country she offers to place in his hands is not an abstraction, as in Edward Dyer's "My mind to me a kingdom is," but a very real place. Furthermore, in this poem Mary goes well beyond the power-sharing arrangement she had in mind with Darnley. According to the memoirs of Lord Herries, Mary objected to her husband signing official papers without her knowledge or consent, because "she thought that although she had made her husband partner in the Government, she had not given the power absolutely into his hands."[119] In "Entre ses mains," on the other hand, Mary places into Bothwell's hands her son, her country, and her subjects. She offers to place power, in short, "absolutely into his hands."

This is an offer that only a queen can make, and yet, paradoxically, Mary uses her position as monarch to undermine her position as monarch. Whereas Henry VIII used the lyric as one of many strategies for increasing his power, Mary uses poetry to articulate her personal subjectivity while destroying her political subjectivity. Moreover, Mary clearly knows this, and her sonnets play on their employment of seemingly cliché devices that suddenly seem very different when articulated by a monarch. Promises of advancement and declarations of loyal service cannot be taken very seriously when given by a struggling courtier; but they have to be taken seriously when put forward by a monarch, even more so when the monarch offers to make the Hepburns Scotland's royal family without the consent of the nobles and Parliament. The same applies to Mary's avowals of loyal service, since they invert the conventional relationship between subject and monarch. Bothwell ought to be declaring *his* desire to serve his queen, not the other way around. Doubtless, many factors contributed to Mary's deposition, yet her verse did its part in ensuring her political demise. When the Casket Letters were finally made public in Buchanan's *Ane Detectioun of the Duinges of Marie, Quene of Scottes* (1571), La Mothe-Fénelon, the French ambassador to England, wrote that "rhymes in French had been added which are worse than all the rest."[120]

---

118. Ibid., 126, 99.
119. Quoted in Bingham, *Darnley,* 120.
120. Quoted in Mahon, *Indictment of Mary Queen of Scots,* 25.

❦ CHAPTER 3

Elizabeth I, Privacy, and the Performance of Monarchic Verse

There is a fascinating disconnect between the lavish praise heaped on Elizabeth's verse by her contemporaries and its subsequent near neglect by literary critics and historians. The dedicatory epistle to Jan Van der Noot's *Theatre for Worldlings (1569),* for instance, proclaims that Elizabeth, instructed by "Apollo and his nine sisters...in the divine Arte of Poetrie...may woorthily be called the second *Sappho*"[1] and George Puttenham, in *The Arte of English Poesie* (1589) extravagantly praised Elizabeth's "learned, delicate, noble Muse [which] easily surmounteth all the rest that have written before her time or since,"[2] a passage that Francis Meres copied, nearly verbatim, into his 1598 "Comparative Discourse of our English Poets with the Greeke, Latine and Italian Poets."[3] To be sure, one of the many enduring mysteries of Queen Elizabeth (to appropriate the title of a an edited collection) concerns the difficulty of understanding the foundation of Elizabeth's reputation. The number of poems we can confidently attribute to her is not great, a problem noted as early as the seventeenth century, when Thomas Heywood wrote in his *Gynaikeion* that he had "seene some" of Elizabeth's "pleasant Fancies, and ingenious Ditties," but had "heard of

---

1. Jan Van der Noot, *Theatre for Worldlings* (London, 1569), sigs. A.iiiir–A5v.
2. Puttenham, *Arte of English Poesie,* 77.
3. Meres, *Palladis Tamia,* 2: 321.

many" more.[4] Marcus, Mueller, and Rose include only fifteen poems in *Elizabeth I: Collected Works,* and Steven May reduces that number to nine for his edition (while including three "possible" poems).[5] Only three poems—all written before she became queen—were published (without Elizabeth's permission) during her life;[6] the rest circulated in manuscript, some during her life, others after; and some poems present almost insoluble problems of attribution. Perhaps as result, very few literary critics have paid significant attention to Elizabeth's verse,[7] even if their projects seem to invite a consideration of this topic.[8]

And yet the small size of Elizabeth's canon and the attendant textual issues should not obscure either the degree of Elizabeth's poetic accomplishment or the importance of her verse for understanding the dynamics of authority during her reign. Like her father, Henry VIII, and her cousins, Mary Stuart and James Stuart, Elizabeth knew how to use verse as a public vehicle for monarchic image-making. The verse exchanges with Sir Walter Ralegh and the German diplomat, Paul Melissus, along with the "hymn" on the sinking of the Armada, reflect and shape Elizabeth's position as queen of England for both the court and an international audience.[9] But unlike the other royal

---

4. Heywood, *Gynaikeion,* sig. Mm2v. The full title of this work is *Gynaikeion: or, Nine bookes of various history, Concerninge women inscribed by ye names of ye nine Muses.*

5. MMR, 45–47, 132–34, 299–309, 409–22; and *Queen Elizabeth I,* ed. May, 1–30.

6. *The Glass of the Sinful Soul,* Elizabeth's 1544 translation of Marguerite de Navarre's *Miroir de l'âme pécheresse,* was first published by John Bale in 1548, and then reprinted in 1568–69, 1582, and 1590. The Woodstock prison poems found their way into John Foxe's 1563 *Acts and Monuments* and the 1587 *Holinshed's 'Chronicles.'* "The doubt of future foes" appeared in Puttenham's *Arte of English Poesie* (1589). Curiously, *The Glass of the Sinful Soul,* composed when Elizabeth was eleven years old and had no assurance (or even idea) that she would become England's queen, has attracted the most critical attention of all her poetic works. See Quilligan, *Incest and Agency,* 33–75; Brown, "Translation and the Definition of Sovereignty"; Shell, *Elizabeth's Glass;* and Prescott, "Pearl of the Valois," 61–76.

7. The few substantive treatments of Elizabeth's verse include Ilona Bell, "Elizabeth Tudor: Poet"; Summit, "'The Arte of a Ladies Penne': Elizabeth I and the Poetics of Queenship"; Jordan, "States of Blindness: Doubt, Justice, and Constancy in Elizabeth I's 'Avec l'aveugler si estrange'"; Marcus, "Queen Elizabeth I as Public and Private Poet"; Mueller, "Elizabeth I: Poet of Dangers"; and Mueller, "Queen Elizabeth I." See also May, "Recent Studies," 283–84.

8. For example, even though Peter Beal and Grace Ioppolo, the editors of *Elizabeth I and the Culture of Writing* (London: British Library, 2007), preface their collection by asserting that Elizabeth I "lived immersed in a culture of writing, one in which she herself participated and which to some degree she helped to create" (xiii), the volume contains no separate analysis of Elizabeth's verse. Montrose (*Subject of Elizabeth*) similarly avoids the topic, as do the contributors to Doran and Freeman, eds., *Myth of Elizabeth.*

9. Frye speculates that "would like have [her poems read] publicly, if only to a private audience" (*Elizabeth I,* 110). But unlike the scenario described by Sir John Harington concerning Henry VIII and his song to Anne Boleyn (see above, chapter 1), we have—with one major exception, the Armada hymn—no evidence that Elizabeth commanded the public performance of her verse.

poets, Elizabeth also wrote for private expression,[10] by which I mean that Elizabeth wrote verse arguably intended either for her eyes alone or for one other person. One might expect that Elizabeth's private views would not differ from her public ones, and that Elizabeth's monarchic position would shape her private, nonpublic thoughts, especially since, as Jonathan Goldberg notes, in the early modern period "the individual derived a sense of self largely from external matrices."[11] And yet Elizabeth seems to have used verse as a repository for emotions and reactions that she banished from the public realm. "The doubt of future foes" reveals an Elizabeth whose private sentiments significantly differ from her public persona and diplomacy, even while the circulation history of this poem suggests how Elizabeth's words could be appropriated to produce a very different monarchic image than the one the queen desired. Similarly, Elizabeth's two ventures into Petrarchan verse, "On Monsieur's Departure" and "When I was fair and young," not only demonstrate Elizabeth's appropriation of Petrarchan discourse for her own purposes, and thus contribute, as Ilona Bell has argued,[12] to the development of a distinctly feminine lyric voice. They also reveal an Elizabeth whose private views on her possible marriage to François Hercule, brother to Henri III, duc D'Anjou and Duc D'Alençon (referred to in the diplomatic correspondence as "Monsieur" or "Anjou"), depart significantly from the expectations of monarchy, even as the poems reflect the tropes and contexts of her matrimonial diplomacy.

Since Elizabeth wrote for two distinct audiences, the public and the private, I organize this chapter accordingly. First, we will consider the private poems: "The doubt of future foes," "When I was fair and young," and "On Monsieur's Departure."[13] We will then deal with Elizabeth's public poetry: in particular, her verse exchanges with Paul Melissus and Sir Walter Ralegh, concluding with her amazing, yet neglected Armada hymn.

I

The standard narrative of the genesis and circulation of "The doubt of future foes" begins with the deposition of Mary, Queen of Scots and her flight into

---

10. I use the term "private" in full knowledge of the extensive bibliography on whether or not interiority as we understand the term existed in the early modern period. See, for example, Maus, *Inwardness and Theater,* and Hanson, *Discovering the Subject.*

11. Goldberg, *James I,* 86.

12. Ilona Bell, *Elizabethan Women,* 108–13.

13. On Elizabeth's "French verses," the long religious poem in French discovered in the Cecil Papers, see Jordan, "States of Blindness," 109–34.

England in 1568. According to this version of events, Mary sent Elizabeth the following sonnet by way of asking for refuge:

> Une seul penser qui me profite et nuit
> Amer et doux, change en mon coeur sans cesse,
> Entre le doubte et l'espoir il m'oppresse
> Tant que la paix et le repos me fuient.
> Donc, chère soeur, si cette carte suit
> L'affection de vous voir qui me presse,
> C'est que je vis en peine et en tristesse,
> Si promptement l'effect ne s'en ensuit.
> J'ai vu la nef relâcher par contrainte
> En haute mer proche d'entrer au port,
> Et le serein se convertir en trouble.
> Ainsi je suis en souci et en crainte,
> Non pas de vous mais quant aux fois à tort
> Fortune rompe voile et cordage double.

> [A single thought that haunts me, day and night,
> Bitter and sweet, torments my heart, without cease,
> Between fear and hope it oppresses me
> So that peace and rest flee me.
> So, dear sister, if this paper reveals
> The desire to see you that oppresses me,
> That is because I live in pain and sadness,
> So long as my suit is not quickly granted.
> I have seen a ship freed from constraint
> On the high seas, near to entering a port,
> And the calm sea turned to storms:
> Likewise, I am troubled and in fear,
> Not because of you, but because Fortune,
> Often wrongly, rips sails and rigging.][14]

---

14. This narrative has its genesis in the poem's first publication in Malcolm Laing's early nineteenth-century *History of Scotland*, vol. 2:, 220–221, where he notes: "This sonnet must have been written when Mary solicited admission to Elizabeth's presence, upon her arrival in England" (220 n. 1). Subsequent critics and editors follow Laing's view, but without his admission of ambiguity. See Travitsky, *Paradise of Women*, 259 n.35; Ilona Bell, *Elizabethan Women*, 61–62; Summit, "'Arte of a Ladies Penne,'" 86–92;. May, *Elizabethan Courtier Poets*, 47–48; Herman, *Reading Monarchs Writing*, 242 n. 19; and Dunn, *Elizabeth and Mary*, 314–15. The modernized text is from *Reading Monarchs Writing*, 242–43; my translation, with the help of Constance Jordan.

Elizabeth did not immediately respond in kind. However, faced with the Northern Rebellion in November 1570 and the ceaseless plotting surrounding Mary, Elizabeth—again, according to the standard narrative—finally answered her cousin's poem with one announcing her knowledge of the various secret plots and predicting their failure. A letter by Sir John Harington, included in *Nugae Antiquae,* reveals how the poem's public life probably began:

> My Lady Wiloughby did covertly get it on her Majesties tablet, and had much hazard in so doing; for the Queen did find out the thief, and chid her for spreading evil bruit of her writing such toyes, when other matters did so occupy her employment at this time; and was fearful of being thought too lightly of for so doing.[15]

Once lifted from Elizabeth's "tablet" (the importance of this term will be discussed below),[16] the poem quickly started appearing in various manuscript collections and miscellanies,[17] and George Puttenham printed a version in his *Arte of English Poesie.*[18] The poem, as edited by Marcus, Mueller, and Rose, reads as follows:

> The doubt of future foes
> Exiles my present joy
> And wit me warns to shun such snares
> As threatens mine annoy.
>
> For falsehood now doth flow
> And subjects' faith doth ebb
> Which should not be if reason ruled
> Or wisdom weaved the web.
>
> But clouds of joys untried
> Do cloak aspiring minds
> Which turn to rage of late repent
> By changèd course of winds.

15. Harington, *Nugae Antiquae,* ed. Harington, vol. 1:, 58.

16. On writing "tablets" generally, see Stallybrass, Chartier, Mowery, and Wolfe, "Hamlet's Tables."

17. For a list, see *Queen Elizabeth I,* ed. May, 9; and May and Ringler, *Elizabethan Poetry,* 2: 1447.

18. Puttenham, *Arte of English Poesie,* 255–56.

The top of hope supposed
The root of rue shall be
And fruitless all their grafted guile,
As shortly you shall see.

Their dazzled eyes with pride,
Which great ambition blinds,
Shall be unsealed by worthy wights
Whose foresight falsehood finds.

The daughter of debate
That discord aye doth sow
Shall reap no gain where former rule
Still peace hath taught to know.

No foreign banished wight
Shall anchor in this port
Our realm brooks no seditious sects—
Let them elsewhere resort.

My rusty sword through rest
Shall first his edge employ
To pull their tops who seek such change
Or gape for future joy.[19]

The poem begins with the speaker worrying about her uncertain condition, how "future foes" could threaten "mine annoy," her personal destruction ("annoy" having a much harsher meaning in the past than in the present). The speaker's personal danger, however, is transformed into national danger in the second stanza with the injection of the term "subjects." The implication is that the speaker is *not* a subject, but a monarch, and the "snares" that threaten signify a revolt against her authority. The monarchic position of the poem's speaker is further underscored when Elizabeth writes: "Our realm brooks no seditious sects." The phrase "our realm" is not an abstraction but refers to the realm that belongs, according to law, to the monarch. In the poem's final lines, Elizabeth takes personal ownership of the sword of

---

19. I have used the version of the poem in MMR, which is based on Folger Manuscript MS V.b.317, fol. 20v, likely the earliest copy.

justice ("My rusty sword through rest / Shall first his edge employ"),[20] and as Jennifer Summit notes, the end of the poem "amounts to a death threat to Mary Queen of Scots."[21]

This version of events depicts the relationship between these two texts as continuing Mary and Elizabeth's previous poetic exchanges, only this time in a fittingly adversarial rather than complementary mode. Elizabeth seems to echo and invert her cousin's nautical language, transforming Mary's description of her self as "a ship freed from constraint / On the high seas, near to entering a port, / And the calm sea turned to storms" into "No foreign banished wight / Shall anchor in this port."[22] As Summit observes, "The interpretive struggle that Mary and Elizabeth enact over the figure of the ship bears witness to each queen's attempt to gain the rhetorical upper hand through figurative poetry."[23]

This interpretation, however, necessarily rests on two assumptions. The first is that Mary wrote and sent Elizabeth "Une seul penser" c. 1568. The second is that Elizabeth deliberately, if coyly, circulated her response through coterie manuscript circulation, which allowed her to condemn Mary "in a way Elizabeth could not officially attempt without risking serious diplomatic repercussions," as Steven W. May points out.[24] To be sure, this narrative holds considerable attractions. If true, it would confirm that Elizabeth's poetic practice—her use of verse to establish and maintain her monarchic authority—continues what we have seen of Henry VIII's and Mary's ventures into "royal poetrie." It would also show Elizabeth consciously taking advantage of the public / private nature of coterie manuscript circulation, "a sphere of restricted circulation that was endowed with cultural prestige,"[25] which overlaps with the conflation of politics and intimacy that characterized Elizabethan courtly culture.[26] Nonetheless, closer examination of the evidence reveals that significant problems with the accepted version of events.

First, the chronology does not quite fit. Elizabeth supposedly wrote this poem c. 1570, approximately two years after Mary's poem, which is a long time for a rebuttal that relies upon the reader's knowledge of Mary's text.[27]

---

20. Puttenham reads "Our rusty sworde" (*Arte of English Poesie,* 256).

21. Summit, "'Arte of a Ladies Penne,'" 74.

22. Ibid., 87–88.

23. Ibid., 90–91.

24. May, 48.

25. Summit, "'Arte of a Ladies Penne,'" 83.

26. Fumerton, *Cultural Aesthetics,* 68.

27. Arbuthnot also notes that Elizabeth's supposed response, "The doubt of future foes," "was not written till many years later" (*Queen Mary's Book,* ed. Arbuthnot, 101 n. 1).

Furthermore, no solid evidence suggests that Elizabeth ever read Mary's poem. Unlike "Adamas Loquitur," the ode that accompanied the heart-shaped jewel,[28] no record of "Une seul penser" exists in Mary's correspondence or the calendars of state papers, English or Scottish, domestic or foreign. Mary did send Elizabeth a letter, dated 1 September 1568, in which she used nautical imagery to describe her plight: "I have said what I had upon my heart to your vice-chamberlain, entreating you not to let me be lost for want of a safe port; for like a vessel driven by all winds, so am I, not knowing where to find a haven, unless, taking into your kind consideration my long voyage, you bring me into a safe harbor."[29] But in this letter Mary does not mention including a poem. Nor does the calendar indicate that one was received. Additionally, the sole manuscript of the poem (undated and unsigned) actually contains two versions of the sonnet, one in French, the other in Italian.[30] Neither poem is in Mary's hand,[31] and while it is possible that Mary wanted to echo their earlier poetic correspondence through a feat of linguistic prowess, her desperate circumstances at this juncture make such a ludic display improbable.[32] While Elizabeth may have had the nautical imagery of Mary's 1568 letter in mind,[33] it is, I think, unlikely that "The doubt of future foes" constitutes a poetic rejoinder similar to Elizabeth's verse responses to Paul Melissus and Sir Walter Ralegh. "The doubt of future foes," in other words, is not part of a verse exchange but stands alone.

If Elizabeth's poem does not respond to "Une seul penser," then what does this poem reflect, and who constituted its intended audience? Regardless of the specific intertexts (since the general import of the poem is certainly clear

---

28. See the discussion in chapter 2.

29. *Letters of Mary, Queen of Scots,* ed. Strickland, 1: 104; *CSPS,* 2, 496, item 797.

30. BL, Cotton MSS, Caligula BV, fols. 323–24.

31. A comparison of the manuscript of "Une seul penser" with Mary's writing at roughly this time (see the reproduction of Mary's 17 May 1568 letter to Elizabeth in Doran, *Mary Queen of Scots,* 132–33) shows significant differences between the two.

32. The eighteenth-century catalogue of the Cotton Collection describes this group of manuscripts as containing "Transacta inter Angliam & Scotiam" (Thomas Smith, *Catalogue,* 35). The pages are not in Mary's hand, although a marginal note labels the poems "Carmina Franca et Gallico scripta per Reginae Scotiae ad Angliae Reginam." There is no date, however, and it is perhaps significant that the online catalogue of the British Library describes this manuscript as "A sonnet, in Italian and French, *said to have been sent* by Q. Mary to Q. Elizabeth" (my emphasis).

33. While historians accept that Mary wrote this poem, they are divided as to the date. John Guy, for example, asserts that Mary wrote the poem in 1562, and that it belongs to the same correspondence that included "Adamas Loquitur" (*True Life,* 152–53). While later editors assume Mary's authorship (see above, note 13), Arbuthnot was more cautious, noting that the poem "is supposed to have been composed by Mary in 1568" (*Queen Mary's Book,* 100 n. 1). Both Arbuthnot and Laing, who discovered the poem, assume that the nautical imagery in Mary's correspondence and "Une seul penser" argue that Mary wrote the two texts at the same time (*Queen Mary's Book,* 100 n. 1). However, if Guy is right, then Mary is recalling her earlier imagery, only now in a much more serious context.

enough), does this poem, as both May and Summit propose, use coterie circulation to condemn Mary to Elizabeth's courtly audience while Elizabeth continues to negotiate with Mary publicly? To answer these questions, which will also help us understand how the poem's circulation altered its meaning, we need to take a closer look at this poem's relationship to Elizabeth's actions and diplomacy concerning Mary between 1568 and 1570.

There can be no doubt that nobody in Elizabeth's court, including the queen, particularly welcomed Mary when she arrived unexpectedly and uninvited in 1568. Elizabeth refused Mary's (repeated) requests for a personal interview, on the grounds that it would not be appropriate for Mary to visit Elizabeth while still under suspicion that she arranged the murder of her husband and Elizabeth's relative. "Whatever my regard for you," Elizabeth wrote on 8 June 1568, "I can never be careless of my own reputation" (*CSPS*, 2, 426, item 692). But at the same time, neither did Elizabeth treat Mary as an avowed enemy and throw her to the mercy of the Scots nobility. In the same letter, Elizabeth also assured Mary: "I shall be so careful of your life and honor, that yourself or any other 'parent' could not have them more at heart" (*CSPS*, 2, 426, item 692). Part of the reason for Elizabeth's solicitousness for her cousin's reputation and welfare (aside from diplomatic politesse) is that Elizabeth and her council had concluded that Mary had to stay in England, and that even if she were to return to Scotland, she could never again enjoy unrestricted possession of the Scots throne.[34] Elizabeth and Cecil also saw a glimmer of diplomatic advantage to keeping Mary on English soil, since her cousin had something Elizabeth very much wanted: assurances that Mary would renounce her claims to the English throne and would ratify the Treaty of Edinburgh. Elizabeth was not going to let Mary out of England until she was satisfied that the Scots queen posed no threat to the English throne. In his report to Cecil (dated 28 July 1568) of Mary's interview with John Maxwell Lord Herries (her ambassador to the English court), Francis Knollys (Mary's keeper at the time) quotes Herries as conveying to his mistress the quid pro quo that Elizabeth demanded in return for Mary's restoration. Before Mary could sit "in hyr seate of regiment and dingnitye regall" (*CSPS*, 2, 465, item 743), she had to fulfill the following requirements, in addition to dealing with the rebellious lords who fled to Scotland:

this Quene shold renownce to clayme or have any present tytle to the crowne of Ynglond, duryng the continuance off hyr hynes and the yssue of hyr bodie: and also upon condition that this Quene leaving the

---

34. Read, *Mr. Secretary Cecil,* 405; Plowden, *Two Queens,* 144.

straight leage with France, shold enter her leage with Ynglond: and also upon condition that this Quene shold abandone the masse in Skotland, and recyve the common prayer after the forme of Ynglond. (*CSPS,* 2, 465, item 743)

Cecil of course doubted that Elizabeth's strategy was realistic, since there was no way of enforcing these provisions once Mary retook the throne ("How they shall be afterwards performed, wise men may doubt," he wrote).[35] My point, however, is once Elizabeth had Mary in custody, she was not about to let her go, regardless of how the Westminster Conference—the event where the Casket Letters were revealed and the charges against Mary adjudicated—turned out, as Mary's envoy at these proceedings, John Leslie, the bishop of Ross, predicted. Elizabeth, Ross wrote, would delay any immediate decision, but "transport you up in the country, and retain you there, till she think time to show you favour, which is not likely to be hastily, because of your uncles in France and the fear she has herself of your being her unfriend."[36]

In short, Elizabeth's strategy up through 1570 and the outbreak of the Northern Rebellion was to keep Mary in English hands, in good part because the English queen recognized the potential advantages of striking a deal with Mary that would not only put to rest permanently the question of her cousin's claim to the throne but would oust an unfriendly power, France, from Scotland, and establish Protestantism as the state religion. It would make no sense at this juncture for Elizabeth to write a poem telling Mary that she had no place in England.

Matters seem to have changed with the 1570 Rebellion and the abortive attempt by Thomas Howard, Duke of Norfolk, to become Mary's husband. Cecil's suspicions of Mary were entirely justified, and on 24 September 1568, Mary wrote her cousin, Elizabeth of Valois, a letter that explicitly invited foreign help to foment a rebellion that would reestablish Catholicism in England and, implicitly, place Mary on the English throne:[37]

For my coming to this country has caused me to make acquaintance, by which I have learned so much of the state of things here, that if I had ever so little hope of succour elsewhere, I would make ours the reigning religion, or perish in the attempt. The whole of this part is entirely devoted to the Catholic faith, and with the right that I have,

---

35. Quoted in Plowden, *Two Queens,* 149.
36. Ibid., 158.
37. *Letters,* 1: 110–11.

for this reason, in my favour, I could easily teach this queen what it is
to intermeddle and assist subjects against princes.

When Elizabeth discovered Mary's complicity in the Norfolk affair and
the Northern Rebellion, she was properly incensed. Elizabeth told Ross
that Mary "had practised with her majesty's subjects to the offence of her
highness' honour and estate" (Ross denied the charge; *CSPS*, 3, 102, item
102), and on 20 February 1570, Elizabeth wrote Mary a long letter accusing
her of "unkindness towards me and my state" (MMR, 121),[38] and of rank
ingratitude:

> Good madame, what wrong did I ever s[eek] to you and yours in the
> former part of my reign, when y[ou] know what was sought against
> me, even to the sp[oil] of my crown from me? Did I invade your coun-
> try and take or detain any part thereof, as all the wo[rld] knoweth I
> might, and as any king or queen of my condition, being so wronged,
> might with justice and ho[nor] have done? (MMR, 122)

After rehearsing all of Mary's offenses against Elizabeth, even as Elizabeth labored on her behalf, the English queen comes to the most recent outrages:

> But if I should remember to you our contrary late dealings by your
> ministers to engender and nourish troubles in my realm, to bolden my
> subjects to become rebels, to instruct and aid them how to continue
> in the same, and in the end to make invasions of my realm, I should
> percase move you to continue in your fear. (MMR, 124)

But Elizabeth's point in this letter is to reassure Mary so that Elizabeth
could get from Mary the diplomatic results she wants. In the next sentence,
Elizabeth writes:

> From the which [Mary's fear of retribution] at this time of compas-
> sion I seek to deliver you, and indeed do earnestly wish you not only
> to be free from the fear expressed in your letters, but that you would
> minister to me hereafter a plain probation and a demonstration how

---

38. See also *CSPS*, 3, 79–82, item 126. The manuscript was damaged, and the square brackets
indicate editorial emendations. The *Calendar*'s editor describes the letter as a draft corrected by Cecil
(82), while Marcus, Mueller, and Rose suggest that Cecil in fact composed it, and that the extent of
Elizabeth's participation "is uncertain" (MMR, 120).

I may be assured of some contrary course, both by yourself and your ministers, in answering with some like fruits of goodwill as mine hath been abundant (MMR, 124)

In other words, while Elizabeth now had good reason not to trust Mary (arguably, she could have had her executed for treason), the English queen's position toward her cousin, surprisingly, did not change at all. At the end of April 1570, Elizabeth met with her council to discuss what was to be done with Mary, and after a week they reiterated the previous position with a few added provisions: Mary would be restored only if she ratified the Treaty of Edinburgh "concerning her pretence to the title and arms of the Crown of England"; she agreed to marry only with Elizabeth's consent; she maintained the Protestant religion; and she agreed to perpetual peace with England "according to the straitest bond that ever has been betwixt England and Scotland."[39] As William Maitland observed to Ross on 15 August 1570, "The Queen of Scots is in the Queen of England's hands, and I think she intends never (with her goodwill) to part with her" (*CSPS,* 3, 310, item 415).

The sentiments and the death threat contained within "The doubt of future foes" directly contradict, therefore, Elizabeth's behavior and diplomacy toward Mary in the aftermath of the Northern Rebellion.[40] Far from denying her safe harbor, Elizabeth sought to keep Mary under English guard, much to Cecil's dismay, since he understood the danger the Scots queen posed. Far from threatening Mary with execution by "rusty sword," Elizabeth refused to allow Parliament to add an "addition" to a new treasons act barring from the succession anyone who makes a claim to the crown during Elizabeth's life or who calls into question Elizabeth's legitimacy.[41] Even the Ridolfi plot and the demands of Parliament in 1572 for Mary's immediate execution did not sway Elizabeth, who twice personally intervened to save her cousin's life.[42]

What therefore are we to make of Elizabeth's "The doubt of future foes"? To understand this poem in its proper context, we must return to Sir John Harington's description of how the poem entered circulation. We learn from his letter that Lady Willoughby "did covertly get it ["doubt of Future Foes"] on her Majesties tablet,"[43] which leads to the question, what is a "tablet"?

---

39. Plowden, *Two Queens,* 170.

40. Cf. Summit, who argues that "the manuscript circulation of 'Doubt of Future Foes' supports Elizabeth's broader strategy for dealing with the Queen of Scots" ("'Arte of a Ladies Penne,'" 83).

41. Plowden, *Two Queens,* 175.

42. Ibid., 179–80.

43. Harington, *Nugae Antiquae,* ed. Harington, 1: 58.

A "tablet," as opposed to "a booke of golde, with leaves in it of paper and parchement to write,"[44] was a popular form of writing technology, imported into England starting in the 1520s.[45] It had three material features: it was small, easily held, and—most important here—"erasable."[46] Apparently, a little moisture sufficed to erase ink "immediately and completely" from a tablet; "graphite was equally easy to erase, while silverpoint left only a slight groove."[47] There would have been nothing at all unusual about Elizabeth owning this type of book, because luxury writing tables "with elaborate bindings were popular as gifts among the aristocracy."[48] In 1584, for example, Lady Layton gave Elizabeth "too payre of writing Tables covered with vellatt with too Claspes of Sylver," and Elizabeth received another gift of tables in 1586.[49] Tables, in sum, were a common item in Elizabethan England, both inside and outside the court, and Elizabethans took care to distinguish between tables and such unerasable technologies as paper and parchment when they described the kinds of mediums people used for writing.

My point, however, is that a "tablet" provides the ideal medium for inscribing thoughts or poems that one intends to keep private by erasing them once you are done, and Harington's specification that Lady Willoughby took the poem from "her Majesties tablet"—as opposed to a piece of paper, or parchment—strongly suggests that Elizabeth had no intention of affording "The doubt of future foes" any kind of permanent status or distributing the poem through coterie manuscript circulation for either private or political goals. Far from a covert threat to both Mary and her disobedient subjects, or, as Summit suggests, a contribution to "a sphere of literary production in which the privacy and enclosure of women's writing coincided with a sphere of restricted circulation that was endowed with cultural prestige,"[50] I suggest that "The doubt of future foes" represents a private, self-revealing moment of intense frustration with Mary. The poem demonstrates that even in her private thoughts, Elizabeth conceived of herself in monarchic terms, but even so, Elizabeth never intended for anyone other than herself to read the poem. It is only an accident that Lady Willoughby happened upon this poem before Elizabeth pressed the early modern equivalent of the "delete" key, erasing the

---

44. The quote describes Sir Henry Lee's New Year's gift to Elizabeth (quoted in Stallybrass et al., "Hamlet's Tables," 402).

45. Stallybrass et al., "Hamlet's Tables," 385.

46. Ibid., 381.

47. Ibid., 382.

48. Ibid., 402.

49. Ibid.

50. Summit, "'Arte of a Ladies Penne,'" 83.

poem from her tablet, as the medium allowed. But once the poem started circulating, Elizabeth had to somehow distance herself from a text that could disrupt her goals (issuing a death threat might not help Mary accept Elizabeth's conditions), and so she dismissed her poem as a mere "toy."[51] Mary's agents already had deep suspicions about Elizabeth's sincerity. Maitland told Ross that whatever "good words" Elizabeth gives you, beware, as "in your hart trust never word scho [she] speakis" (*CSPS* 3, 311, item 415). "The doubt of future foes," if acknowledged, would only confirm those suspicions, and render Elizabeth's diplomatic goals all the more remote.

Whatever Elizabeth's original intentions, once the poem entered the realm of manuscript circulation, it took on a life of its own. In *The Subject of Elizabeth,* Louis Montrose notes that Elizabeth's image was subject to "a ceaseless and casual process" of appropriation by subjects who would fashion the queen's image and words for their own purposes,[52] and I suggest we can see some of this process in the circulation of "The doubt of future foes" in manuscript and print. As noted above, many Elizabethans were far more willing to execute Mary Stuart than was Elizabeth, and the English queen's seemingly inexplicable resistance to employing her "rusty sword" caused significant frustration among those who espoused a harsher policy. While one cannot always intuit a reason or a politics for why a particular item appears in a commonplace book,[53] it is nonetheless highly suggestive that "The doubt of future foes," by far the most popular of Elizabeth's poems, would appear in manuscripts that otherwise indicated an interest in prosecuting Mary to the fullest extent.

For example, Folger MSS V.b.317, compiled c. 1577 (and serving as the copy text for Marcus, Mueller, and Rose), includes "Verses made by the Q. majestie" (fol. 20v) as well as "Reasons to move the Q. Majesties conscience to procede with severitie in the case of the Q. of S[cots]" (fol. 1),[54] Elizabeth's poem providing further reason to "procede with severitie." Similarly,

51. Cf. Summit, who notes that poems "were commonly referred to as 'toyes'" ("'Arte of a Ladies Penne,'" 75–76). The term, however, was often used as a pejorative dismissal of poetry. See Herman, *Squitter-wits and Muse-haters,* 46–47.

52. Montrose, *Subject of Elizabeth,* 2.

53. For example, in the Arundel manuscript, "The doubt of future foes" (recorded as "The dread of future foes") is one lyric among very many, and there is no obvious reason, other than the poem's charms, for its inclusion (*Arundel Harington Manuscript,* 276–77). However, all the manuscripts containing Elizabeth's poem note her authorship, even when the other items are anonymous. The Arundel manuscript, for example, concludes with "ffinis / Elizabethā Regina" (277), and the version in Bodleian Rawlinson Poetical 108 has the headnote "verses made by the Quenes [majesty]" (fol. 44v). See the transcription of variants in Herman, *Reading Monarchs Writing,* 269–79.

54. I am grateful to Georgianna Ziegler of the Folger Shakespeare Library for this information (e-mail message to author, 7 August 2007).

a manuscript compiled by someone in Elizabeth's court who resided in the Inner Temple (one of the Inns of Court) between 1578 and 1588 contains "The doubt of future foes" along with "A speech made by her ma[jes]tie tochinge the treasons of the Quene of Scotte,"[55] a speech in Parliament by one "F. A." defending himself against the imputation that he favored Mary,[56] and Elizabeth's 1586 speech, which finally admitted the necessity of executing Mary, Queen of Scots.[57] To be sure, a great deal of other material in this manuscript that does not concern Mary (curiously, the manuscript also includes a version of Elizabeth's poem to Sir Walter Ralegh, "Ah silly pug," which is crossed out),[58] yet the inclusion of Elizabeth's poem with these other, anti-Marian texts appropriates the poem for the project of justifying the queen's later actions toward Mary. The poem not only provides a kind of backstory for why Elizabeth should either proceed with severity against Mary or have her executed, by providing evidence of treasonous plotting as early as 1570, but also helps create an image of a consistently hawkish Elizabeth who warned her cousin to cease and desist. This image is not a mirror up to nature, but a reflection of how at least some would have preferred Elizabeth to have acted.

Puttenham's *Arte of English Poesie offers another example of this process.* To be sure, Puttenham's treatment of Elizabeth and her poem continues his project of justifying Mary's execution, defending it in terms of occlusion and revealing:[59] he writes so that "no part of her Majesties behaviour or doings therin should be covered or hidden."[60] However, Puttenham's section in the *Arte* on "The doubt of future foes" also participates in another aspect of the political imaginary. In his description of both the poem and its author, Puttenham stresses two aspects of Elizabeth's imagery: her beauty and her omniscience. Just as the queen's "selfe being the most gorgeous and bewtifull,"[61] so does her poem exemplify "the most bewtifull [and gorgeous] figure of speech";[62] and because Elizabeth perceives "how the Sc. Q. [Scots Queen] residence within this Realme at so great libertie and ease...bred secret factions among her people,"[63] she writes a poem "to declare that she was nothing ignorant [of]

55. Inner Temple Library, Petyt MS 538, vol. 10, fol. 6v; "The doubt of future foes" is on fol. 3v. See also Summit, "'Arte of a Ladies Penne,'" 84.

56. Inner Temple Library, Petyt MS 538, vol. 10, fol. 6.

57. Ibid., fol. 6b.

58. Ibid., fol. 3v. The marginal note "per Reginam / Walter Rawley" is also crossed out.

59. Summit, "'Arte of a Ladies Penne,'" 77–78.

60. "A Justification of Queene Elizabeth in Relacion to the Affaire of Mary Queene of Scots," in *Accounts and Papers,* 68.

61. Puttenham, *Arte of English Poesie,* 255.

62. Ibid., 254.

63. Ibid., 255.

those secret favours, though she had long with great wisdome and pacience dissembled it."[64] It should be noted that Puttenham adjusts history to fit his purpose. At no point was Mary "at so great libertie and ease," although she certainly "bred secret factions." Nonetheless, Puttenham's version of the royal image strikingly anticipates the image of Elizabeth in the c. 1600–1603 "Rainbow" portrait (fig. 15). In both Puttenham's *Arte* and this portrait we find combined the queen's youthful, beautiful features and a plethora of eyes, mouths, and ears adorning her dress. The point of this combination is to present an image of Elizabeth that emblematizes her mastery of intelligence, or control over her subjects through the powers of surveillance.[65] This concept, as Louis Montrose has shown, permeated sixteenth- and seventeenth-century thought.[66] Elizabeth nicknamed the earl of Leicester her "eyes" and Sir Christopher Hatton her "liddes," and this language marked the correspondence surrounding Mary, Queen of Scots in particular.[67] Thomas Morgan, for instance, Mary's sometime secretary, referred to Henry Howard as Mary's "speciall Eye."[68] We see the appropriation of this imagery for the purposes of the "Rainbow" portrait, which also participates in the extraordinary series of images of the aging Elizabeth as a young "Queen of Beauty,"[69] and I suggest we see the same in Puttenham's recasting of "The doubt of future foes" as exemplifying Elizabeth's omniscience and her beauty. Like the portrait, Puttenham's treatment of Elizabeth's poem emphasizes its "knowledge-power" nexus,[70] and again as in the case of the portrait, Puttenham's aim is to create an idealized image of Elizabeth that combines the feminine and the political, a queen who is both "gorgious" and "nothing ignorant,"[71] that is, a queen whose gorgeousness in part depends upon her omniscience, and whose omniscience contributes to her gorgeousness.

II

The next two poems, "When I was fair and young" and "On Monseiur's Departure," require a caveat since, as Elizabeth's editors Marcus, Mueller, and Rose admit, the provenance of these lyrics rules out absolute certainty about

---

64. Ibid.

65. Montrose, "Idols of the Queen," 140–41.

66. Ibid., 140.

67. Ibid., 142.

68. Quoted in Montrose, "Idols of the Queen," 142.

69. Strong, *Cult of Elizabeth,* 46–55. The phrase "Queen of Beauty" is the title of a miniature by Nicholas Hilliard.

70. Montrose, "Idols of the Queen," 142.

71. Puttenham, *Arte of English Poesie,* 254, 255.

FIGURE 15. "Rainbow" portrait, c. 1600–1603 (Hatfield House, Hertfordshire, reproduction courtesy of the Marquess of Salisbury)

their authorship and their context. "On Monsieur's Departure" exists in five manuscripts, none written during Elizabeth's lifetime.[72] Even so, Marcus, Mueller, and Rose posit that this poem "is almost certainly hers,"[73] and Steven W. May agrees: "The lack of contemporary copies of this love lament

---

72. For details of the manuscripts, see MMR, 302 n. 1; and *Queen Elizabeth I,* ed. May, 13.
73. MMR, 302 n. 1.

casts some doubt on its authenticity, yet each of the extant manuscripts attributes it to the Queen."[74] "When I was fair and young," on the other hand, does exist in an Elizabethan copy (Henry Stanford's commonplace book),[75] but Stanford does not specify the poem's author, and a later manuscript ascribes it to the Earl of Oxford. Even so, Marcus, Mueller, and Rose assert that the majority of the evidence points toward Elizabeth's authorship; and again, May concurs: "Perhaps Oxford could have written this love lament from a woman's viewpoint, yet the attributions to Elizabeth on two lines of textual descent tip the scale in her favor."[76]

Significantly, a strand within the manuscript tradition for both poems binds them to the unsuccessful courtship of Elizabeth by Anjou.[77] May notes that "three of the five manuscripts associate" this poem with Elizabeth and "Monsieur," as he was commonly known;[78] and Marcus, Mueller, and Rose write that "On Monsieur's Departure" was "almost certainly... written in connection with Monsieur's final leave-taking."[79] As for "When I was fair and young," Marcus, Mueller, and Rose add the tantalizing detail that in the version of this poem recorded in the commonplace book of the Jacobean courtier John Finet, we find the ascription "Verses made by the queen when she was supposed to be in love with Monsieur."[80] Although the heading is struck through, Marcus, Mueller, and Rose suggest that discretion rather than doubt is the likelier cause (although they do not speculate as to why a Jacobean courtier would feel the need for delicacy about a failed courtship over twenty years old).[81]

Furthermore, there are strong indications that Elizabeth did not intend these poems for any sort of public readership. No record of either work exists in the copious diplomatic correspondence surrounding this match, including but not limited to letters from Elizabeth, Anjou, Walsingham, and Simier, plus Burghley's memoranda and summaries of council meetings.[82]

---

74. *Queen Elizabeth I,* ed. May, 13.

75. MMR, 303 n. 1. See *Henry Stanford's Anthology,* ed. May, 129, item 202. Stanford also includes "Now Leave me and Let Me Rest" (155, item 222) and a speech by Elizabeth dated 15 March 1575 (84–88, item 112). Only the speech is attributed to Elizabeth.

76. MMR, 303 n. 1; *Queen Elizabeth I,* ed. May, 13.

77. Frye dates this poem to sometime in the 1590s, and she argues that Elizabeth directed "When I was fair and young" at the courtiers who incessantly pestered her with their "importuning." The "clear if ironic message to her 'suitors,'" Frye points out, "is to leave her alone" (*Elizabeth I,* 110).

78. *Queen Elizabeth I,* ed. May, 13.

79. MMR, 302 n. 1.

80. Quoted in MMR, 304 n. 1. The manuscript is Rawlinson Poetical 85, fol. 1r.

81. MMR, 304 n. 1.

82. See in particular *CA* and *HMC.* A selection of the correspondence is included in MMR.

If Elizabeth gave Anjou "On Monsieur's Departure," someone would have noted it. Additionally, Elizabeth and Anjou conducted their correspondence in French, while "On Monsieur's Departure" is in English. So far as I know, Anjou did not know English, and so it would make little sense for Elizabeth to hand her suitor a gift he could not understand. The diplomatic record also contains no record of "When I was fair and young," and Stanford's access to "the very highest courtly circles" started in the late 1580s, approximately a decade after the collapse of the French match.[83] While Stanford's editor, Steven W. May, does not specifically address the question of when Stanford included this poem in his manuscript, he notes that Stanford copied his entries in chronological order, and several poems coming before "When I was fair and young" date from "about 1590."[84] In sum, there is no evidence for the circulation of either poem between 1579 and 1581, namely, at the (probable) time of their composition. While we do not know exactly how these poems came into the hands of their later copyists, or where they resided until they did (two more "mysteries of Elizabeth"), the evidence collectively suggests that Elizabeth did not intend these works to be read by anyone other than herself.

Consequently, while I intend to analyze these poems in the context of Elizabeth's relations with Monsieur, I acknowledge that both context and authorship remain probable, not certain. This section, therefore, is something of a thought experiment: assuming that Elizabeth did indeed write these poems, and that they reflect her courtship with Anjou, what follows? How are these examples of "royal poetrie"? As we will see, the answers to these questions are complex and suggest why Elizabeth may have wanted to keep these poems very close.

In January 1579, the marriage negotiations between Elizabeth and Monsieur revived, and Jean de Simier, Monsieur's representative, arrived in England to arrange the match. As numerous historians have noted, the initial impetus for restarting negotiations was not love, but the concatenation of self-interest and foreign policy;[85] it served Elizabeth's interest to marry Anjou because his intervention in the Netherlands could balance the growing power of Catholic Spain, and it served his interests because Elizabeth could subsidize his intervention. The marriage also served the interests of the French

---

83. *Henry Stanford's Anthology,* ed. May, xvii.

84. Ibid., xxxix, xxiv.

85. I have relied upon Read, *Mr. Secretary Walsingham,* 2: 1–117; Doran, *Monarchy and Matrimony,* 154–94; and Neale, *Queen Elizabeth I,* 237–56.

crown because Henri III would have fobbed off his troublesome brother along with his expensive wars against England while simultaneously gaining an ally against Spain and possibly expanding French rule to England, and the marriage served the interests of the English crown because of the possibility of an heir. Everybody, it seems, had something to gain from this match, and so "the wooing continued," as Read explains, "because it was mutually profitable."[86] Even so, Elizabeth's courtiers worried about how the queen's previous courtships might have poisoned the waters, as it were. Sir Francis Walsingham, Elizabeth's ambassador to the French court, worried to Sir Christopher Hatton that their queen's previous courtships had significantly eroded her good name—"I would to God her Majesty would forbear the entertaining any longer the marriage matter. No one thing hath procured her so much hatred abroad as these wooing matters, for that it is conceived she dallieth therein."[87]

But while politics may have been uppermost in everyone's mind, that does not mean that personal relations were completely ignored. In his notes dated 7 October 1579, Burghley recorded that the first question that must be answered before going on to dealing with the trickier issue of religion is "if she shall so lyke the Duke's person as to marry him" (*HMC*, 271). If not, "it were but labour lost to pursue the matter further" (*HMC*, 271). Furthermore, the council proposed a face-saving measure that clearly indicates the primacy of this condition: "If there should be any cause of misliking on her part towards him, it should be alleged as the cause of breaking off the marriage, but that the articles of religion should bear the burden" (*HMC*, 271). Rather than acknowledging that Elizabeth found Anjou so unattractive that she could not bear the thought of marrying him, they would let it be known that religion rather than personal chemistry was the cause. The council need not have worried, however, since Elizabeth and Anjou seemed quite smitten with each other (*HMC*, 159). Elizabeth carried around Anjou's miniature in her prayer book and addressed him in her letters as "mon trécher" or "my very dearest"[88] (*HMC*, 281). As for Anjou, he termed himself "the most affectionate and faithful slave on this earth" (le plus fidelle et affectionne esclave qui puyse aytre sur la terre, *HMC*, 265), and his infatuation with Elizabeth was common gossip in the French court (*HMC*, 159).

After she met Anjou, Elizabeth decided to marry, and she was furious with her council for not immediately supporting her. When informed of

---

86. Read, *Mr. Secretary Walsingham*, 4.
87. Nicolas, *Sir Christopher Hatton*, 93; see also Read, *Sir Francis Walsingham*, 6.
88. See the translation of letters of Elizabeth and Anjou in MMR, 237–39.

their reservations, Elizabeth (according to Burghley's report) "uttered many speeches, and that not without shedding of many tears, that she should find in her Councillors by their long disputations any disposition to make it doubtful whether there could be any more surety for her and her realm than to have her marry and have a child of her own body to inherit, and so to continue the line of Henry the Eighth" (*HMC*, 272). Even further, "her majesty's answers were very sharp in reprehending all such as she thought would make arguments against her marriage" (*HMC*, 273). To be sure, Elizabeth never unambiguously committed herself: "she thought it not meet to declare to [her counsellors] whether she would marry with Monsieur or not" (*HMC*, 273); and in answer to the question of whether she "liked" Anjou, Elizabeth said "that she will never any (if she shall marry) but hym"(*HMC*, 272). Yet Burghley had no doubt about the direction of his queen's affections: "And most of those about her know that she never speaketh of him but with great allowance of his nature and conditions; and lastly, she seemeth not pleased with any person or with any argument appearing to mislike of the marriage" (*HMC*, 272).

Elizabeth, however, had much to mislike, as opposition to the match came fast and furious. In Elizabeth's council, Leicester led the antimarriage faction and perhaps arranged for Sir Philip Sidney to write his "Letter to Queen Elizabeth touching her marriage to Monsieur." Outside the court, the reaction was vehemently against. In London, preachers delivered sermons and organized public prayers against the match.[89] The most famous polemic against Anjou was written by the unfortunately named John Stubbs, who gave his work a verbose, yet pointed title: *Discoverie of a Gaping Gulf, whereinto England is like to be swallowed by an other French marriage, if the Lord forbid not the banes, by letting her Majestie see the sin and punishment thereof.* Thousands of copies were printed and widely distributed. Fifty copies were sent to one Richard Grenville in Cornwall to distribute among his friends.[90] Elizabeth punished both the author and the man who distributed the book with public mutilation and with dubious legality, but the spectacle only served, according to William Camden, to further harden attitudes toward the match:

> Some Lawyers murmured that the sentence was erroneous and voyd by reason of the false noting of the time wherein the law was made, and that the Act was only temporary, and dyed with Queene *Mary.* . . . Hereby

89. Doran, *Monarchy and Matrimony,* 164.
90. Ibid.

Stubbs and *Page* had their right hands cutt off with a cleaver driven through the wrist with the force of a beetle, upon a scaffold in the market place in *Westminster*. The Printer was pardoned. I remember (being present thereat,) that when *Stubbs,* having his right hand cut off, putt off his hatt with his left, and sayd with a loud voyce, *God save the Queen,* the multitude standing about, was altogether silent, either out of horror at this new and unwonted punishment, or else out of pitty towards the man being of most honest and unblameable report, or else out of hatred of the marriage, which most men presaged would be the overthrow of Religion.[91]

Resistance to the Anjou match, however, was also carried on iconographically. As Susan Doran notes, "The idea of Elizabeth as the Virgin Queen was given pictorial representation for the first time during the debate on the Anjou marriage in the series of some seven 'Sieve' portraits painted between 1579 and about 1583."[92] In the earliest of these portraits, attributed to George Gower, the viewer's attention is clearly drawn to the sieve (fig. 16).

These paintings constitute an early example of what Louis Montrose terms "instrumental adoration": praising Elizabeth in terms that seek to persuade the queen to adopt a position.[93] The sieve represents virginity, as both Montrose and Roy Strong note,[94] and the globe in the upper-left constitutes an imperial motif that will become more prominent in subsequent versions of this painting.[95] Taken together, the paintings homologize Elizabeth's virginity and England's imperial destiny, positing that each relies on the other. But as all commentators on these portraits agree, the paintings also contain a coded warning: losing one (virginity) necessarily means losing the other (imperial destiny). Thus the "Sieve" portraits seek not only to praise the queen or predict England's imperial destiny, but to persuade Elizabeth not to marry Anjou. Ignoring the problem of succession, these paintings claim that England's future requires a virgin queen.

---

91. Camden, *History of the Most Renowned and Victorious Princess, Elizabeth,* bk. 3, sig. Bb2v. Camden assigns this incident to 1581. Stubbs's book, however, was published in 1579, and the punishment occurred on 3 November 1579 (Doran, *Monarchy and Matrimony,* 166).

92. Doran, *Monarchy and Matrimony,* 171. See also Strong, *Gloriana,* 101–7.

93. Montrose, *Subject of Elizabeth,* 89–90.

94. Ibid., 125; and Strong, *Gloriana,* 105. Montrose and Doris Adler also note that the sieve has other connotations, discernment in particular. However, the placement of the sieve next to Elizabeth's vagina strongly suggests that virginity is the paramount meaning. See Montrose, *Subject of Elizabeth,* 90; and Adler, "Riddle of the Sieve," passim.

95. Montrose, *Subject of Elizabeth,* 123.

FIGURE 16. George Gower, "Sieve" portrait, c. 1579 (By permission of the Folger Shakespeare Library)

It is in this context that I want to place Elizabeth's lyric "When I was fair and young":

When I was fair and young, and favor graced me,
Of many was I sought unto, their mistress for to be.
But I did scorn them all, and said to them therefore,
"Go, go, go seek some otherwhere; importune me no more."

But there fair Venus' son, that brave, victorious boy,
Said, "What, thou scornful dame, sith that thou art so coy,
I will so wound thy heart, that thou shalt learn therefore:
Go, go, go seek some otherwhere; importune me no more."

But then I felt straightway a change within my breast:
The day unquiet was, the night I would not rest,
For I did sore repent that I had said before,
"Go, go, go seek some otherwhere; importune me no more."[96]

Assuming that this poem was indeed written c. 1579, when the queen, as John Finet puts it, "was supposed to be in love with Monsieur,"[97] there are autobiographical overtones to what may seem a conventional lament. The opening stanza seems to glance at the history of Elizabeth's courtships, all of which failed for a variety of reasons.[98] In addition, the opening words, "When I was fair and young," implicitly recognize that the speaker is no longer fair and young, something that was very much on the minds of Elizabeth's counsellors when debating the merits and dangers of the Anjou match. Burghley, for example, noted the fact that Anjou "is much younger than the Queen" (*HMC*, 270) among the negatives of the marriage, and Sir Ralph Sadler opposed the match because Elizabeth was too old to bear a child while Anjou was "in his best lust and flourysshing age."[99] Whether or not Elizabeth "sore repented" rejecting her previous suitors, the poem indicates that someone has captured the queen's affections, an interpretation supported by Elizabeth's anger at her council for their lukewarm endorsement of the match.

---

96. MMR, 304–05. MMR print two versions of this poem. The first comes from Stanford's commonplace book, and as it is the earliest extant version of the poem, I have to chosen to base my analysis on this text. The second version comes from the commonplace book of John Finet and dates from the seventeenth century. Finet's version has an additional stanza.

97. Quoted in MMR, 304 n. 1. The manuscript is Rawlinson Poetical 85, fol. 1r.

98. See Doran, *Monarchy and Matrimony*, passim.

99. Quoted in Doran, *Monarchy and Matrimony*, 173.

Her "shedding of many Teares" and her sharp "reprehending of all such as she thought wold make Arguments ageynst hir Mariadg"[100] strongly indicate that something more than political expediency governed her thinking.

But more than indicating Elizabeth's emotional engagement, this poem engages in a very monarchic if implicit rejoinder to the "instrumental adoration" of the "Sieve" portraits. Against their invocation of virginity as the sine qua non of imperial greatness, Elizabeth posits a counternarrative of herself as a desiring woman whose object may or may not reciprocate. Far from emphasizing inaccessibility, the speaker in this lyric regrets that she did "scorn them all, and said to them therefore, / 'Go, go, go seek some otherwhere; importune me no more.'" And far from representing herself as "remote, self-sufficient and desirable,"[101] this poem represents the speaker as vulnerable and subject to a power much greater than her own, "Venus' son, that brave, victorious boy" (a resonance we will return to below). Elizabeth thus answers the tide of verbal and iconographic arguments against the marriage with a lyric that justifies the Anjou match not on the grounds of geopolitical expediency, but of desire. What is more, Elizabeth also breaks with the tradition of women writers using Petrarchan rhetoric to guarantee their chastity by becoming the first English woman to write a love lyric not addressed to God[102]—an innovation made possible, one imagines, by her superior position as queen.

Yet as the spectacle of Mary Stuart amply demonstrated, the public articulation of desire could also destroy her monarchy, and for very similar reasons. Like the speaker in Mary's sonnets, the speaker in Elizabeth's lyric abandons her superior monarchic position and submits. She subordinates herself first to "Venus' son, that brave, victorious boy," who can now count Elizabeth herself among his conquests, and by implication, to the lover whose "importuning" she now grants. What makes this seemingly innocuous lyric so politically charged is that like Bothwell, Elizabeth's object of desire was vehemently opposed by a great many of her subjects. But Elizabeth, to state the obvious, was much more politically astute than her cousin, and we can see her acumen reflected in this poem in two ways. First, Elizabeth's lyric focuses on her interior drama. The change happens "straightway . . . within my breast," and her desire remains unknown outside the confines of her mind: the speaker may "sore repent that I had said before, / 'Go, go, go seek some otherwhere; importune me no more,'" but her repentance does not lead to

100. Doran, *Monarchy and Matrimony,* 173.
101. Frye, *Elizabeth I,* 107.
102. Ibid., 109. See also Jones, *Currency of Eros.*

any further action, any "importuning" of the beloved. Unlike Mary, Elizabeth addresses Amor, not her inamorato. Her submission is thus restricted to the pretty room of this sonnet; while Elizabeth may try to resist the pressure of the "geopolitical imaginary," to invoke another of Montrose's terms, she does so in a counternarrative that emphasizes privacy and interiority. Second, Elizabeth seems to have ensured that this poem remained private. The fact that "When I was fair and young" emerged approximately twenty years after its composition strongly suggests that its author kept this poem very close, perhaps having learned from Mary Stuart's sonnets to Bothwell what could happen when a queen abandons her monarchic position, even in the space of a lyric.

Of course, Elizabeth did not marry Anjou, and her initial enthusiasm for the match notwithstanding, after Anjou left England she started to temporize. The sticking point, or the excuse, was the problem of religion. The marriage negotiations allowed some space for Anjou and his train to worship privately in the manner of their choosing, but the marriage's opponents would not allow even this small concession, and in a letter written in late December 1579 / early January 1580, Elizabeth explained to Anjou, "in tones of deep regret,"[103] that she could not overcome her subjects' scruples in the matter of religion:

> I promise you on my faith, which has never yet sustained a spot, that the public exercise of the Roman religion sticks so much in their hearts that I will never consent to your coming among such a company of malcontents with your being pleased to consider that the commissioners loosen the strict terms that Monsieur Simier offered us...I entreat you to give great consideration to this, as a thing so hard for the English to bear that you would not be able to imagine it without knowing it.[104] (MMR, 243)

Elizabeth's strategy for temporizing is significant: rather than asserting that she herself finds the matter of religion insurmountable, Elizabeth situates the

---

103. Doran, *Monarchy and Matrimony*, 175.

104. The original can be found in *HMC,* 299. Anjou's response highlights the difference between France's absolutist political system and England's mixed monarchy, in which the monarch's powers are more limited: "Such is her Majesty's judgment," Anjou writes, "and so great the obedience of her people, that they will always consent to what is agreeable to her, inasmuch as their contentment depends entirely on her own" (*HMC,* 307). Elizabeth took precisely the opposite tack, arguing that her contentment depended on that of her people.

pressure elsewhere and claims that while she might wish otherwise, she cannot defy such opposition.

We find the same paradigm after the Estates offered Anjou sovereignty over the Netherlands in June 1580, which meant that Anjou would now be carrying on France's war with Spain. Elizabeth could have used this development as an excuse to withdraw from the marriage, but instead she complained that her subjects would not fund her husband's wars, and therefore, it would be best to shift the negotiations from marriage to a defensive league with France against Spain, even as she allowed her diplomats to negotiate a marriage contract that specified the form of the marriage service.[105] The cause for the shift from marriage to league, however, is not Elizabeth herself, but her subjects. In his letter to Burghley, Walsingham wrote that he told the French king "how ingratefull it would be to her [Elizabeth's] subjects to have her marriage accompanied with a War," and later in the letter, that the cost of the war "could not but breed a discontentment in her Subjects" (*CA,* sigs. Aaa4v, Bbbv). Elizabeth's temporizing had the effect of further undermining her credibility with the French. Walsingham reported to Elizabeth that Henri III was not impressed and that he had doubts "of your Majesties perseverance in the performing and due observation of the said League ... fearing lest when he should be imbarqued, your Majestie would slip the Collar" (*CA,* sig. Aaa2). In a subsequent letter, dated 13 August 1581, Walsingham told Elizabeth bluntly that she must conquer "the difficulty in your own nature," meaning her indecision, and that her temporizing had wasted her diplomatic capital: the French now think "that your Majestie dallieth with them (both in marriage and League) [which] greatly exasperate them against you" (*CA,* sig. Ddd3r). A week later, Walsingham expressed to Burghley his own exasperation with his mistress: "I would to God her highness would resolve one way or other touching the matter of her marriage, the uncertain course that is now held in that behalf" (*CA,* sig. Ggg2v).

Anjou, however, was nothing if not persistent, and in the autumn of 1581, with the campaigning season over and his funds running low, he decided to

---

105. The "Form of Celebration and Solemnization of Marriage between the Queen of England and the Duke of Anjou" is a fascinating document. First, it specifies that the marriage between the two shall be performed "by two bishops, one of the Reformed Anglican religion, the other of the so-called (*pretense*) Catholic," which is, to my knowledge, the first "interfaith" marriage ceremony on record that brings together clergymen of different persuasions. Second, Elizabeth promises her husband "fidelity and conjugal dues" and to "show thee conjugal obedience" in health and sickness. While the phrase "conjugal obedience" is conventional, in this context it may be intended to limit Elizabeth's obedience to the domestic sphere. Sex and breakfast, in other words, but not delivering England's wealth to France or freeing Mary, Queen of Scots. The document is reproduced in *CSPF,* 190–91, item 205.

return to England to pursue his marriage suit in person.[106] There followed an event that amazed and confounded everyone. According to Bernardino de Mendoza, the Spanish ambassador,

> On the following day Alençon and all his company displayed, not discontent alone, but entire disillusionment as to the marriage taking place. On the 22nd [of November] however, at eleven in the morning, the Queen and Alençon were walking together in a gallery, Leicester and Walsingham being present, when the French ambassador entered and said that he wished to write his master, from whom he had received orders to hear from the Queen's own lips her intention with regard to marrying his brother. She replied, "you may write this to the King: that the Duke of Alençon shall be my husband," and at the same moment she turned to Alençon and kissed him on the mouth, drawing a ring from her own hand and giving it to him as a pledge. Alençon gave her a ring of his in return, and shortly afterwards the Queen summoned the ladies and gentlemen from the presence chamber to the gallery, repeating to them in a loud voice, in Alençon's presence, what she had previously said. (*CLSP*, 3, 226, item 173).

Mendoza believed that the whole scene was contrived, or as he expressed it, "artful and conditional," largely because of Elizabeth's earlier refusals to fully commit herself: "If she had really desired to marry, she would not have wasted time as she have done" (*CLSP*, 3, 227, item 173). But most others were convinced of the queen's sincerity, for both good and ill. Camden reported: "Some leaped for joy, some were astonished, and some were caste downe with sorrow. [Leicester, Hatton, and Walsingham] fretted as if the Queene, the Realme, and Religion were now undone."[107] Bonfires were lit in Antwerp, and Henri III announced that as soon as his brother was crowned king of England he would become "a nasty thorn" in Spain's side.[108]

Yet the international response, necessarily delayed, was mistaken, for almost as soon as Elizabeth had finished with this scene, the antimarriage faction went into high gear. Leicester, Walsingham, Hatton, and Thomas Norton all pressured Elizabeth to reverse herself. Norton even landed in the Tower for "his overmuch and undutiful speaking touching this cause."[109] Elizabeth's

---

106. Doran, *Monarchy and Matrimony*, 186.
107. Camden, *History*, bk. 3, sig. Bbv.
108. Quoted in Doran, *Monarchy and Matrimony*, 187.
109. Ibid.

ladies-in-waiting added their voices to the antimarriage chorus by wailing "and by laying terrors [of marriage?] before her, did so vexe her mind with anguish, that she spent the night in doubtfull care without sleepe, amongst her women which did nothing but weepe."[110] The strategy worked, as the next day, in a private conversation, Elizabeth retracted her promise. Anjou reacted as one might expect: after "withdrawing himselfe to his Chamber, cast the ring from him, and soone took it againe, taxing with one or two quippes the lightnesse of women, and the inconstancy of Ilanders."[111]

It is at this point that Elizabeth likely penned the lyric conventionally known today as "On Monsieur's Departure":[112]

I grieve and dare not show my discontent;
I love, and yet am forced to seem to hate;
I do, yet dare not say I ever meant;
I seem stark mute, but inwardly do prate.
    I am, and not; I freeze and yet am burned,
    Since from myself another self I turned.
My care is like my shadow in the sun—
Follows me flying, flies when I pursue it,
Stands, and lies by me, doth what I have done;
His too familiar care doth make me rue it.
    No means I find to rid him from my breast,
    Till by the end of things it be suppressed.
Some gentler passion slide into my mind,
For I am soft, and made of melting snow;
Or be more cruel, Love, and so be kind.
Let me or float or sink, be high or low;
    Or let me live with some more sweet content,
    Or die, and so forget what love e'er meant.

As Ilona Bell and Gregőry Szönyi have noted, Elizabeth's poem draws on the tradition of paired oxymorons to describe a lover's internal state. The

---

110. Camden, sig. Bbv.

111. Ibid. While Elizabeth's passion for Anjou seems to have been genuine and the basis for "On Monsieur's Departure," she cooled decidedly in the immediate aftermath of the ring incident. Certainly, by 1582, according to Mendoza, Elizabeth did everything she could to get Anjou off English soil and out of her life: "The Queen has adopted every human artifice to get him gone as speedily as possible to the Netherlands" (*CLSP,* 3, 280, item 209).

112. Ilona Bell also tentatively dates the poem's composition to the aftermath of the betrothal ceremony (*Elizabethan Women,* 111). See also MMR, 302 n. 1.

tradition begins with Catullus's *Carmen* 85 (Odi et amo, quare id faciam, fortasse requires? / nescio, sed fieri sentio et excrucior)[113] and poem 134 of Petrarch's *Rime Sparse* (Peace I do not find, and I have no wish to make war; and I fear and hope, and burn and am of ice; and I fly above the heavens and lie on the ground; and I grasp nothing and embrace all the world).[114] But it is not quite right to say that "Elizabeth's imagery seems virtually indistinguishable from these classic oxymorons,"[115] because the queen makes several very significant changes. Unlike other English versions of this sonnet (e.g., the "freezing fires" of Sir Philip Sidney's *Astrophil and Stella* 6 and Joannes Baptista's poetic riddle "Of his straunge love,"—"In fire I freeze, in Froste I frie: / How so, wouldst knowe? a lover I"[116]), Elizabeth does not describe an inner landscape riven by intolerable paradoxes such as "I fear and hope" (temo et spero).

Ilona Bell posits that once Elizabeth became queen, "poetry became not only admonitory but also performative and efficacious, for she was clearly in a position to make it so by saying so."[117] Yet the crux of "On Monsieur's Departure" is that Elizabeth is *not* in a position to make it so. Quite the opposite, in fact, as the conflict lies between the speaker's inner desires and unnamed outward pressures that force the speaker into a public position at odds with her true feelings. Elizabeth transforms the Catullan "I hate and I love" (Odi et amo) into "I love, and yet am forced to seem to hate" (2), just as Petrarch's infamous paradox of simultaneously freezing and burning becomes in Elizabeth's hands "I freeze and yet am burned" (5), in both cases the sudden use of the passive voice obscuring the question of precisely who or what burns the speaker or forces her to hate. Similarly, Elizabeth transforms Petrarch's "I have no tongue and yet cry out" (non ò lingua et grido) into "I seem stark mute, but inwardly do prate" (4). Elizabeth grieves, but she "dare not show [her] discontent" (1), thus transforming the Petrarchan landscape of inner division into the drama of outside forces silencing her inner thoughts and squelching her desires.

The beginning of the second stanza returns to a more conventional expression of Petrarchan self-division: "My care is like my shadow in the sun— / Follows my flying, flies when I pursue it" (7–8). But in the third line

---

113. *Catullus,* ed. Quinn, 78. The following is my rough translation: "I love and I hate. Why do I do it, perhaps you ask? I do not know, but I feel it happening, and I am tortured." On the early modern reception of Catullus generally, see Blevins, *Catullan Consciousness.*

114. *Petrarch's Lyric Poems,* trans. Durling, 272. All subsequent references to Petrarch are to this text.

115. Bell, *Elizabethan Women,* 113.

116. *Astrophil and Stella,* ed. Herman, 131; and Kendall, *Flowers of Epigrammes,* 97.

117. Bell, "Elizabeth Tudor: Poet," 17.

of the stanza, the focus shifts from Elizabeth's "care" to the "care" shown by someone else, and Elizabeth shifts from channeling Petrarch to echoing the angry Laura of *Canzone* 23. The "care" that causes pain is now her lover's importuning, which Elizabeth seems to both welcome and revile: "His too familiar care doth make me rue it / No mean I find to rid him from my breast" (10–11). The stanza's final line only intensifies the ambiguity: "Till by the end of things it be suppressed" (12), as it is entirely unclear whether "it" refers to her lover's "too familiar care" or to her own "care," which follows her like a shadow in the sun. In the final stanza, Elizabeth returns to an exploration of her inner divisions, and the poem concludes with the speaker begging for some kind (any kind!) of certainty: "Let me or float or sink, be high or low; / Or let me live with some more sweet content, / Or die, and so forget what love e'er meant" (16–18). Echoing Petrarch's speaker in *Rime Sparse* 129, Elizabeth in this poem is a queen whose "state is uncertain" (stato è incerto), who depicts herself as "soft, and made of melting snow" (14).

To be sure, this lyric's description of vacillation and incertitude generally recalls Elizabeth's own uncertain policy toward the Anjou match, the alternation between enthusiasm and doubt that drove her counsellors to distraction.[118] As much as Elizabeth draws on Petrarch for the poem's rhetoric, the queen also echoes the self-division evident in her correspondence. Elizabeth's striking line "Since from myself another self I turned" has analogues not only in Petrarch, but also in her letter to Monsieur dated 17 January 1580, in which she exclaims: "See where the love that I bear you carries me—to act against my nature" (MMR, 246); and in a letter to her ambassador to the French court written c. August 1580, the queen writes: "O Stafford! I think not myself well used, and so tell Monsieur that I am made a stranger to myself" (MMR, 248). It might seem that by first appropriating Petrarch for her diplomatic correspondence and then reusing the same language in her verse, Elizabeth gives new meaning to the term "Petrarchan politics," yet in fact Elizabeth does something very different in this poem.

As we have seen, before Anjou's second visit to England, the queen and her diplomats regularly invoked the hostility of Elizabeth's subjects to justify their breaking off marriage negotiations with Monsieur in favor of a defensive league. In the letter to Sir Edward Stafford cited above, Elizabeth reiterates how outside pressures have rendered the match impossible, and how she will not sacrifice the public good for her private happiness: "God forbid that the banns of our nuptial feast should be savored with the sauce

118. Bell, *Elizabethan Women*, 108–13.

of our subjects' wealth. O what may they think of me, that for any glory of my own would procure the ruin of my land?" (MMR, 248). In this letter, it seems that the decision is an easy one: "Hitherto they have thought me no fool; let me not live the longer the worse: the end crowneth all the work.... My mortal [foe can] no ways wish me a greater loss than England's hate; neither should death be less welcome unto me than such mishap betide me" (MMR, 248).[119]

Yet Elizabeth reverses this position in her poem. While the private lyric repeats the public position of personal desire thwarted by outside forces, the connotation is the opposite. In her public diplomacy, Elizabeth seems to embrace the opportunity to once again emphasize her devotion to England's welfare, even at the cost of her personal happiness. But in the lyric, the outside influences that result in inner paradoxes cause her agony: "I grieve and dare not show my discontent; / I love, and yet am forced to seem to hate / ... / I freeze and yet am burned" (1–2, 5).[120] When in her letter to Stafford Elizabeth writes "Tell Monsieur that I am made a stranger to myself" (MMR, 248), she means that Anjou's acceptance of the sovereignty of the Netherlands while in the middle of negotiating for Elizabeth's hand has made a fool of her: "Suppose now how this may make our people think well of him and of me—to bring them to the possession of such neighbors!" (MMR, 247–48). But when Elizabeth returns to this phrase in her poem—"Since from myself another self I turned" (6)—she uses the paradox to express a self rent in half, torn, it seems, between existence and extinction: "I am, and not" (5). Whereas "When I was fair and young" engages the political imaginary by proposing an alternative to the construction of Elizabeth as the Virgin Queen (i.e., Elizabeth as the "desiring Queen"), "On Monsieur's Departure" seems to record the cost of Elizabeth's policy toward Anjou, and the price seems to be much more than personal travail, as this poem undoes Elizabeth's monarchy in two ways that perfectly overlap.

First, she undoes her image as a monarch who commands. In her response to a parliamentary petition to marry, Elizabeth first writes that it is "a strange thing that the foot should direct the head in so weighty a cause,"

---

119. The square brackets enclose the editors' conjecture because of a tear in the MS.

120. Elizabeth's position in this poem recalls her 1572 exchange with Sir Thomas Heneage in which she complains bitterly of how she must sacrifice her personal happiness for the common good. The poem consists of a Latin epigram and the queen's translation of the same: "I serve the rout and all their follies bear; / I suffer pride and sup full hard assays; / To others' will my life is all addressed, / And no way as might content me best" (MMR, 299–300). The last line of Elizabeth's Latin epigram is even more pointed: "Vixi ad aliorum arbitrium, non ad meum" (I live to be the ruler of others, not for myself, MMR, 299; my translation). See also May, *Elizabethan Courtier Poets,* 342–43.

and concludes with an even harsher restatement of the same: "I will deal therein [marriage] for your safety and off it unto you as your prince and head, without request. For it is monstrous that the feet should direct the head" (MMR, 96, 98). Yet the speaker in this poem occupies precisely the opposite position. She grieves but "dare[s] not show [her] discontent," and the choice of "dare not" implies that the speaker fears unspecified consequences if she articulates her grief. She loves "yet [is] forced to seem to hate"; she means (precisely what is unclear), but again "dare[s] not say" she ever meant. The poem contravenes the expectations of monarchic verse by portraying the queen as passive and powerless, a subject rather than a monarch—in other words, a woman rather than a man.

As many have observed, Elizabeth had to confront the general misogyny of the age (consider, for example, the homily on matrimony's infamous description of woman as "a weak creature, not endued with like strength and constancy of mind...sooner disquieted, and they be the more prone to all weak affections and dispositions of mind"[121]) as well as the particular controversy over the viability of female rule. The basis for John Knox's opposition to female "empire" is that women, by nature, are "weake, fraile, impacient, feble and foolishe."[122] Therefore, as Knox puts it, woman "was made to serve and obey man, not to rule and command him."[123] Faced with these views, Elizabeth adopted a strategy of balancing admissions of female weakness with assertions of masculine power.[124] The most famous example would be the Armada speech at Tillbury in 1588, when Elizabeth declared: "I have the body of a weak and feeble woman, but I have the heart and stomach of a king, and of a king of England too" (MMR, 326). One can find instances of such rhetoric much earlier. In 1563 the queen started a response to a parliamentary appeal to marry thus: "The weight and greatness of this matter might cause in me, being a woman wanting both wit and memory, some fear to speak and bashfulness besides, a thing appropriate to my sex," (MMR, 70); and in her 1566 response to Parliament: "As for my own part, I care not for death; for all men are mortal. And though I be a woman, yet I have as good a courage, answerable to my place, as ever my father had" (MMR, 97). But in "On Monsieur's Departure," Elizabeth depicts herself as weak and malleable.

---

121. "Homily of the State of Matrimony," 174.

122. Knox, *First Blast of the Trumpet,* sig. B2.

123. Ibid., sig. B5r.

124. See Marcus, "Shakespeare's Comic Heroines," passim; and Jordan, "Representing Political Androgyny," passim. See also Schleiner, *"Divina virago,"* and Heisch, "Queen Elizabeth I," the two classic treatments of this theme.

When she writes, "For I am soft, and made of melting snow" (14), Elizabeth does more than echo the shifting, unstable body of the lover in Petrarch's *Canzone* 23, she also confirms the cultural stereotype of women as yielding and frail. Equally, when Elizabeth writes in the first stanza that she obeys the injunctions preventing her from showing discontent, to dissemble love and to maintain silence, even though she "inwardly do prate" (4), she confirms rather than challenges the general expectations of gender roles. However, Elizabeth's confirmation of gender stereotypes and her abandoning, even in the space of a lyric, her position as "head" cannot be severed. Each necessarily involves the other, and Elizabeth's confirmation of gender stereotypes necessarily means the abandonment of rule. Given these resonances, it is no wonder that Elizabeth did not circulate the poem during her lifetime. The last time a queen described herself thus in verse, the poems contributed significantly to her political destruction.

III

Sometime around 1590, Elizabeth decided to write a long poem in French on the state of her soul and the process of her salvation that found its way into the Cecil Papers at Hatfield House.[125] The immediate cause of Elizabeth's decision to engage in spiritual reflection is not clear,[126] and the poem seems so uncharacteristic of her (and at times, the French so poor) that Steven W. May and Anne Lake Prescott have proposed that "Avec l'aveugler si estrange" must be a translation of a lost original.[127] Indeed, at first glance the poem does not fit easily with our assumptions. Elizabeth, as Constance Jordan reminds us, "is not known to have been much interested in profound or mystical religious experience,"[128] and therefore, this poem has little precedent. Furthermore, the speaker often uses highly unmonarchic language to describe herself. At different points in this poem, the speaker refers to herself as "a sad sinner" (triste pecheur, 205), as someone who is "lost" (perdu, 21), and as "childlike" (Comme'L'enfant, 41).

---

125. The poem was discovered by Steven May (see *Elizabethan Courtier Poets,* 41–68), who along with Anne Lake Prescott published a prose translation and transcription in *English Literary Renaissance* 24.1 (1994): 9–43, which was reprinted in Farrell and Swaim, *Mysteries of Elizabeth.*

126. Jordan argues that Elizabeth uses the poem to reflect upon and confirm her treatment of Mary, Queen of Scots ("States of Blindness," 125–33). I am indebted throughout this section to Jordan's fine analysis.

127. May and Prescott ("French Verses of Elizabeth I," 98–99) consider this poem a translation of a lost original, while MMR believe "this poem is a complete, original composition" (413). While I find MMR's position more persuasive, perfect certainty is not possible.

128. Jordan, "States of Blindness," 111.

And yet the French verses exhibit a number of parallels with Elizabeth's previous writings. First, there are moments in the French verses when Elizabeth invokes the same rhetoric of self-division that marked her earlier writing about the Anjou match. In 1580, as we have seen, Elizabeth wrote to Sir Edward Stafford asking him to "tell Monsieur that I am made a stranger to myself" (MMR, 248), and the poem includes at least two striking descriptions of self-alienation. The poem begins thus: "With the blinding so strange, / So contrary to my name / . . . / So far was I from me" (Avecq l'aveugler si estrange / Si au rebours de mon Nom / . . . /So Loing ~~que~~ je fus de moy ~~mesme~~, 1–2, 10);[129] and later, Elizabeth writes: "Remembering my baptism, / I acknowledged that so far / I was always from myself" (Et me souVenant de La baptesme / le Cognu que si Loing / l'estois touriours de moymesme, 83–85). Similarly, the Petrarchism of "On Monsieur's Departure" finds its analogue in Elizabeth's description of spiritual torment: "Knowing better, that in joy / I had to suffer, / I turned myself to so many tears / That a thousand times my comfort / Renewed my pains" (Scachant que / Mire ~~estant~~ en Joye / Je duis patir / tournois / Me ~~mettoit~~ tant depleurer, 196–200).

The difference, however, between the earlier rhetoric and the French verses is that in this poem the self-divisions are resolved. Elizabeth describes the initial stage of her conversion as the start of her self-recognition: "Seeing myself, who at dawn, / Begin to understand myself" (Moy Voyant qui a l'aube / Je Commence a m'entendre, 61–62). Turning away from sin and becoming "newly made" (nouvellement faict, 111) results in Elizabeth "Ceasing to be a stranger" to herself (Laissant d'estre estrangier, 121). But for Elizabeth, the process of self-understanding and conversion, while drawing on Pauline terms, really means the process of becoming a monarch, because for Elizabeth, there is no meaningful distinction between her inner being, including her spiritual being, and her political position as queen.[130]

The poem begins with a paradox, "With the blinding so strange, / So contrary to my name" (Avecq l'aveugler si estrange / Si au rebours de mon Nom, 1–2); and with a seeming recognition of her common humanity: "Although

---

129. For the translation of this poem, see MMR, 413–21. For the original French, see *Elizabeth I: Autograph Compositions,* ed. Mueller and Marcus, 85–94; I reproduce the strikethroughs and superscripts shown in the latter.

130. The conflation is evident even in her private devotions. In a 1588 prayer on the defeat of the Armada, for example, Elizabeth addresses God as both His "devoted servant" (MMR, 423) and as England's queen, thanking him for fulfilling "our desires" and protecting "our army from foes' prey and from sea's danger," "our" meaning both "England" and Elizabeth. Indeed, in another prayer dated 1588, Elizabeth conceives of creation in governmental terms. God, Elizabeth writes, "didst divide into four singular parts the form of all this mold, which aftertime hath termed elements, they all serving to continue in orderly government the whole of all the mass" (MMR, 424).

every evil deceives me / By this share in being man" (bien che tout Le mal me deçoit / de ce part que fus homme, 3–4). While Elizabeth certainly recognizes her mortality, she still sees herself as occupying a fundamentally different position than the rest of us. "Mon Nom" may refer to the false etymology by which Elizabeth means, according to William Camden, "Peace of the Lord or quiet rest of the Lord, the which England hath found verified in the most honored name of our late sovereign."[131] However, it is likelier that Elizabeth uses "name" here not to denote appellation, but her reputation as "a very Debora, to execute justice, equity and truth,"[132] and her rank as queen (a usage now obsolete but current in the late sixteenth century).[133] The poem begins, therefore, with the admission that spiritual blindness is not compatible with her position (her "name") as ruler.

The poem continues by using distinctly political language to talk about her parlous spiritual state. In the second stanza, the speaker admits that while she wanted to "put myself to the proof" (Alors de m'espreuver, 17), she decides that she is unworthy: "Not finding myself to reign / In my kingdom, I hold back" (Ne me trousVant pour regner / En mon Royaulme Je me garde, 19–20). Granted, it was commonplace to talk about one's inner state using the language of government, but Elizabeth uses a term that connotes, as William Kennedy points out, "a general domain of governance."[134] Nicot, in his *Thresor de la Langue Française* (1606), defines "royaume" as "regnum," and indeed, Mary, Queen of Scots used this term to dismiss a possible suitor, Archduke Charles, because she found nothing worthwhile in his realm: "Auquel elle ne trouvoit aucune commodité pour son royaulme."[135] Elizabeth conceives of her inner "kingdom," her soul, as it were, as if it were her outer "royaulme," meaning, of course, England; and her spiritual crisis reveals "that I did not know how to govern well" (que ne scaVois bien gouVerner, 65).

Once she confronts "the state of her heart" (L'estat de mon Coeur, 112), Elizabeth ceases "to be a stranger" (Laissant d'estre estrangier, 121) and becomes a monarch once more. She raises "up the sword" (J'enhaussas Le Countrepoint, 125), which, as Jordan and May and Prescott note, is simultaneously God's sword and the sword of justice, which Elizabeth wields

---

131. Quoted in MMR, 413 n. 2. See also May and Prescott, "French Verses of Elizabeth I," 105 n. 1.

132. John Prime, *A Sermon briefly comparing the estate of King Salomon and his subjects together with the condition of Queen Elizabeth and her people,* sig. B3r; quoted in Walsham, "'A Very Deborah?'" 12.

133. For example, in Thomas Dekker's *Shoemaker's Holiday* (1599), when Dodger tells Lincoln about the news in France, he says that the casualties are "four thousand English, and no man of name" (Sc. 8.l.9). See also the *OED*, s.v. "name" 2.b: "A title of noble or ecclesiastical rank."

134. Kennedy, *Site of Petrarchism,* 102.

135. Quoted in Mignet, *History of Mary, Queen of Scots,* 80.

as God's deputy.[136] God, Elizabeth writes, has converted her (Et puis me Convertist, 130), and then "transformed [her] / Into my ordained rank" (et tranfourmé / En mon ordre ordonné, 132–33). At this point, Elizabeth surveys the workings of her "three similar souls" (trios Ames ressamblans, 136), meaning the workings of Reason, Will, and Fantasy, and she finds that her spiritual recovery entails a political recovery. Elizabeth's inner "royaulme"—disordered by its monarch's sin—becomes a well-ordered state: "I saw my realm well governed / By reason and not by [decree]"[137] (Je Vi mon regne bien gouverne / Par raison et non par [decre], 134–35).

While Elizabeth says that she "saw the whole government / So very near to perfect" (Et Vi tout Le Government / Si pres d'estre parfaict, 58–59), what constitutes perfection in the Will is surprising:

> I saw the Will give responsibility
> Absolute and ordinary,
> By which her retinue increased
> To something extraordinary.
>
> [Je Vi La Volunte donner charge
> Absolu et Ordinaire
> Qui par accroistre Sa Suite
> Jusques a l'extraordinair.]
> (161–64)

"Absolute and ordinary," however, is a highly charged phrase with a very long history, as Francis Oakley has demonstrated.[138] While the terms seem to have their origin in the distinction between the courts of Chancery and the common law courts,[139] Tudor lawyers, as the legal historian Alan Holdsworth explains, used them to distinguish "between the doing of such acts

---

136. See *Autograph Compositions,* ed. Mueller and Marcus, 89 n. 7.

137. While both May and Prescott and MMR have "degree," a strong argument can be made for emending the word to "decree." MMR do not gloss this line, but May and Prescott also note that "degree" makes little sense in this context, and that "decree" fits better both contextually and thematically ("French Verses of Elizabeth I," 117 n. 10). Kingdoms are not ruled by "degrees" but can be ruled (badly) by "decree." Also, May and Prescott note Elizabeth's carelessness in other parts of this poem (see 119 n. 16), and the manuscript is filled with Elizabeth's own emendations and corrections. Therefore, I have decided to emend "degree" to "decree."

138. Oakley, "Jacobean Political Theology." I have relied heavily on Oakley in this section. Cf. May and Prescott, who gloss "ordinaire" as implying that the Will "is on the 'ordinary' list of the prince's permanent servants" ("French Verses of Elizabeth I," 123 n. 17).

139. Oakley, "Jacobean Political Theology," 324.

as to which [the monarch] had an unfettered discretion, and the doing of such acts...for which the law had prescribed limitations."[140] The notion that monarchs may have "unfettered discretion" would, of course, become a hallmark of James's political writings, but this concept was not unknown in the Tudor era. In 1528, for example, Henry VIII instructed his diplomats in Rome to tell the pope that while he "perhaps" could not grant a divorce "using his ordinary power," yet he could do it "of his mere and absolute power, as a thing in which he may dispense above the law" (*LP*, 4.2, 1158, item 4977). Significantly, Henry VIII claims these powers for the pope, not for himself, doubtless because he knew (perhaps he remembered the abortive attempt to alter the coronation oath[141]) that English monarchs could not be "above the law."

In 1539, Cromwell's propagandist and Erasmus's translator, Richard Taverner, who also, not coincidentally, had attended the Inns of Court and was therefore schooled in English law,[142] put together a short florilegium of classical learning, called *The Garden of Wysdome*. In this book, Taverner praises Antigonus, King of "Macedonie," because he rejected absolute power, and adds this authorial comment:

> And wold god the eares of chrystian rulers were not tykled with lyk tales, and yf they be, that they wolde with luke severitie rejecte them. For what other thynge saye they, which singe them this note, *Quod principi placuit legis, habet vigorem:* that is to say: That lyketh the prynce hat the strengthe of law: which saye that the prynce is not bounde to lawes, which gyve hym two maner powers, an ordinarie power, and an absolute power, whereof the one can do what the lawes, pactes, and leages demaunde, the other what so ever it lusteth. (sig. D1r-v)

In 1571 in a debate in Parliament over monopolies that very quickly turned into a debate over royal power, Sir Humphrey Gilbert worried that Elizabeth might follow the example of "Louis of France," who said that "other kings had absolute power, as Denmark and Portugal, where, as the crown became more free, so are all the subjects thereby rather made slaves."[143] And Sir Thomas Smith, in *De Republica Anglorum* (1582), declared that if any

---

140. Holdsworth, *History of English Law,* 4: 206–7; see also Oakley, "Jacobean Political Theology," 326–27.

141. See chapter 1.

142. See Andrew Taylor's biography of Taverner in the *Oxford Dictionary of National Biography.*

143. Quoted in Cromartie, *Constitutionalist Revolution,* 107–8.

body has absolute power, it is Parliament, not the monarch: "The most high and absolute power of the realm of England, is in the Parliament"; and the legitimacy of the laws produced by Parliament derives from the joint approval of both parties, not one or the other: "and upon mature deliberation every bill or law being thrice read and disputed upon in either house . . . and after the Prince himself in presence of both the parties doeth consent unto and alloweth. That is the Princes and whole realm's deed: whereupon justly no man can complain, but must accommodate himselfe to find it good and obey it."[144]

Elizabeth was evidently quite mindful of this rejection of absolutism. Unlike James, she never claimed to be above the law in her speeches to Parliament, even when the occasion seemed to call for such a claim. For example, when Parliament objected to the queen's proceedings against Mary, Queen of Scots, Elizabeth allows that she "did not deal by the course of the common law of the realm" (MMR, 188). But Elizabeth does not argue that Mary is above the law. Indeed, she exclaims: "God forbid that the ancient law should be defective to punish a person which should offend in so high degree" (MMR, 188). Rather, she altered Mary's jury from "twelve men in Staffordshire," which Elizabeth says would be "absurd," to have "her tried by the most honorable and ancient nobility of the realm, against whom and whose proceedings no exception might or can be taken" (MMR, 188–89). And the printed version of the "Golden Speech" to Parliament in 1601 has Elizabeth explicitly rejecting absolutism: "You must not beguile yourselves nor wrong us to think that the glosing luster of a glittering glory of a king's title may so extol us that we think all is lawful what we list" (MMR, 343).[145]

And yet Elizabeth not only claims for inner "royaulme" powers "Absolu et Ordinaire" but credits them with her Will's success: they allow her retinue to increase "to something extraordinary" (Jusques a l'extraordinair, 164). Nevertheless, Elizabeth seems to recognize that this sort of power requires great delicacy. Thus she writes that the Will "went along very gently" (Elle alla tout bellement, 165).[146] We are also now in a better position to understand why Elizabeth would write that a "well-governed" (Bien gouverne, 134) realm is a realm governed "by reason and not by decree" (Par raison et non par [decree], 135). To rule by decree means ruling without Parliament;

---

144. Sir Thomas Smith, *De Republica Anglorum,* 78.

145. Both the journal of Hayward Townshend and the copy in the Egerton Papers have Elizabeth asserting that she is not enticed by "the glorious name of a king or royal authority" (MMR, 339, 342).

146. May and Prescott have "moved softly."

it means that the ruler "is not bounde to lawes" and so can do whatever the ruler "lusteth," as Taverner puts it. It would mean being so dazzled by "royal authority" that "all is lawful what we list." Therefore, in her French verses, while it is apparent that Elizabeth may sympathize with absolutism, she recognizes that granting the monarch such powers in both the inner and the outer kingdoms requires many self-imposed limits.

The manuscript of this poem records one instance, in the following stanza, of Elizabeth emending her draft to impose such limits on herself and her royal authority:

> I saw that when Justice
>   Went away, compelled by Discord
> That compelled by my Malice,
>   Seeking Mercy,
> I made her ask for Justice.
>
>   *(231–35)*

According to Constance Jordan's summary of this confusing stanza, "Elizabeth saw that when Justice, exiled from her kingdom by discord, was asked to grant mercy to malice, or the evil engendered by sin (her own or that of another), she . . . insisted on Justice. In other words, she tells herself that she recalled Justice from exile and reinstituted it in her government—both her self-government and that of her people."[147] Elizabeth, however, makes a key revision:

> Je Vi quant ~~ma~~ la Justice
>   Alla forze et de discord
> Que a forse de ma malice
>   Cherchant misecorde.

As monarch, Elizabeth knew that she was ultimately responsible for the administration of justice in both her inner and outer kingdoms. In, for example, her response to a petition from Parliament urging the execution of Mary, Queen of Scots, Elizabeth asserts that she applies justice with "indifference":[148] "And for the course of justice, I protest that I never knew difference of persons—that I never set one before another but upon just cause, neither

---

147. Jordan, "States of Blindness," 123.

148. On "indifference" and the Ancient Constitution, see Patterson, *Reading 'Holinshed's Chronicles,'* ix.

have preferred any to office or other place of ruling for the preferrer's sake, but that I knew or was made to believe he was worthy and fit for it. Neither did I ever lend mine ear to any person contrary to order of law to pervert my verdict" (MMR, 198).

However, in the French verses, Elizabeth first writes "ma," but then strikes it out and writes "la," thereby turning "Justice" into an abstract concept or entity that is independent of Elizabeth's person—a move that has significant analogues in Elizabeth's earlier private and public utterances. In a prayer on the administration of justice, dated 1563, Elizabeth reveals that while she, as the queen, must render judgment, "Justice" is not her's, but the Lord's: "Grant that this crown, which Thou hast placed on my head, I may always put beneath Thy feet, and the regal scepter placed in my hand may serve Thy glory, and the justice and equity of Thy people" (MMR, 154).[149] Consequently, while Elizabeth claims "absolute and ordinary" power in her "royaulme," she qualifies that power by granting that while she may rule over England, God rules over her. The French verses are thus not only a window into Elizabeth's soul, but a window into Elizabeth's views of herself as a monarch, the two being one and the same, or as Elizabeth's motto expresses it, "Always one," *Semper eadem.*[150]

IV

Not all of Elizabeth's poems, of course, were private. And while "The doubt of future foes," "When I was fair and young," and "On Monsieur's Departure" diverge in various ways from the paradigms of "royal poetrie," her verse exchanges with the German diplomat and poet Paul Melissus and with her favorite, Sir Walter Ralegh, demonstrate that Elizabeth certainly knew how to use verse as a public vehicle for diplomacy and monarchic image-making.

In 1580, Melissus published *P. Melissi Mele sive Odae…Epigrammata,* a collection of his epigrams. The collection included a poem he wrote to Elizabeth and the queen's response ("Reginae Responsum").[151] The verse exchange itself took place c. 1577.[152] The exchange, as James E. Phillips

---

149. See Jordan, "States of Blindness," 124.

150. Camden, *History and Annalls of Elizabeth,* sig. F2.

151. On the background, see Phillips, "Elizabeth I as a Latin Poet," 289–98; and Revard, "Latin Ode from Elizabeth I," 156–69.

152. MMR, 301. I use MMR for the English translation of Melissus's poem and Elizabeth's response, and Phillips, "Elizabeth I as a Latin Poet," for the Latin of each. MMR note the possibility that "Melissus may have altered her verses before publishing them," but as my analysis shows, if Melissus did alter Elizabeth's poem, his ministrations were probably technical, as they did not affect

notes, with the concurrence of Marcus, Mueller, and Rose, occurred within the context of negotiations between Elizabeth and the German Protestant princes for a Protestant league to defend Henry of Navarre against Catholic depredations.[153] While the poems (so far as I can tell) do not comment on or allude to the precise details of this diplomacy, neither is Elizabeth's "responsum" innocent of monarchic politics, as the English queen answers Melissus's epigram with a poem that constitutes a significant diplomatic performance in its own right. Within the confines of a twelve-line Latin epigram, Elizabeth manages to display her intellectual virtú, acknowledge the panegyrical discourses surrounding her, appropriate these discourses for her own purposes, and make a statement on England's political identity and the nature of monarchy.

In his poem, Melissus first offers his books to Elizabeth, and then proceeds to offer himself:

> Not books alone I give and consecrate:
>> Myself I offer, goddess, to your genius.
> Known as a German man of Frankish stock,
>> I place myself beneath your royal yoke.
> Make me your bondsman, lady, and be mistress
>> To a freeborn slave who ever sings your praises.
>>>> (5–10)

> [Non solos, inquam, tibi dono [sic] sacroque libellos:
>> Ipsum me Genio dedico Diva tuo;
> Germanumque hominem Francâque propagine cretum
>> Regia me dedo sub juga servitii.
> Vtere me servo domina; ingenuoque ministro
>> Sis hera, qui laudes incinat usque tuas."]
>>>> (Phillips, "Elizabeth I as a Latin Poet," 289–90)

In her reply, Elizabeth gratefully thanks Melissus but declines his offer:

> Welcome your song, most welcome your gift, Melissus—
>> More welcome its sweet image of your spirit.
> But what cause moves you so, what urge impels you,
>> That you, a free man, wish to be a slave?

---

the poem's content. May does not accept Elizabeth's authorship of these verses (*Queen Elizabeth I,* ed. May, xxxvi n. 7).

153. Phillips, "Elizabeth I as a Latin Poet," 295; MMR, 301 n. 1.

'Tis not our custom poets to mure up,
> Or cause them to suffer the least loss of rights.
Rather you would be freed, your patroness
> Loosing the bonds that held you as a servant.
>> (*"The Queen's Answer," ll. 3–9*)

[Grata Carmena tua est, gratissima dona, Melisse:
> Gratior est animi dulcis imago tui
At quae tanta movet te causa, quis impetus urget,
> Ex homine ingenuo servus ut esse vellis [sic]?
Haud nostrum est arctis vates includere septis,
> Aut vel tantillum deminuisse caput.
Tu potius liber fieres, laxante patrona,
> Vincula, si famula conditione fores.]
>> (*Phillips, "Elizabeth I as a Latin Poet," 290*)

Elizabeth's poem gracefully recalls a number of controversies. First, there is the place of poetry itself. When she writes, "'Tis not our custom poets to mure up, / Or cause them to suffer the least loss of rights," or as Phillips renders this line, "It is by no means our custom to keep poets within narrow confines, or to restrict their rights even in the smallest degree,"[154] in all likelihood, she has in mind the humanist controversy over the freedom of the poet, and probably also the controversy in England over the morality of verse. While one can find praise abounding for verse in the early modern period, yet at the same time, as G. Gregory Smith pointed out long ago, "Elizabethan criticism arose in controversy,"[155] and the controversy over poetry has long, deep, and intellectually formidable roots stretching from Plato's *Republic* and *Laws* to early sixteenth-century continental humanism.[156] The Spanish humanist Juan Luis Vives, for example, wrote a dialogue entitled "Truth Dressed Up: To What Extent Poets May Be Permitted to Vary from the Truth,"[157] written, as Vives states in the prefatory letter to the first version of this work (1514), "to recall certain young men from their devotion

---

154. Phillips, "Elizabeth I as a Latin Poet," 290 n. 3.

155. G. Gregory Smith, *Elizabethan Critical Essays,* ed. Smith, 1: xiv.

156. In the tenth book of the *Republic,* Plato famously bans poets from his ideal state because they constitute a disruptive force ("If you grant admission to the honeyed Muse in lyric or epic, pleasure and pain will be lords of your city instead of law," 607a), and Plato forcefully reiterates this view in the *Laws* (7, 817a-d). On antipoetic sentiment generally, see Herman, *Squitter-wits and Muse-haters.*

157. Herman, *Squitter-Wits and Muse-haters,* 36–36.

to vain, impure poetry."[158] The dialogue concludes with a ten-point contract between "Truth" and "False" that allows "False" (really, "Fiction") very little room to maneuver. The first article declares that he who makes up the whole of what he tells is thought a fool, or rather a liar, than a poet," and article 7 reads: "In the exposition of arts and learning, whether in verse or in prose, no deviation from Truth is permitted save for the use of metaphor."[159] This controversy heated up in England with the publication of Stephen Gosson's *School of Abuse* in 1579, which likely sparked Sir Philip Sidney's *Apology for Poetry* (c. 1579) and his famous defense of the poet's freedom to invent: "Only the poet, disdaining to be tied to any such subjection, lifted up with the vigor of his own invention, doth grow in effect another nature in making things either better than nature bringeth forth, or quite anew, forms such as never were in nature."[160] By decidedly siding with the poets, Elizabeth manages to implicitly repudiate the local Muse-haters while promoting England as a haven for poets (a description that Edmund Spenser, in the October Eclogue of the *Shepheardes Calender*, might dispute). Whatever the reality, constructing England as friendly toward the Muses has the distinct advantage of accruing cultural, thus diplomatic, capital on the international stage.

There is, however, even more going on here, as Elizabeth casts her response in distinctly political terms. When Melissus writes, "I place myself beneath your royal yoke" (Regia me dedo sub juga servitii), followed by a request that Elizabeth make him "your bondsman," that is, a "slave," he (perhaps unknowingly) asks for something that is fundamentally antithetical to English identity. Elizabeth thus responds with seeming incomprehension: "What urge impels you, / That you, a free man, wish to be a slave?" The distinction between a free man and a slave, between those subject to a "royal yoke" and those independent of such encumbrances, raises the issue of the subject's liberty, a central concept in English political thinking from at least the Magna Carta onward. As Christopher Hill has shown, the term "yoke" came to symbolize tyranny and a sense of lost rights during the English Revolution, but it carried these connotations in the sixteenth century as well.[161] Thomas Churchyard, for example, in his 1579 poem *The Miserie of Flaunders*, compares England's happiness with the parlous state of its neighbors and competitors abroad: "O ENGLANDE, thou art blest in deede, / Thy

---

158. Vives, "Truth Dressed Up," 66.

159. Quoted in Nelson, *Fact or Fiction*, 46, 47.

160. *Sir Philip Sidney: "An Apology for Poetry,"* ed. Herman, 64. Later in the *Apology*, Sidney asserts that poets do indeed need to be curbed: "Yet confess I always that as the fertilest ground must be manured, so must the highest-flying wit have a Daedalus to guide him" (112).

161. Hill, "Norman Yoke," 60–61, 64–73.

necke is free from yoke."[162] As for slavery, that too is antithetical to the native liberty of the English subject, as evidenced by Sir Philip Sidney's comparison of himself to a "slave-born Muscovite" (Astrophil and Stella 3).[163] Melissus thus asks Elizabeth to do something contrary to the very essence of English political identity, and granting his request, even poetically, would have marked her as a tyrant. Therefore, she not only rejects Melissus's request to become her slave; she assures him that in England his rights are inviolable, thus affirming England's political identity as a country where the subject's liberty is sacrosanct.

These lines take on further point when one considers Elizabeth's employment of the pronoun "us" (nostrum) when she writes, "'Tis not *our* custom poets to mure up, / Or cause them suffer the least loss of rights." The first-person plural refers to the English people generally (her meaning can be summarized as "Here in England we do not enslave people"), yet "nostrum" also constitutes a use of the royal "we." Consequently, when Elizabeth assures Melissus that "'Tis not our custom poets to mure up," she speaks both for and *as* the nation, a position only possible if one is England's monarch.

In the final two lines of her poem, however, Elizabeth plays with the same distinction between subject and monarch that Mary Stuart confronted to such disastrous effect in the Casket Letters (published in 1571), and that Elizabeth employs in "On Monsieur's Departure." But where Mary used her verse to literally make herself a subject to the Earl of Bothwell,[164] in the process handing over the keys to the kingdom to him, Elizabeth—unlike the stance she adopts in "On Monsieur's Departure"—allows herself to be a subject only for the duration of a clause or two: "But you are the prince of poets, I, a subject [ego vati subdita] / To a poet when you choose me as the theme / Of your high song" (9–11). Significantly, Elizabeth does not allow her subordinate status to continue, for she knows (in anticipation of Louis XV's courtier, who responded to the king's request that he be made the subject of a joke: "Le roi n'est pas sujet"[165]) that the monarch is never a subject.Consequently, the poem concludes with Elizabeth reasserting her royal position. If she raises Melissus to the rank of prince, albeit prince "of poets,"[166] Elizabeth makes sure that she reinscribes her superiority by referring to herself as a semideity *before* Melissus's poetic ministrations: "What

162. Churchyard, *Miserie of Flaunders,* sig. Eiiiiv.
163. See Archer, "Slave Born Muscovites," 167.
164. See above, chapter 2.
165. Quoted in Kastan, "'Proud Majesty Made a Subject,'" 110.
166. "Sed vatum es princeps." Phillips, "Elizabeth I as a Latin Poet," 290.

king would shame to cherish/ A poet who, from demigods, makes us gods?"
Granted, Melissus does call Elizabeth "goddess" (6), but it is significant that
in her answer, Elizabeth does not say that the poet transforms monarchs from
humans into divine beings; rather, the poet transforms "demigods" ("semideis" in the original) into gods. Elizabeth starts off, in other words, already
superior to mere mortals, and goes up from there.

Elizabeth's references to herself as a "demigod" ("semideis") has two further resonances. First, this passage shows Elizabeth actively participating in
the formation and dissemination of her image. As many have pointed out,
Elizabethan courtiers and poets regularly associated the queen with such
demigods and full-fledged goddesses as Ceres, Diana, Juno, Venus, and Pallas.
One finds the same association in paintings, although, as "in *iconic* representations... this identification tended to be made obliquely."[167] As Louis Montrose has brilliantly shown, those associating the queen with divine figures
usually did so in order to enlist Elizabeth in their cause (the process dubbed
by Montrose "instrumental adoration"). For example, in the 1578 Norwich
pageant, Elizabeth was treated to a song in which each of the goddesses
strives to "claime the highest place above." Jove, however, puts an end to this
contest when he declares: "A soveraigne wight there is that beareth life, / In
whose sweete hart I have inclosde you all."[168] The point of all this praise was
not simply to flatter Elizabeth (although doubtless that formed no small part
of the intention), but to convince the queen into siding with the Reformists,
and the organizers of the pageant were successful. As the anti-Catholic cru-
sader Richard Topcliffe writes: "Shortly after, a great sort of good preachers,
who hadd beene longe comaunded to silence for a lytell nyceness, [were] and
again commanded to preache."[169]

However, as much as I am indebted to Montrose's analysis here and throughout this book, I differ on one key point. In *The Subject of Elizabeth,* Montrose
emphasizes Elizabeth's relative passivity: "Elizabeth Tudor was a privileged
agent in the production of the royal image, but she was not its master."[170]
Montrose analyzes the manipulation of Elizabeth's image by others, arguing that Elizabeth was a queen more acted upon, than acting; in this poem,
however, we can see Elizabeth taking full charge of her image, appropriating
the panegyrical discourse that had become central to the Elizabethan political

---

167. Montrose, *Subject of Elizabeth,* 88–95.
168. Ibid., 88; Garter, *Joyfull Receyving,* 261.
169. Quoted in Montrose, *Subject of Elizabeth,* 87.
170. Montrose, *Subject of Elizabeth,* 2. My objection is restricted to this particular poem. In the
larger sense, Montrose is absolutely correct. See below, chapter 4.

imaginary, confirming it, and disseminating her image as semidivine to project and enhance her authority for her own ends. What those ends might be brings us to the second resonance in her self-reference as a "demigod."

By explicitly raising the issue of rights and freedoms, and by referring to herself as a "demigod," Elizabeth intervenes in the debates over resistance theory that very much occupied the circle of "hot" Protestants to which Melissus belonged, a group that included Sir Philip Sidney, Daniel Rogers, and George Gilpin, all of whom served as intermediaries between Elizabeth and Melissus.[171] Widening the circle, this group would include Hubert Languet, Philippe de Plessis-Mornay, and Robert Dudley, the Earl of Leicester. All of these figures strongly advocated a muscular response to Spain, and they participated in the development of resistance theory to justify the subject's taking up arms against a Catholic monarch. While we do not know Melissus's position on these matters, it is reasonable to assume, given the company he kept, that he shared their views, and that Elizabeth knew that he shared these views.

While Elizabeth may have supported the idea of a Protestant league as a bulwark against Catholic tyranny and persecution, the view of monarchic authority and monarchic accountability—that is, the monarch, while anointed by God, nonetheless must honor the covenants between the monarch and God, and between the monarch and the people; breaking that covenant by becoming a tyrant justified rebellion[172]—growing out of this movement may not have been to her liking. Indeed, Elizabeth understood monarchy in a fundamentally different way. In a letter to King James VI of Scotland a few years later, Elizabeth reveals that she shares her cousin's conception of monarchy as divinely instituted, and the monarch's authority as superior to the clergy's: "Since God hathe made kinges, let them [the Kirk] not unmake ther [the monarch's] authorite, and let brokes and smal rivers acknowledge ther springes, and flowe no furdar than ther bankes. I praise God that you uphold ever a regal rule."[173] Elizabeth's use of the term "regal" is particularly significant, because, as Sir John Fortescue writes in his highly influential tract, "The Governance of England," "there are two kinds of kingdoms, one of which is called in Latin *dominium regale,* and the other is called *dominium politicum et regale.*"[174] In the former, the monarch's will is law;

171. Phillips, "Elizabeth I as a Latin Poet," 294.

172. For an excellent general survey of the development of Protestant resistance theory, see Kingdon, "Calvinism and Resistance Theory," 193–218.

173. Elizabeth I and James VI/I, *Letters,* 27.

174. Fortescue, *On the Laws and Governance of England,* 83.

in the latter, no laws may be imposed without the people's assent. Elizabeth's wish that James will "uphold ever a regal rule" goes well beyond politeness: she is indicating her preference for a particular theory of kingship, one in which the monarch is universally acknowledged as supreme, accountable to no one other than God.

When, therefore, Elizabeth constructs herself as a "demigod," in addition to acknowledging her widespread reputation as Cynthia and Diana, she is also putting Melissus and his circle on notice that while she may support the idea of a Protestant league, she does not agree with their notions of kingship. For Elizabeth, the monarch is a "demigod"; for such "hot" Protestants as Sidney and the monarchomachs, the monarch may be anointed by God but is certainly accountable to the "brokes and small rivers" that symbolize the monarch's subjects.[175] Elizabeth's response to Melissus constitutes an implicit rejoinder to the political philosophies of the French Calvinists whom she is trying to organize into a league against the Catholic powers—a subtle, yet pointed reminder that while Elizabeth shared their diplomatic goals, she did not share their view of monarchs as accountable to those below them. For Elizabeth, a monarch is, as her cousin James would later put it, "the supremest thing on earth," exercising "a manner or resemblance of divine power upon earth."[176] I think she wanted Melissus and his circle to know that.

In 1587, in her verse exchange with Sir Walter Ralegh, Elizabeth plays with her monarchic position similarly. The substance of Ralegh's poem is nicely summed up by the title it was accorded sometime in the 1640s, when both poems were published as a broadside ballad: "The Lover's Complaint for the Loss of His Love."[177] Most of the stanzas strike the conventional note of the lover pining for the mistress who has rejected him:

In vaine, mine eyes, in vaine you wast your tears;
In vaine, my sighes, the smokes of my despairs,
In vaine you serch the earth and heaven above,
In vaine you serch, for fortune keepes my love.

(9–12)[178]

---

175. This different conception of monarchy may also help explain the differing treatments of the ambassadors sent by the king of Navarre in 1577. To one, Elizabeth gladly "made large promises, agreeing to lend Duke John Casimir 50,000 crowns with which to raise troops in Germany for the Huguenots"; but to the other, Duplessis-Mornay, the likely author of the *Vindiciae Contra Tyrannos,* Elizabeth was "not at all generous" (Read, *Mr. Secretary Walsingham,* 1: 298).

176. "A Speech to the Lords and Commons," Wootton, 107.

177. MMR, 307 n. 1.

178. For Ralegh's poem and Elizabeth's response, I refer to May, *Elizabethan Courtier Poets,* 318–19. May includes modernized versions of both in *Queen Elizabeth I Selected Works,* 14–18.

Ralegh's poem, however, draws on the intertwining of love and politics characterizing the language of politics in the Elizabethan court,[179] the seeming failure of his amorous suit figuring, as Steven W. May has shown, Ralegh's fear that the rise of Robert Devereaux, the Earl of Essex, threatened his position at Elizabeth's favorite.[180] In his poem, Ralegh blames Fortune, who represents both Essex and the goddess, Fortuna, rather than the beloved for his condition. Fortune, Ralegh's speaker declares, rules over all, even monarchs: "Fortune conquers kings, / Fortune that rules on earth and earthlie things / Hath ta'en my Love in spite of vertue's might, / So blind a goddesse did never vertue right" (18–21). With the speaker asserting, "No fortune base shall ever alter me" (24), which simultaneously declares the constancy of his love (it will never alter), the poem implicitly accuses Elizabeth of inconstancy (her love for Ralegh has altered) and, ironically, given Ralegh's nonaristocratic origins, denounces his rival as "base," meaning both evil and lowborn.

Elizabeth's response begins by reassuring Ralegh that her heart still belongs to him: "Ah silly pug, wert thou so sore afraid? / Mourne not, my Wat, nor be thou so dismaied" (1–2). The next line of Elizabeth's response, though, turns to the issue of monarchic power. Significantly, throughout his poem Ralegh's terms deny his "Love" any agency: "Fortune hath taken thee away my princess, / ... / Fortune hath taken all away from me, / Fortune hath taken all by taking thee" (3, 5–6). In her response, however, Elizabeth immediately reclaims agency. Fortune, she writes, cannot "force my harte to thinke thee any ill" (4), and further: "No, no, my pug, though fortune weare not blind, / Assure thie selfe she could not rule my mind" (7–8). Elizabeth will choose her favorites, not have them chosen for her. To Ralegh's assertion that "fortune conquers kings" (17), Elizabeth agrees, but then adds a significant qualification: Fortune "*sometimes* doth conquer kings, / And rules and raignes on earth and earthlie things" (13–14; my emphasis). Elizabeth, however, is stronger than fortune: "But never thinke that fortune can beare sway, / If virtue watch and will not her obay" (15–16).

Elizabeth's assertion, however, does more than echo a truism, for in asserting virtue's independence from the vicissitudes of fortune, Elizabeth appropriates for her own purposes the language of royal panegyrics, which regularly focused on the queen as the embodiment of various virtues, such as justice

---

179. See Marotti, "'Love is not love,'" 398–99; Tennenhouse, "Sir Walter Ralegh," 238; and May, *Elizabethan Courtier Poets,* 117–18. But this phenomenon was noted much earlier than the advent of the New Historicism. Read, for instance, observes that "Elizabeth was shrewd enough to see that rules framed for chivalrous love-making might very aptly be applied to diplomatic purposes, and for that reason she always liked to mingle an element of love-making in her diplomacy" (Mr. Secretary *Walsingham,* 2: 4).

180. May, *Elizabethan Courtier Poets,* 119; see also Ilona Bell, "Elizabeth Tudor: Poet," 14.

(Astraea) or chastity.[181] Indeed, they personified the queen as "Virtue."[182] Thus the line "virtue...will not her [Fortune] obay" emends the allegory in which "Fortune" signifies Essex to include "virtue" signifying the queen, and so should be construed as "Elizabeth...will not her [Fortune] obey." Elizabeth responds to Ralegh by explicitly referring to her power ("it passeth fickle fortune's power and skill / To force my harte to thinke thee any ill," 1–2) and her regal position. Simply put, the queen does not obey others, including Fortune; others obey the queen, including Fortune.

Appropriately, Elizabeth ends her poem by issuing a series of instructions in the form of commands:

> Plucke up thie hart, suppresse thie brackish teares,
> Torment thee not, but put away thie feares,
> Thie Love, thie Joy, she loves no worthlesse bands,
> Much lesse to be in reeling Fortune's hands.
>
> Dead to all Joyes and living unto woe,
> Slayne quite by her that never gave wiseman blow,
> Revive againe and live without all dread,
> The Lesse afrayde the better shalt thou spead.[183]
>
> *(17–24)*

Certainly, these lines (which contrast significantly with the passivity of "On Monsieur's Departure") deliver a critique of the Petrarch courtiership that had become a convention of Elizabeth's court. Yet they also serve to further establish the queen's dominant position by not unqualifiedly pledging her support to Ralegh. When Elizabeth enjoins Ralegh to stop acting the forlorn, Petrarchan lover, with "Dead to all Joyes, and living unto woe," she adds, "Slayne quite by her that never gave wiseman blow." The phrase "Slayne quite by her" continues Elizabeth's ironic allusions to Ralegh's Petrarchan rhetoric, while the clause "that never gave wiseman blow" suggests that even as Elizabeth is encouraging Ralegh to drop the pose, she is reminding him that he had better remain a "wiseman." Otherwise, he could expect a "blow,"

---

181. Strong, *Gloriana,* 99; Montrose, *Subject of Elizabeth,* 104–13.

182. For example, in *Elizabetha Triumphans* (1588), James Aske writes: "The royall state of famous English soile, / (Right happy made by this their noble Quéene,) / Declares the vertues of a heavenly mind, / Adorn'd with all the gifts which Nature can / Bestowe, on any of her déerest Nimphes" (sig. B1r).

183. Ilona Bell, "Elizabeth Tudor: Poet," 17.

namely, the rejection he so fears. Elizabeth's response to Ralegh does more than reassure a jittery courtier of her continued favor; the poem also serves to reinforce the queen's place at the top of the hierarchy.

V

Elizabeth's final public poem represents perhaps her finest work. In 1588, she composed a hymn "in manner of a thanksgiving to God for her and our deliverance from the invincible Navie of the Spaniard... which thanks and praise was performed at Saint Pauls crose in London."[184] In this remarkable "song," Elizabeth rehearses the imagery and rhetoric surrounding the sinking of the Spanish fleet. When she writes, "He made the windes and waters rise," and God "kept the Saints from Pharoahs rod" by drenching "the honour of the proud," she endorses and reinforces the frequent comparison in popular and official discourse between Spain and the Egyptians drowned in the Red Sea. In the anonymous "Song for Thanksgiving," published in *A Song Or, Story, For the Lasting Remembrance* (2nd ed., 1626), for example, the author first describes how "Egypts King did them [the Israelites] pursue, / Into the red Seas heart" (sig. C2v), and then asks, "What better type of Englands blisse, / Saved from Spanish furie?" (sig. C3v). But Elizabeth alters the conventional rhetoric surrounding the Armada in one crucial detail. In the various texts giving praise and thanks for England's deliverance from the Spanish threat, one finds a consistent emphasis on "us" or "we." For example, Oliver Pigge, in *Meditations Concerning praiers to Almightie God, for the safetie of ENGLAND* (1589), writes: "For whatsoever want was in *our* praiers, yet hast thou heard *us* in that for which *we* cried.... The least benefit that *we* receive from thee, deserveth infinite thanks from *us*. For, what are *wee* of *Englande,* that thou shouldst consider *us?*" (sig. c6v-r; my emphasis). In 1588, Robert Humston, in *A Sermon Preached at Reysham* (printed in 1589), also uses the first-person

---

184. Rhodes, *Countrie Mans Comfort,* sig. D6. The title page's assertion that the book originally appeared in 1588 finds confirmation in the Stationers Register. The 1588 edition, however, is lost (*Queen Elizabeth I,* ed. May, 20). The poem survives in two versions: the first is found in a manuscript at the National Maritime Museum in England, and the second is in Rhodes's book; the two differ significantly in a number of places. Rather than using the contemporary edited version of this poem in MMR, 410–11, and in *Queen Elizabeth I,* ed. May, 22–23, I rely on the version in Rhodes. In so doing, I depart from May, who privileges the manuscript version over Rhodes. While the manuscript may or may not be truer to what Elizabeth actually wrote (it is not in her hand), Rhodes undoubtedly reflects the text circulating under Elizabeth's name. Why Rhodes decided to include two examples of Elizabeth's poetry in his compendium of popular religious verse is something of a mystery. Even so, the presence of this poem in such a work argues that the poem and its companion, a prayer in the form of a psalm, circulated widely and publicly.

plural: "The Lord of hoastes managed of late to strech the lyne of Samaria over the Realme of England, and to sound *our* Cities and measure *our* families with the Plummet of the house of Ahab . . . wherein *our* enemies came against *us* as fierce as the Wolves in the evening" (sig. C8r; my emphasis).

In her poem, however, Elizabeth emphasizes the first-person singular in her poem. Rather than speaking (or singing) in terms of "we" or "us," the emphasis in this poem is on "I," "me," and "mine." Elizabeth asks God to "bow downe thine ear," not to view England in prayer but to "see / Thy handmaid." While Elizabeth notes the "Priests offring to thee," she puts herself first among them, offering God "My selfe, and scepter, [as] sacrifice." In Elizabeth's poem, unlike the other prayers and sermons, God does not destroy England's enemies, but *"mine* Enemies." In other words, throughout her hymn of thanksgiving, Elizabeth also reminds both the original audience (and subsequent readers) of her position as monarch. This emphasis is especially evident in the last two lines, in which Elizabeth moves from invoking God's terrible vengeance on the Egyptians to the more pacific language of the Song of Songs: "He hath preserved now in love, / The soule *of me* his turtle dove" (my emphasis). If Elizabeth had written, as the sole manuscript of this poem has it, "The spirit of *his* turtle dove" (again, my emphasis), then one could argue that the "turtle dove" represents either England or, as the gloss in the Geneva Bible would have it, Christ's church. But in the printed version of this poem, the version that circulated, the emphasis is not on England or the church, but on *Elizabeth* as the *embodiment* of England or the church. In this poem, in other words, Elizabeth uses the occasion of the Armada's destruction to create a hymn that simultaneously thanks God for preserving England and subtly yet unmistakably serves to underscore the authority of her royal position.

And yet this poem is more than a mere reminder of who is boss. As A. N. McLaren has shown, the rhetoric surrounding Elizabeth's special relationship with God, her role as God's "handmaid," as she says in this poem and elsewhere, reflects in small the difficulties of being a queen in a fundamentally patriarchal culture. In the ocean of unsolicited opinion bombarding the queen up through the 1580s, one reads over and over again "that Elizabeth is most godly when she eschews her own will, acting instead as the instrument of God's will as identified by her male subjects."[185] Asserting Elizabeth's special relationship with God, in other words, has the paradoxical effect of subordinating the queen's authority to both her masculine subjects and her masculine God. For example, in the third volume of *The Monument of*

---

185. McLaren, *Political Culture*, 25.

Matrons, entitled The Third Lampe of Virginitie; Conteining sundrie formes of divine meditations & Chrsitian praiers, penned by the godlie learned, to be properlie used of the QUEENES most exellent Majestie (1582; the title itself is remarkable—can one imagine any of the "godlie learned" having the nerve to prescribe similar prayers for Henry VIII?), Thomas Bentley regularly insists upon Elizabeth's subordinate status as queen. In a prayer Bentley puts into Elizabeth's mouth, the queen is supposed to acknowledge herself as God's "handmaid prostrate here before the throne of thy divine Majestie...a subject and servant to thy most high and sacred Majestie, and a child depending alone and wholie upon thy divine and fatherlie providence for all things" (sig. Aa7r). The gender issue here is overt: "As I saie, it is thy good will, not my deserts,...to appoint me a fraile woman thy Lieutenant here on earth: and to give power unto thy *Queene* to judge the ends of thy dominions" (sig. Bb2.v). When, therefore, Bentley invokes the language of the Song of Songs, when he has Elizabeth call God "my heavenlie Bridegroom and spirituall spouse" (sig. Bb5v), the purpose is to emphasize Elizabeth's feminine powerlessness, and her appropriate subordination to masculine authority. According to Bentley's prayers, Elizabeth is a passive vessel for the Lord's desires: "Because that without thee I can do nothing, neither is it possible to please thee, do thou O father of light, from whome all good gifts doo come and proceede, vouchsafe to power downe plentifullie of thy principall spirit upon me, and so ravish my hart with the flame of the love of thee and thy people..., that with Joseph I may carefullie and faitfullie provide for thy people" (sig. Bb4r).

McLaren argues that Elizabeth negotiated this positioning through an implicit quid pro quo: she will allow herself to be cast as "'Deborah,' eschewing her own will to serve as God's instrument, if (implicitly when) her subjects perform the analogous move by enacting the absolute obedience to her stewardship enjoined by divine example."[186] The Armada hymn provides a slightly different form of the positioning McLaren proposes, since Elizabeth takes the rhetoric exemplified by Bentley and puts her own spin on it. Certainly, Elizabeth constructs herself in these verses as God's "handmaid," and she doubtless includes herself among the princes whose spirits God "restraineth." But she balances her subordination to God in this poem with assertions of her earthly position. First, it is worth noting that unlike Bentley and others, Elizabeth predicates her subordination to God in political rather than gendered terms. God "restraineth" the spirits of *all* princes, regardless of their sex; King Philip of Spain is as subject to God's power as Queen Elizabeth of England.

---

186. Ibid., 32.

Furthermore, Elizabeth offers God service in terms that remind the audience not of her supposedly proper role as a passive woman, but of her position as England's queen. She asks God to look down and see her "among thy Priests offring to thee . . . / My self, and scepter, sacrifice." She offers God not only herself, but the one gift only she can offer, her "scepter" as well, thus reminding the audience that it is a queen who composed these verses, and a queen who speaks. Similarly, God does not destroy England's enemies, but *hers:* "He made the windes and waters rise: / And did destroy mine enemies." In these lines, Elizabeth conflates herself with England. But in a reversal of the process by which the husband absorbs the woman's identity, the state becomes Elizabeth rather than Elizabeth becoming the state. God did destroy "mine enemies," not God did destroy "England's enemies."

In the final line, Elizabeth, like Bentley, invokes the Song of Songs: "He hath preserved now in love, / The soule of me his turtle dove." Again, however, the point is not to emphasize Elizabeth's position as a kind of royal *femme couverte,* married to God, and so, submerging her will in His. The phrase "of me" crucially emphasizes that it is not England that is God's favorite, but Elizabeth herself.

Even further, by identifying herself as God's "turtle dove," Elizabeth is doing much more than shifting to erotic and irenic imagery. Protestant commentary on the Song of Songs regularly associated the dove with the Reformed church, and so, when Elizabeth writes, "He hath preserved in love, / The soule of me his turtle dove," this could echo the conventional rhetoric of God preserving the English church through his destruction of the Spanish Armada. But as I have just noted, Elizabeth emphasizes that she is the "turtle dove" whose soul God has preserved, not England. Consequently, the poem also intervenes in the delicate matter of Elizabeth's authority in church government. As, again, McLaren notes, in order to calm waters roiled by the prospect of a female head of the church, at the start of her reign Elizabeth and her counsellors arrived at a compromise: she would be the Supreme Governor of the Church of England, not Supreme Head. That is to say, she would be in charge administratively, but not doctrinally. Yet "there is evidence that Elizabeth's disclaimer of the title of Supreme Head was partial and occasional. She seemingly adopted a rhetorical strategy of claiming headship of the church in her own person when it appeared she could carry the point, falling back on the well-established trope of the prince as head of the body politic when she could not."[187] I suggest that Elizabeth's very

---

187. Ibid., 19.

precise identification of herself as the "turtle dove" God has preserved is just such a moment: by casting herself as the turtle dove preserved by God, she uses the language of biblical allegory to reassert herself as the embodiment, and thus the Supreme Head, of the Church of England.

Finally, the reference at the beginning of the final stanza to "Jacob's Head" highlights both Elizabeth's monarchic position and, paradoxically, her equivocal status as an author. "Jacob's Head" obviously refers to God, and the entire line, "This Jacob's Head, this Israel's God," continues the powerful identification in Armada discourse between England and the Israelites. Yet one must ask, why Jacob? especially since the manuscript of this poem has "This Joseph's Lord" rather than "Jacob's Head." What is at stake here? Elizabeth also points to her royal authority when she chooses to describe God as "This Jacobs Head." As others have noted, Jacob in Reformist discourse represented election, chosenness;[188] and so, Jacob fits, because he typologically represents England, God's chosen nation. Yet as a woodcut representing Jacob in a 1578 biblical paraphrase, *The Historie of Jacob,* shows, Jacob's iconography was distinctly monarchic (fig. 17). Consequently, the phrase "Jacob's Head" creates, as James Nohrnberg describes it, "a quasi-Biblical parallelism";[189] inasmuch as Jacob equals Israel, and typologically England, Jacob also is to Israel as Elizabeth is to England: both are monarchs, and Elizabeth invokes Jacob in part to emphasize her monarchic position.

As we have noted, Elizabeth casts the Spanish as her personal adversaries: God "made the windes and waters rise: / And did destroy *mine* enemies" (my emphasis) Constance Jordan has argued that Elizabeth's "body natural found a figurative dimension in her body politic, distinct yet not to be divided from her body natural."[190] In this poem, however, the body politic finds a figurative dimension in Elizabeth's "body natural." As much as the phrase "mine enemies," as well as the other instances of "my" and "me," point to Elizabeth herself, her personal identity, her natural body, now includes all of England, not by creating a single collective unit, but by absorbing England into herself. With this phrase, Elizabeth reverses the process by which her identity, her agency, is erased, and she becomes a vessel for masculine authority; the state becomes Elizabeth rather than Elizabeth becoming the state.

This process is especially evident in the poem's final lines, where Elizabeth invokes the Song of Songs: "He hath preserved now in love, / The soule of me his turtle dove." While these lines may appear to reinscribe Elizabeth's

---

188. Ephraim, "Jewish Matriarchs," 303.
189. James Nohrnberg, e-mail message to author, 15 September 2005.
190. Jordan, "States of Blindness," 115.

FIGURE 17.   Detail from woodcut in *The Historie of Jacob,* 1578 (Reproduced by permission of the Huntington Library, San Marino, California)

subordinate status, reducing her to a symbol of peace, without power, preserved by an appropriately masculine God, the resonances of this couplet are manifold and complex. First, Protestant commentary on the Song of Songs regularly associated the beloved with the Reformed church,[191] and so the metaphor of Elizabeth as God's "turtle dove" could be construed as

---

191. For example, the headnote for the Geneva translation reads: "In this Song, Salomon by most swete and comfortable allegories and parables describeth the perfite love of Jesus Christ, the true Salomon and King of peace, and the faitful soule or his Church, which he hathe sanctified and appointed to be his spouse, holy, chast, and without reprehension" (*Geneva Bible,* 281).

echoing the conventional rhetoric of God preserving the English church through his destruction of the Spanish Armada. This identification is further supported by the Geneva Bible's gloss on the phrase "turtle dove" in Psalm 74.19 as signifying "the Church of God, which is exposed as a prey to the wicked."[192] Doubtless, that interpretation is part of the intended effect, yet there is more.

As she does with so much of this poem's imagery, Elizabeth draws on the contemporary rhetoric surrounding her queenship only to turn it to her advantage. Bentley, for example, also invokes the Song of Songs when he has Elizabeth call God "my heavenlie Bridegroom and spirituall spouse" (sig. Bb5v), but the effect of the two allusions is quite different. Whereas Bentley uses the Song of Songs to emphasize Elizabeth's feminine powerlessness, her appropriate subordination to masculine authority, Elizabeth uses the allusion to emphasize her special relationship to God. The crucial phrase, "of me," emphasizes that it is not only England—or the Reformed church—that God has preserved, but Elizabeth herself.[193] She is the turtle dove, she is God's beloved, and she represents England. Far from subsuming her identity in the larger nation-state, Elizabeth subsumes the nation-state into her own identity.

There is yet another resonance, and perhaps an unexpected one. Unlike Henry VIII, Elizabeth produced this poem after the resurgence of the Muse-haters in early modern culture: many of poetry's detractors believed that writing verse was not appropriate for Protestant nobility, who should be devoting themselves to statecraft, not cultivating the Muses.[194] By associating herself with the "turtle dove" of the Song of Songs, Elizabeth signals that her hymn is verse of another order. In his sermons on the Song of Songs, Theodore Beza contrasts the songs of the "turtle dove with the "unchaste and filthie poemes which men bring us even hither, so stinking that never came greater infection out of the dungeons of the most infamous brothel-houses that ever were."[195] The songs of the turtle dove, on the other hand, are

---

192. *Geneva Bible,* 250.

193. It is possible that Elizabeth's choice of "turtle dove" also points specifically toward her. The English phrase "voice of the turtle dove" is a translation of the Latin "vox turturis." "Turtur" (turtle dove) is a masculine noun, and so, by comparing herself to a "turtle dove," Elizabeth is implicitly creating a hermaphroditic image that recalls her self-description in the Armada speech: "I know I have the body but of a weak and feeble woman, but I have the heart and stomach of a king and of a king of England too" (MMR, 326).

194. See Herman, *Squitter-wits and Muse-haters,* 31–59, on Protestant antipoetic sentiment generally. On Beza's conflicted relationship with poetry, see Herman, 55–58; and Prescott, "English Writers and Beza's Latin Epigrams," 83–117.

195. Beza, *Master Bezaes Sermons,* sig. Ll2v.

those songs "which God teacheth unto the heart & putteth in the mouth of those who are his." Even more specifically, the voice of God's spouse is "but his holy worde which hath rong in the world, & hath in most divine sort charmed his Church" (sig.Ll2r). By casting herself as the "turtle dove," Elizabeth is not only associating herself as God's beloved, but implicitly defending her verse as religiously correct and asserting that her song constitutes a sign of divine election.

Elizabeth's hymn implicitly provides an answer to A. N. McLaren's question, "What, then, of the queen? How did she negotiate the role of 'Deborah'?"[196] This poem demonstrates that Elizabeth negotiated that role consciously and skillfully. "Looke and bow downe thine ear, O Lord" shows that Elizabeth was completely aware of the rhetoric surrounding her and the Armada, and that she used the occasion of this hymn to appropriate that rhetoric for her own ends, that is to say, she produced a hymn that simultaneously advertised her subordination to God and asserted her role not only as England's monarch, but as England herself (and I use the pronoun deliberately). Elizabeth's Armada hymn is a remarkable performance. To paraphrase her godson, Sir John Harington, no other than such a queen could have written such a sonnet.

---

196. McLaren, *Political Culture,* 31.

❧ Chapter 4

King James VI/I and the Scene of Monarchic Verse

Like Henry VIII, Mary Stuart, and Elizabeth I, James Stuart had a penchant for writing verse, and like his royal cousins, he knew how to use manuscript circulation for both entertainment and political advantage (mainly, as we shall see, to help his quest to be named Elizabeth's successor).[1] But unlike the other royal poets we have examined so far, James wrote in a much wider variety of genres,[2] and he actively sought out print publication, bringing out two books of poetry while king of Scotland, re-printing his short epic, the *Lepanto,* upon his accession to the English throne, and sponsoring its translation into French and Latin.[3] As Sandra Bell has demonstrated, James intended his first book, *The Essayes of a Prentise* (1584), as an intervention in Scotland's domestic politics, its publication forming "part of a larger movement by both James and Parliament to reestablish

---

1. There is little evidence, however, that James's poetry circulated in manuscript without his permission or knowledge. See below, note 63.

2. In addition to love poetry, the epic, elegy, and Petrarchan verse, James also translated the Psalms. On the complexities of the latter, see Doelman, "Reception of King James's Psalter"; and Sharpe, *Remapping Early Modern England,* 167–68.

3. On this point, I differ with Daniel Fischlin, who suggests that James's poem "effectively [sig-nals] how extraordinary it was to be both a poet and a sovereign" ("'Like a Mercenary Poët,'" 552). Given the poetic output of Henry VIII, Mary Stuart, and Elizabeth I, there is nothing extraordinary about monarchs writing verse. What is extraordinary is James's decision to publish his verse, a point I will explore at greater length later in this chapter.

the authority of the monarch, and to identify the monarch once more with the Scottish nation."[4] On the one hand, James's use of "royal poetrie" was brilliantly successful in that he became widely known as a poet-king whose verse enhanced his royal authority, and whose royal authority enhanced his verse. Yet at the same time, James VI/I also represents the limits of "royal poetrie," since in two cases (one dating from before James ascended to the English throne, the other from near the end of his reign) the king's attempt to use verse as an instrument of diplomacy or (in the latter case) as an assertion of monarchic power failed. I will demonstrate first how James's previously ignored sonnet to Elizabeth and his elegy for Sir Philip Sidney constitute attempts at buttressing his position in England, and I will investigate the parallels between the (literal) ambivalence of the *Lepanto* and his foreign policy as well as the resonances of James's decision to republish the *Lepanto* as a separate piece when he became king of England in 1603. In so doing, we will also see how the publication history of the *Lepanto* contributes to the history of authorship and how James took advantage of the growing author-ity of authorship to enhance his position as England's monarch. Finally, I will look at James's attempt to answer a manuscript poetic libel with a widely circulated manuscript poem of his own. In this work, as we shall see, James reiterates his view of monarchy as absolute, even God-like, but, as we shall also see, to no avail.

I

The sonnet James penned for Elizabeth sometime in 1586 especially dem-onstrates how monarchic verse could be employed for diplomatic purposes. Throughout much of that year James and Elizabeth haggled over the terms of the Anglo-Scots treaty, the primary sticking points being the size of James's pension and whether or not Elizabeth would sign an "instrument" guaranteeing his place next in line to the English throne. In March, Elizabeth rejected James's request to sign this document with firm but gentle irony:

> Tochinge an "instrument," as your secretarye terme it, that you desiar to have me signe, I assure you, thogh I can play of some, and have bine broght up to know musike, yet this disscord wold be so grose as wer not fit for so wel-tuned musike. Must so great dout be made of fre good wyl, and gift be so mistrusted, that our signe Emanuel must

---

4. Sandra Bell, "Kingcraft and Poetry," 161.

assure? No, my deere brother. Teache your new rawe counselars bet-
tar manner than to advis you such a paringe of ample meninge. Who
shuld doute performance of kinges offer? What dishonor may that be
demed? Folowe next your owne nature, for this never came out of your
shoppe. But, for your ful satisfaction, and to plucke from the wicked
the weapon the wold use to brede your doubt of meanings, thes the be.
First, I wil, as longe as you with ivel desart alter not your course, take
care for your safety, help your side, and shun al actes that may damnifie
you in any sort, ether in present or future time; and for the portion
of relife, I minde never to lessen, though, as I see cause, I wil rather
augment. And this I hope may stand you in as muche assuranse as my
name in parchement, and no les for bothe our honors.[5]

James, however, was not assured. He wanted something in writing, not a
verbal promise of future "performance," and he tactfully responded that he
did not want a signed document for himself, but for others:

And as for the instrument, quhairunto I desyre youre seale to be affixit,
think not, I pray you, that I desire it for any mistrust, for I protest before
God that youre simple promeis wolde be more then sufficient to me, if
it waire not that woulde have the quole worlde to understand how it
pleacith you to honoure me above my demeritis, quhich favore and innumerable otheris, if my evill happ will not permitt [me] by action to
acquye, yett shall I contend by goode meaning to contervayle the same
at her handis, quhome, committing to the Almichties protection, I pray
ever to esteeme me.[6]

James reportedly had a fit when he read Elizabeth's reply (now lost), turning
various shades of red and swearing "By God" that had he known "what little
account the queen would make of him, she should have waited long enough
before he had signed any league, or disobliged his nobles, to reap nothing
but disappointment and contempt."[7] James apparently told Elizabeth so in
a letter (sadly, also lost), but the queen replied in a more temperate fashion,
wondering "how possiblie my wel-ment letter, prociding from so fauteles a
hart, could be ether misliked or misconstred," and she reassured James of her
esteem and constant care for him. Yet despite the sweet words, she refused

5. *Letters of Queen Elizabeth and King James VI*, ed. Bruce, 30–31.
6. Ibid., 32.
7. Ibid., 33.

to raise the offered pension, and she refused to sign the instrument, because such a document "fitted not our two frindeships."[8] James realized that he had gotten as much as Elizabeth would give him, and so he "digested all," signing the treaty in July.

According to G. P. V. Akrigg, sometime during 1586 James wrote a letter to Elizabeth that included a sonnet. Because both the letter and the sonnet are very important and as yet have passed without notice, I quote them in full:

> Madame and dearest sister,
>
> Notwithstanding of my instant writing one letter unto you yet could I not satisfy my unrestful and longing spirit except by writing of these few lines, which, albeit they do not satisfy it, yet they do stay the unrest thereof while the answer is returning of this present.
>
> Madame, I did send you before some verse. Since then Dame Cynthia has oft renewed her horns and innumerable times supped with her sister Thetis. And the bearer thereof returned, and yet void of answer. I doubt not ye have read how Cupid's dart is fiery called because of the sudden ensnaring and restless burning; thereafter what I can else judge but that either ye had not received it, except the bearer returned with the contrary to report; or else that ye judge it not to be of me because it is *incerto authore*. For which cause I have insert[ed] my name to the end of this sonnet here enclosed. Yet one way I am glad of the answer's keeping up, because I hope now for one more full after the reading also of these presents and hearing this bearer dilate this purpose more at large according to my secret thoughts. For ye know dead letters cannot answer no questions; therefore I must pray you, how unapparent soever the purpose be, to trust him in it as well as if I myself spake it unto you face by face (which I would wish I might) since it is specially and in a manner only for that purpose that I have sent him. Thus, not doubting of your courtesy in this far, I commit you, madame, and dearest sister, to God's holy protection, the day and dates as in the other letter.
>
>> Your more loving and affectionate
>> brother and cousin than (I fear)
>> yet ye believe.
>> James R.

---

8. Ibid., 34. Even so, Elizabeth adds: "[I] have sent you a lettar that I am sure containes all you desired in spetiall wordes, I trust it shal content you" (34). To my knowledge, this letter has been lost, although Willson assumes that it contained "a revised statement concerning the succession" (*King James VI and I*, 72).

[Sonnet enclosed with letter]
Full many a time the archer slacks his bow
That afterhend it may the stronger be.
Full many a time in Vulcan'[s] burning stow
The smith does water cast with careful ee.
Full oft contentions great arise, we see,
Betwixt the husband and his loving wife
That sine they may the firmlyer agree
When ended is that sudden choler strife.
Yea, brethren, loving others as their life,
Will have debates at certain times and hours.
The winged boy dissentions hot and rife
Twixt his lets fall like sudden summer showers.
Even so this coldness did betwixt us fall
To kindle our love as sure I hope it shall.

Finis J.R.[9]

Given the correspondence between Elizabeth and James, it seems probable that this poem originated in James's desire to get beyond his anger at Elizabeth for refusing to sign the "instrument" and to ameliorate Elizabeth's annoyance at his persistance, the reference to "dissentions" and "contentions" echoing Elizabeth's reference to musical "disscord" in her letter of March 1586. As such, James's sonnet represents more than an interesting diversion: when he first arrived in Scotland, the England agent Thomas Randolph reported that "the King still follows his hunting, riding and writing in metre."[10] The poem argues that occasional strife only strengthens a relationship, and therefore he and Elizabeth are better allies for having had this argument. The sonnet thus demonstrates James using the medium of poetry to achieve a diplomatic goal, in this case, helping to smooth out the relationship between Elizabeth and himself after their quarrels over money and the "instrument."

Yet the poem fascinates for a number of additional reasons. First, the imagery in this sonnet and the rhetoric of the accompanying letter demonstrate James's awareness of, and desire to appropriate for his own benefit, the politicization of erotic discourse permeating Elizabeth's court. Second, the letter demonstrates James's sensitivity to the importance of authorship, since he makes absolutely sure that Elizabeth knows that the sonnet comes

---

9. *Letters of King James VI & I*, ed. Akrigg, 71–72.
10. Quoted in Willson, *King James VI and I,* 72.

from *his* pen, and is not *"incerto authore,"* and further ensures that Elizabeth knows*by* signing this copy with his initials. Finally, while I recognize the danger of arguing from silence, Elizabeth's refusal to acknowledge James's effort, let alone write a verse reply, even though she engages in a mock-debate in verse with Sir Walter Ralegh at precisely this time, remains among the most intriguing aspects of both the letter and the sonnet.

As many literary critics and historians have noted,[11] the rhetoric of love in the Elizabethan court became deeply entwined with the rhetoric of politics. James clearly knew about these developments, and in order to further ingratiate himself with Elizabeth, whose political and financial favor he depended on as much any of Elizabeth's courtiers, he evidently decided to try to write using the tropes of political Petrarchism in both his poetry and his prose, with unique results. In no other letter, either before or after, does James use allegory ("Dame Cynthia has oft renewed her horns and innumerable times supped with her sister Thetis," meaning it has been a long time since I sent the poem to you[12]) or invoke "Cupid's dart"(which we will return to below). Additionally, this letter nuances Foucault's deconstruction of the author. The speaker's identity matters intensely to James because Elizabeth's silence might be explained by her not knowing the poem's source (unlikely, to be sure). As James writes, she might "judge it not to be of me because it is *incerto authore* [meaning James had not signed the original manuscript]. For which cause I have insert[ed] my name to the end of this sonnet." Yet remarkably, James's attempt to speak the erotic language of the Elizabethan court fails. Elizabeth ignored the poem the first time James sent it, and so far as we can tell, she ignored it the second time as well. I want to offer two possible explanations for Elizabeth's declining to play along.

First, as Arthur Marotti, Louis Montrose, and others have argued,[13] courtiers assimilated Petrarchan language easily because the relationship between the lover and the beloved closely mirrors the relationship between the courtier seeking favor from a distant, witholding sovereign. The gender relationship between the lover and his beloved also mirrored (at least rhetorically) the relationship between the courtier and the queen, the male being in the subservient position of *asking* for favor, which the woman (i.e., Elizabeth) can give or withhold.

But as we have seen in chapters 1–3, the status of the speaker makes all the difference in the world, and what might be unexceptional from a courtier

---

11. See the introduction.
12. I am grateful to Anne Lake Prescott for her help with this reference.
13. See the introduction.

has very different resonances and consequences when articulated by a monarch. James thus transgresses the conventions of courtier verse even as he attempts to follow them, at least in part because of his position as a monarch. In other words, James's status as king precludes his using the rhetoric of courtiership, for several reasons.[14] When his mother used this language, she offended by putting herself in a subservient position not compatible with her position at the top of the social hierarchy, with predictable results when the poems were made public. James, though, has the opposite problem. First, as a monarch treating with another monarch, in theory the two are equal, and both considered themselves God's anointed on earth.[15] Yet nearly all the examples James uses in his sonnet are not only explicitly hierarchical, but gendered as well. There is no mutuality between the "archer" or the "smith" (conventionally male, I think) and their instruments, the early modern division of power between "the husband and his loving wife" needs no rehearsing, and the same gender relations obtain between lovers under the influence of "The winged boy." In other words, archer is to bow what husband is to wife, and smith is to furnace what the male lover is to the female beloved. When, therefore, James writes, "Even so this coldness did betwixt us fall," he does more than compare their political disagreements to a lovers' spat; he implicitly compares his relationship with Elizabeth to a series of *un*equal relationships, with *himself* as the dominant partner. He adopts the opposite poetic strategy from the one his mother applied in "Adamas Loquitur," in which Mary addressed Elizabeth as an equal, not as her superior.[16] Given the poverty of James and his court as well as his status as a petitioner for the English throne, let alone English gold, Elizabeth might very well have decided not to respond because the poem implicitly figures her as an inferior, the bow to James's archer, the water to James's smith, the subservient wife to James as husband. The poem thus inverts the actual power relations between the two, as well as serving to remind Elizabeth of the cognitive dissonance surrounding a powerful female monarch ruling "a stratified society in which authority is everywhere invested in men—everywhere, that is, except at the top."[17] James, in other words, has made a tactless blunder.

---

14. See Perry's analysis of the tensions between James's status as monarch and Petrarchan poetics in James's early love poems (*Making of Jacobean Culture,* 1–23).

15. In letter XVII, Elizabeth explicitly endorses James's theory of absolute kingship: "Since God hathe made kinges, let them not unmake ther authorite, and let brokes and smal rivers acknowledge ther springes, and flowe no furdar than ther bankes. I praise God that you uphold ever a regal rule" (*Letters of Queen Elizabeth and King James VI,* ed. Bruce, 27).

16. See chapter 2.

17. Montrose, "'Shaping Fantasies,'" 31.

In addition, the erotic rhetoric in the letter and the sonnet invokes connotations that James might not have intended, but that probably resonated very badly for Elizabeth. In both texts, James adopts the persona of the amorous lover. In the letter, he compares his apprehension at the lack of response to not hearing from one's lover: "I doubt not ye have read how Cupid's dart is fiery called because of the sudden ensnaring and restless burning." The poem culminates in a similar image: "The winged boy [Cupid] dissentions hot and rife / Twixt his lets fall like sudden summer showers. / Even so this coldness did betwixt us fall / To kindle our love as sure I hope it shall."[18] In virtually all their previous (and subsequent) correspondence, however, James and Elizabeth consistently invoke close family relationships to describe each other. In letter XVI, for example, James begins by calling Elizabeth "madame and deirest sister" and concludes by calling himself "Your trewest and assured brother and cousin."[19] Elizabeth in turn replies by addressing him as "right deare brother" and "my deerest brother and cousin the king of Scots."[20] In an earlier letter, James even calls Elizabeth "Madame and mother," signing himself as "your most loving and devoted brother and son, James R."[21]

The letter with the sonnet begins as most of the others do—"Madame and dearest sister"—but then James does something very unusual by veering into erotic allegory and concluding with a more passionate ending than usual— "your more lovinge and affectionate brother and cousin than (I fear) yet ye believe" (as opposed to "your most loving and devoted brother and sonn" in letter XIV, or "Youre most loving and affectionat brother and cousin" in letter XXXII)—along with (re)enclosing a sonnet comparing himself and Elizabeth as lovers. While James doubtless intended Elizabeth to read this unprecedented use of erotic language as a witty invocation of common tropes and as a demonstration of his ability to "talk the talk" of the Elizabethan court, the concatenation of amorous and familial terms might very well have sounded suspiciously like something that haunted Elizabeth from her earliest days: incest.

Elizabeth owed her existence to the putatively incestuous relationship between her father, Henry VIII, and Katherine of Aragon. Without that

---

18. Akrigg avers that lines 11 and 12 "are unintelligible as they stand. Apparently the King, when copying his poem, carelessly left out some word such as 'joys' after 'his'" (*Letters of King James VI & I*, ed. Akrigg, 72). Craigie, however, using a later copy of the poem (which he dates 1604) from a different source (Hatfield MSS, *Historical Manuscripts Commission,* 393), gives exactly the same reading (*Poems of James VI,* ed. Craigie, 2: 171), suggesting that "his" means "the lovers belong to Cupid" rather than referring to Cupid's "joys" or whatever.

19. *Letters of Queen Elizabeth and King James VI,* ed. Bruce, 24–25.

20. Ibid., 27, 28.

21. *Letters of King James VI & I,* ed. Akrigg, letter 15 (3 August? 1585), 64.

"scruple," Henry VIII would not have married Elizabeth's mother, Anne Boleyn. But then, Anne herself fell, and Henry charged her with incest with
her own brother Lord Rochford (some even said that Anne was Henry's
illegitimate daughter, making Elizabeth's mother guilty of double incest).
And Thomas Cranmer, the archbishop of Canterbury, argued for Elizabeth's
illegitimacy on the grounds of Henry's affair with Anne's sister, Mary Carey,
since the definition of incest also included marriage to a former mistress's sister.[22] While Elizabeth regularly "portrayed herself in multiple kinship roles"
when dealing with other monarchs,[23] James actually was related to Elizabeth by blood.[24] The references to "brother," "sister," and "cousin," in other
words, are not purely rhetorical. Consequently, when James shifts gears and
suddenly starts comparing himself and Elizabeth to lovers, he raises an issue
that Elizabeth would have likely found most unwelcome, since it constituted
one of the prime grounds for the challenges to her legitimacy.

Furthermore, Marc Shell argues that "it is at the level of incest both spiri-
tualized and secularized that Elizabeth as monarch later established herself as
the national virgin queen who was at once the mother and the wife of the
English people."[25] Therefore, when he writes, "The winged boy dissentions
hot and rife / Twixt his lets fall like sudden summer showers," or describes his
agony at waiting for a response to "the sudden ensnaring and restless burning"
of Cupid's fiery dart, James implicitly (and probably unwittingly) *despiritual-
izes* incest. It is one thing for a courtier, like Hatton, to use these terms when
writing for Elizabeth. He was not actually related to her. But when James
uses them, he sets in motion an entirely different set of connotations. Elizabeth evidently believed that the best response to such rhetoric was to pretend
it hadn't happened, and James got the message. He never used such language
with Elizabeth again.

II

One year later, on 21 September 1586, Sir Philip Sidney died, and about five
months after that, in February 1587, Alexander Neville edited a volume of
Latin verse commemorating Sidney, titled *Academiae Cantabrigiensis Lachrymae*

---

22. Shell, *End of Kinship,* 109–10.
23. Shell, *Elizabeth's Glass,* 69.
24. Henry VII's daughter, Margaret, was James's grandmother.
25. Shell, *End of Kinship,* 113. Shell expands this argument in the introduction to *Elizabeth's Glass,* 3–73.

Tumulo Nobilissimi Equitis, D. Philippi Sidneii Sacratae.[26] The publication of Neville's volume gave James an opportunity to move monarchic verse beyond the court and manuscript transmission, but like the Elizabeth sonnet, James's contribution demonstrates his use of verse for political ends (although more successfully, and certainly more appropriately). Neville's volume includes English and Latin versions of James's epitaph for Sidney as well as contributions from Lord Patrick Gray, Sir John Maitland, Colonel James Halkerston, Lord Alexander Seton, and the Earl of Angus, none of whom are known today as poets, but all of whom were deeply involved with James's highly slippery diplomacy toward England. Significantly, James's mother, Mary, lost her head on 8 February, about two or three weeks before Neville's volume appeared, and, I propose, her death may have constituted the precipitating factor in James's decision to deliver contributions from himself and his courtiers. The printer, John Windet, clearly added the Scots contributions after the compositor set the volume in type: unlike the rest of the volume, the pages with the Scots elegies are not numbered, the signatures for their poems start at "K" even though the final pages of Neville's preceding letter are signatures H3r-v (thus missing "I" and "J"), and the first poem after the Scots elegies, by G. H. (Gabriel Harvey?), is on—using the actual pagination—page 1, sig. A1v. Also, Windet or the compositor put the volume's title and an ornamental design above G. H.'s poem,[27] and the page preceding it, signature A1r, repeats the title page. Taken together, these details of book production suggest that the Scots elegies arrived after Windet had completed the volume, which in turn suggests that the Scots wrote and published their poems less out of concern for the late Sir Philip than in reaction to Mary's very recent execution.[28]

James's contribution is neither particularly distinguished nor especially deep:

> Thou mighty Mars the Lord of souldiers brave,
> And thou Minerve, that dois in wit excell,
> And thou Apollo, that dois knowledge have,
> Of every art that from Parnassus fell
> With all you Sisters that thaireon do dwell,

---

26. All citations below refer to the facsimile reproduction of this text in *Elegies for Sir Philip Sidney (1587)*, ed. Colaianne and Godshalk.

27. There are in fact two sets of "K" signatures, which caused me no end of confusion when I tried to find James's poem.

28. Baker-Smith, "Great Expectations," 94.

Lament for him, who duelie serv'd you all
Whome in you widely all your arts did mell,
Bewaile (I say) his inexpected fall,
I neede not in remembrance for to call
His race, his youth, the hope had of him ay
Since that in him doth cruell death appall
Both manhood, wit and learning every way,
  But yet he doth in bed of honor rest,
  And evermore of him shall live the best.

But again, like the Elizabeth sonnet, the fact of its author eclipses all aesthetic considerations. We have already seen James's concern for rendering explicit his authorship, and the typography suggests that James (or one of his ambassadors) and the printer collaborated on presenting his sonnet as a monarchic performance. The poem comes first (thus indicating the social and political preeminence of its creator), appears in English (all the other elegies are in Latin or Greek), and Windet further highlights it by using italic type and a slightly larger font than in the rest of the volume. Furthermore, Windet gives it the following title (the first line of which appeared in the larger font):

IN *PHILIPPI SIDNAEI*
interitum, Illustrisimi Scotorum
Regis carmen

Whereas Windet ascribes all the other poems to individuals (either through initials or full names), this one originates from an institution: it is a poem not by "James Stuart," but by the most illustrious king of the Scots (Illustrisimi Scotorum / Regis). As such, the poem seems nothing more than a royal tribute to Sir Philip Sidney, and the political/diplomatic resonances are complex.

Dominic Baker-Smith suggests that James's elegy for Sidney can be partly explained by their common interest in a "specifically Christian poetics."[29] Yet I know of no extant evidence suggesting that Sidney and James ever discussed poetry (despite their common interest in Guillaume Du Bartas), nor do I know of any evidence proving that they ever met in person. Furthermore, Baker-Smith does not take into account the ideological gulf separating James and Sir Philip, in particular their different views concerning the role of

---

29. Ibid. 94. See also Campbell, "Christian Muse," 45–49.

the monarch. By at least 1580, James thought that a king should be absolute, ruling by divine right, and he expressed these views to Walsingham at their first meeting in 1583 (for which Walsingham roundly rebuked him),[30] while Sidney sided more with Buchanan and the French resistance theorists. Nor was James, as we shall see, as hot a Protestant as Sidney might have liked. The mystery of why James would go to such trouble to write an elegy and to commission elegies for someone with whom he had deep ideological differences lifts when we remember the dictum that nations do not have friends, but interests.[31]

Therefore, as Baker-Smith point outs, however much James actually mourned Sidney, the poem also served James's desire to "commend his own name to those, in England and abroad, who looked for a fit successor to Elizabeth, one equipped to serve the Protestant interest."[32] In other words, James uses the occasion of Sidney's death to strengthen his claim to the English throne. Yet the matter is murkier than Baker-Smith allows, for if this poem shows James trying to ingratiate himself with Sidney's father-in-law, or more importantly, Elizabeth's trusted Privy Counsellor Walsingham, while implicitly advertising himself as Elizabeth's heir, he was also exploring his options with England's Catholic enemies. In sum, this poem should not be taken as a simple declaration of principle or ambition, as Baker-Smith suggests, but as one more example of the slipperiness of James's diplomatic maneuvering and his penchant for using verse to further his goals.

While Sidney and James might very well have liked each other had they met, their relations were more diplomatic than personal. Sidney's involvement with James dates back to 1585, when, as Roger Howell notes, his name starts to "figure prominently in Scots affairs."[33] Specifically, Sidney was deeply involved with Walsingham's negotiations over the amount of Elizabeth's pension for James. Of course, Sidney's activities on James's behalf formed part of his Protestant activism, as a large grant "would not only strengthen the Protestant cause north of the border but it would also help to thwart the

---

30. Read, *Mr. Secretary Walsingham,* 2: 212–13. According to Willson, Walsingham "told James that his power was insignificant, that he was too young to judge affairs of State, that he should rejoice in such as friend as Elizabeth, and [most interestingly] that young kings who sought to be absolute were apt to lose their thrones" (*King James VI and I,* 51).

31. It is worth noting that James's opinion of Sidney's poetic accomplishments shifted considerably after James's accession. In 1618–19, well after James had any need to praise Sidney for diplomatic advantage, he told Ben Jonson that "Sir P. Sidney was no poet" (quoted in *Poems of James VI,* ed. Craigie, 2: 234).

32. Baker-Smith, "Great Expectations," 93, 94.

33. Howell, *Sir Philip Sidney,* 106.

machinations of the continental powers."[34] And although neither Howell nor Baker-Smith mentions it, Sidney knew enough about James's interests to send him a gift of bloodhounds (not poems), for which James instructed his English ambassador to be sure to thank him.[35] While the negotiations for an Anglo-Scots alliance were ultimately successful (although James did not get as large a pension as he would have liked, nor, more importantly, an unequivocal statement about the succession), we need to remember that Elizabeth consistently resisted those who were unqualifiedly in favor of James.

The reason why is not hard to find, for if James appeared to Sidney as pro-English and (no doubt) pro-Protestant, the king was also treating with the Catholic powers. In 1585 (the same year that Sidney sent James the dogs), not only did the king refuse to keep the Catholic Earl of Arran in prison and out of favor, but—as Walsingham writes with considerable disgust—the Jesuits and the Guise were in Scotland with their own offers for James's "loyalty":

> For myself I give over all hope of Scotland otherwise than by force. I see no reason to think that Bellenden and Maitland's credit (now that Arran and Gray are reconciled) shall be able to prevail to keep the King in good terms with her Majesty. There are lately arrived in that realm one Hay, general of the Jesuits of the Scottish nation and one Durye that hath written against the ministers in Scotland....They are sent from the Duke of Guise with very large offers unto the King....I see so great treachery in that nation as I have no desire at all to have any extraordinary dealing with them.[36]

In another letter, Walsingham concluded that "the best is to deal warily with them all, for they are all born under one climate," and clearly Elizabeth agreed, for, Walsingham continued, "I can by no means persuade her Majesty to write to Gray, neither will she, in respect of the jealousy had of the King's cunning and unsound dealing, yield unto him the pension promised."[37] We therefore cannot regard James's elegy as unequivocal evidence of his devotion to Protestant humanism or of his undying devotion to the Leicester-Walsingham-Sidney faction's hostility toward Spain, as Baker-Smith argues,[38]

---

34. Ibid.
35. Letter to Lewis Bellenden, dated 12 April 1585, in *Letters of King James VI & I*, ed. Akrigg, 62.
36. Quoted in Read, *Mr. Secretary Walsingham*, vol. 2: 246.
37. Ibid., 248.
38. Baker-Smith, "Great Expectations," 95.

since James clearly adhered to one principle alone: his self-interest (we will return to James's dealings with Catholic powers below).

Of course, the "letting slip" of the pro-English Ruthven lords completely changed matters, and James finally signed the Anglo-Scots alliance that Sidney and Walsingham, among others, labored to bring about on 5 July 1586. But then, Walsingham brought to light the Babington plot, which would lead to the execution of Mary, Queen of Scots, and James once more consistently played a double game.

While reports famously vary regarding James's reaction to his mother's death,[39] James clearly tried to keep all his options open, not knowing "whether Protestant or Roman Catholic" would eventually win.[40] James may very well have intended, as Baker-Smith argues, his elegy for Sidney as an implicit endorsement of the Anglo-Scots treaty, a reassurance that both he and his chief advisors remained committed to England. This interpretation accords with James's secret understanding with Leicester that he would not break the alliance if his mother were executed, since that would mean losing the throne of England.[41] Furthermore, James continued his friendship with Henry of Navarre and delighted in the company of his favorite poet, the very Protestant Du Bartas. Yet at virtually the same time, James refused to receive Elizabeth's ambassador for several months, and he sent letters to Henry III, Catherine de Medici, and the Guises asking for support.[42] James's chancellor, Maitland, who also wrote in memory of Sidney, several months later made a speech in Parliament vowing "vengeance for Mary's blood."[43] In consequence, we need to regard the Sidney elegy not so much as a contribution to the making of the Sidney legend, but as another front in James's duplicitous diplomacy, an attempt—through the medium of verse—to reassure his English allies while he secretly negotiated with their enemies.

III

James wrote his mini-epic, the *Lepanto,* in 1585. The poem clearly meant more to him than anything else he wrote, since he included it in his 1591 volume, *His Majesties Poeticall Exercises,* along with a translation into French by

---

39. See the summary of the various reports of James's reactions, which range from being entirely unmoved to implicitly swearing revenge for his mother's death, in Stafford, *James VI of Scotland,* 17.

40. Stafford, *James VI of Scotland,* 17.

41. Ibid., 13.

42. Ibid., 18.

43. Ibid., 21.

Du Bartas. James then republished the *Lepanto* in 1603, followed by a Latin version by Thomas Moray in 1604 (entitled *Naupactiados*), both clearly part of his monarchic self-presentation in England, as they (obviously) coincided with his accession to the English throne. Consequently, James's continuing interest in his mini-epic probably stemmed from more than his estimation of the poem as his masterpiece. The *Lepanto* partakes of three distinct (if overlapping) sets of contexts, and as we will see, this text performs very different political work in 1585, 1591, and 1603. Furthermore, James alters his authorial self-presentation in accord with these different contexts.[44]

According to the hierarchy of genres popular in the early modern period, the epic—or "Heroicall song," as James terms it—ranks the highest. "The heroical," Sir Philip Sidney observes in his *Apology for Poetry*, "is not only a kind, but the best and most accomplished kind of poetry."[45] Consequently, writing an epic is a perfectly appropriate task for a poet-king (indeed, it might be the only genre worthy of a king). Yet when James turned to this subject in 1585, there was nothing obvious about his attraction to either the subject matter or the genre itself.

To be sure, the story of the Battle of Lepanto (1571) seems ideally suited for epic treatment: Don Juan, leading a fleet of 208 galleys sailing under the flag of a "Holy League" organized by Pope Pius V, the Spanish monarchy, and the Venetian republic, destroyed the Turkish fleet in one day of fighting, and the victory of the Christian forces over the Islamic "Other" was very quickly transformed into the subject of chronicles in Spanish, Italian, and Latin.[46] The victory did not mean very much strategically, however, as within one year the Turks had rebuilt their navy and were making "new incursions on the Spanish protectorate of Tunis, overtaking the town for good in 1574."[47] While, as Ferdinand Braudel remarks, "This victory seemed to open the door to the wildest hopes,"[48] and while seventeenth-century writers would depict this conflict as a heroic event, people closer to the battle itself recognized that the hopes led nowhere.[49] Furthermore, given James's lifelong aversion

---

44. On the thematics of book production and editing, see Kastan, Shakespeare after Theory 23–42, and his *Shakespeare and the Book*. See also Marcus, *Unediting the Renaissance,* 1–37.

45. Sidney, *Sir Philip Sidney,* ed. Herman, 92.

46. *Poems of James VI,* ed. Craigie, 1: lix–lx; Appelbaum, 186.

47. Appelbaum, 188; Wernham, *Counter-Reformation and Price Revolution,* 252–53, 353–54.

48. Braudel, *Mediterranean and the Mediterranean World,* 2: 1103; Appelbaum, 188.

49. Michel de Montaigne, for instance, uses this battle as an example of why we should not use earthly events as indicators of divine will: "It was a notable Sea-battle, which was lately gained against the Turkes, under the conduct of Don John of Austria. But it hath pleased God to make us at other times both see and feele other such, to our no small losse and detriment" (*Essayes of Montaigne,* 172). Donald Frame translates this passage from Montaigne as follows: "It was a fine naval battle that was

to both figurative and literal military exploits (his son, Prince Henry, distinguished himself from his father by adopting an explicitly chivalric and bellicose persona[50]), the king's decision to write the poem in the first place and then republish it requires more explanation than a desire to write an exciting story or to demonstrate expertise in a variety of genres on James's part.

The ideological work behind James's composition of the *Lepanto* becomes clearer when one takes into consideration his very tenuous hold on political power in 1585. The year before, James had Parliament pass bills asserting "the royal authority in the state, both in theory and in practice," no mean feat given the resistance, both in theory and in practice, of both the aristocracy and the clergy.[51] The clergy were furious at James for ending the Presbyterian system in Scotland, and a number had fled to England. The return of the banished Ruthven lords along with an army of 10,000 men added to James's troubles, and we have already noted the tense relations between the young king, Elizabeth, and Walsingham. "Estranged from Elizabeth, menaced by the exiled lords and ministers, and aware of discontent in Scotland,"[52] James chooses this moment to write an epic, and as Fischlin argues, the *Lepanto* could be construed as "an empowering literary response to the contingencies of sovereign rule by a monarch struggling to achieve a modicum of internal political stability."[53] In other words, James composed and distributed the *Lepanto* as part of his (at times desperate) project of asserting monarchic authority within and without Scotland by representing himself through the highest, most "noble" genre. While it would be absurd to assert that James actually thought that he would become Elizabeth's heir and subdue his recalcitrant clergy and aristocracy by writing epic poetry, James likely intended his poem to strengthen his prestige by interjecting himself "into the literary pantheon that contributes to [monarchic and poetic] authority."[54]

In addition to demonstrating James's attempt to add some luster to his crown by appropriating the cultural authority of the epic poet, the *Lepanto* exemplifies James's sometimes clumsy, sometimes adept strategy throughout his Scottish reign of balancing Catholic interests against those of the Protestants. First, James calls Don John (in the poem, "Don Joan") a "Generall

---

won these past months against the Turks, under the leadership of Don John of Austria; but it has certainly pleased God at other times to let us see others like it, at our expense" (*Complete Essays,* ed. Frame, 160).

50. See Strong, *Henry, Prince of Wales,* 115; and Herman, "'Is this Winning?'" 2.
51. Lee, *Great Britain's Solomon,* 64.
52. Willson, *King James VI and I,* 51.
53. Fischlin, "'Like a Mercenary Pöet,'" 547.
54. Ibid., 550.

great" (207) and depicts him as an ideal leader, who knows "the names of speciall men" and, somewhat like a nautical Henry V, rows about his troops, urging them on.[55] James also highlights Don John's nationality, consistently referring to him as "the Spanish Prince" (481, 798), and once uses orthography to emphasize the point: "The SPANIOL Prince" (497). Given the presence of Spain in Scots affairs at this point, it would be hard not to read these references as a deliberate compliment, just as the Sidney elegy could be construed as a declaration of loyalty to the Protestant side. As such, it would be hard for some of the hotter Protestants in Scotland not to take offense, but James takes them into consideration as well.

The poem itself splits neatly down the middle in its valuation of the anti-Turkish forces' religion. On the one hand, in the main body of the epic, James pointedly refuses to condemn either Don John's religion or his nationality. In the Job-like scene at the start of the poem, Christ says to Satan:

> I know thou from that City comes,
>   CONSTANINOPLE great,
> Where thou hast by the malice made
>   The faithless Turkes to freat [fret].
> Thou hast inflamde their maddest mindes
>   With raging fire of wraith [wrath],
> *Against them all* that doe professe
>   My name with fervent fayth.
>   (*49–56; my emphasis*)

Christ seems to care only about the profession of his name; none of the doctrinal quarrels dividing Christianty matter very much to him. Similarly, James consistently calls the anti-Turkish force and the inhabitants of Venice Christians rather than Catholics, thus once more submerging or erasing doctrinal and theological differences in favor of a larger unity. Even God, while not endorsing all forms of observance, nonetheless declines to dwell on these distinctions in his answer to Christ:

> *All christians* serves [sic] my Sonne though not
>   Aright in everie thing.
> No more shall now these *Christians* be
>   With Infidels opprest
>   (*79–82; my emphasis*)

---

55. All citations from *Lepanto* refer to Craigie's edition, *Poems of James VI,* vol. 1: 198–258.

The Turkish conquest of Cyprus "moo'ved each Christian King / To make their Churches pray for their / Relief in everie thing" (150–52); urged on by Gabriel's rumor campaign, the town's population and the Venetian senate implore "The Christian Princes" (190) for aid in the conflict "twixt the Turkes / and Christians" (195–96); and the entire fleet, made up of Spanish and Italian ships, are a "Christian Navy" (292).

Yet the angelic chorus at the poem's end displays no such ecumenicism. Its odd argument (rather, James's odd argument) is that if God gives victory to such *deficient* Christians, indeed, to people who barely deserve the title at all, imagine what he could do for Protestants:

> But praise him more if more can be,
>   That so he loves his name,
> As he doth mercie shew to all
>   That doe professe the same:
> And not alanerlie [only] to them
>   Professing it aright,
> But even to them that mixe therewith
>   Their own inventions slight:
> As specially this samin time
>   Most plainly may appeare,
> In giving them such victory
>   That not aright him feare:
> For since he shewes such grace to them
>   That thinks [sic] themselves are just,
> What will he more to them that in
>   His mercies onelie trust?
>
> (957–72)

One could dismiss these shifts in emphasis as another example of James's lack of skill, but they are entirely consistent with his refusal to choose unequivocally between Catholicism and Protestantism, or—perhaps more to the point—between the Catholic powers of Spain and France and the Protestant power of England.

In 1580–81, Esmé Stuart, the Earl of Lennox, dominated James's thinking and affections, and while he might have remained ignorant of the details concerning Lennox's intrigues with the Catholic powers, he nonetheless absorbed their lessons well. As David Harris Willson describes it, "He stood on the periphery of them, understanding their general drift, and was introduced to the subtle courses of a double diplomacy."[56] And James soon acquired a nasty reputation for two-facedness. Elizabeth, for instance, exclaimed with no end of annoyance: "That false Scotch urchin! What can be expected from the double dealing of such an urchin as this?"[57] James's strategy of playing Catholics off Protestants and vice versa intensified starting in 1584 and continued through 1585, exactly the period during which James composed the *Lepanto.* We have already noted James's highly tenuous hold on power because of various domestic problems, and opportunely in 1584 James received a letter from the Catholic Duke of Guise offering friendship and protection. James regarded this letter as a means of shoring up his crumbling authority, and he responded so positively that the Spanish king, Philip, noted, "He is quite ready to confess them himself"; Philip thought, in other words, that James would convert to Catholicism, a concept that James encouraged by writing to the Pope: "I trust to be able to satisfy your Holiness on all other points, especially if I am aided in my great need by your Holiness."[58] At the same time, James is negotiating with Elizabeth over the fate of his mother, and in May 1585, just before James started the *Lepanto,* Elizabeth opened up negotiations for a league with Scotland.

Ultimately, James realized that his interests lay with England and Protestantism, not with Spain, but he also realized that he could gain even more by keeping both in play. Consequently, as Willson observes, "Even while he sought aid from Catholic powers he strove tenaciously to improve his relations with England";[59] or one can restate this from the opposite perspective, that is, that James strove tenaciously to improve his relations with the Catholic powers while seeking a treaty with England. The matter is more evenly balanced that Willson's rhetoric allows, for, as Willson himself points out, James's negotiations with foreign Catholic powers, along with his refusal to curb his domestic Catholic lords, served to enhance "his bargaining

---

56. Willson, *King James VI and I,* 39.

57. Quoted in Willson, *King James VI and I,* 39, who also cites these other examples of English exasperation regarding James's "diplomacy": "'The King's fair speeches and promises,' wrote an English noble, 'will fall out to be plain dissimulation, wherein he is in his tender years better practised than others forty years older than he is. He is holden among the Scots for the greatest dissembler that ever was heard of for his years'" (39). Indeed, reading over their correspondence and Walsingham's various reports of his negotiations with James, it is hard not to have the sense that during the early years of James's reign Elizabeth considered him an intensely annoying little twerp who exasperated her beyond all measure.

58. Both quotes are cited in Willson, *King James VI and I,* 51.

59. Ibid., 52.

power with Elizabeth, formed a counterpoise to the Kirk, and offered hope of survival in case of Spanish victory."[60] At the time of its composition, therefore, the *Lepanto* participates in James's domestic and foreign diplomacy by exemplifying his attempts to keep all his cards in play. The main body of the text serves to assure the Catholic powers of his esteem for both their military heroes and their religion, and the angelic chorus serves to assure the Kirk and the English Protestants who happen to read the poem that James is really on *their* side. James, in other words, does not so much make a poetic attempt at forging a *via media* between the two opposing poles of Christianity as invent a strategy for maintaining maximum diplomatic advantage while avoiding a firm committment to either side.

By 1591, however, when James publishes the *Lepanto* as part of his *Poeticall Exercises,* both the domestic and the foreign contexts had shifted considerably. James had signed the treaty with England, the crisis over his mother's execution had passed, and he now clearly favored England and Protestantism. The formation of a moderate party within the Kirk made accommodating them easier,[61] and James continued to advertise his preference for Protestantism through his disputation with the Jesuit James Gordon, his marriage to the Protestant Anne of Denmark, and his eventual containment of the Catholic northern earls with George Gordon, Earl of Huntly's defeat in 1589. While James continued to infuriate with his refusal to completely repress the Catholic lords or to unequivocally sever his ties with Spain,[62] he recognized that his interests lay with Protestantism and England, not Spain and Catholicism, and acted accordingly.

But the shift in contexts created a problem for the *Lepanto,* which carefully endorses both sides because this strategy made diplomatic sense at the time of the poem's composition. James asserts, as so many authors in this period do, that the poem has circulated in manuscript without his knowledge: "For although till now, it have not bene imprinted, yet being set out the the publick view of many, by a great sort of stoln Copies, purchast (in truth) without my knowledge or consent" (198).[63] Even so, James concerns himself

---

60. Ibid., 81.

61. Ibid., 71.

62. Even though James threw the Spanish agent, Colonel Semple, in prison after the defeat of the Armada ("with great Protestant zeal," as Willson says), he nonetheless allowed him to escape (Willson, *King James VI and I,* 84).

63. There is no evidence that the *Lepanto* underwent unauthorized manuscript transmission, which suggests that James is making up this scenario of uncontrolled transmission. Furthermore, James's poetry rarely appears in contemporary miscellanies, and an entry in Stephen Powle's commonplace book suggests that James rather tightly controlled the copying of his lyric verses. Concerning "In Sunny beames the skye doth shewe her sweete," Powle writes that the poem was "Geaven

less with unauthorized transmission than with unauthorized *interpretation:* "It falles out often, that the effects of mens actions comes [sic] cleane contrarie to the intent of the Author. . . . It hath for lack of a Praeface, bene in somethings misconstrued by sundry" (198). In all likelihood, sundry *have* read the poem correctly, but now—in 1591—the original, evenly balanced meaning no longer serves James's interest, and so the "Author" adds a preface in an attempt to "guide" the reader to a more politically correct interpretation. Don John, which the text unambiguously declares a Christian hero, James now calls "a forraine Papist bastard," and he announces that "I name not DON-JOAN neither literally nor any waies by description" (198), even though James most certainly does name Don John both literally and by way of description. Furthermore, James explicitly denigrates Don John's military accomplishments and Catholicism: "Next followes my invocation to the true God only, and not to all the He and She Saints, for whose vaine honors, DON-JOAN fought in all his wars" (200). The preface, in other words, accommodates the change in political/diplomatic circumstances by trying to tip the poem's careful balance toward Protestantism, even if this means contradicting what the poem actually says.

We have already seen, in his 1586 letter to Elizabeth, James's sensitivity to the question of ascription, and he adopts a similar strategy in this text by highlighting his position as monarch. The (putative) misconstruction of the poem bothers James, but the offense against his royal dignity really annoys him:

And for that I knowe, the special thing misliked in it, is, that I should seeme, *far contrary to my degree* and Religion, like a Mercenary Poët, to penne a worke, *ex professo,* in praise of a forraine Papist bastard. . . . *For as it becomes not the honour of my estate,* like an hireling, to pen the praise of any man: *becomes it far lesse the highness of my rancke and calling,* to spare for the feare of favor of whomseoever living, to speake or write the trueth of anie. (198–200; my emphasis)

In a manner analogous to Henry VIII's warbled question, "Who shall me let?" and to Mary's "Entre ses mains," James invokes his degree, his estate, the highness, as he says, of his rank and calling to impose his interpretation on his poem. These references unmistakably mark the speaking "I" of the preface as a royal "I," and James offers his interpretation/corrections not just as evidence of authorial intention (i.e., I wrote the poem, so I know what it means

---

me by Master Britton who had been (as he sayed) in Scotland with the Kinges Majesty: But I rather thinke they weare made by him the the person of the Kinge" (quoted in Marotti, *Manuscript,* 14).

better than you), but of the absolute monarch's will. As Jonathan Goldberg suggests, in the preface "the powers of poet and king are parallel.... They exercise the discourse of power and the power of discourse."[64] The position James adopts, in other words, is that of king, not simply author, speaking to the reader, with the implication that the reader better pay attention.

Yet, ironically, in doing so James draws not just on his vision of God-like royal authority, but on the growing authority of authorship itself, and we can trace this development through an examination of the title pages, organization, and page layout of his books. During this period, as J. W. Saunders notes, gentlemen simply did not publish poetry.[65] Manuscript transmission was perfectly acceptable, even a mark of aristocratic identity, but because of the associations of print publication with the marketplace and commerce, publishing one's verse "could damage rather than enhance social status."[66] John Selden expresses this marvelously:

> 'Tis ridiculous for a Lord to print Verses; 'tis well enough to make them to please himself, but to make them public, is foolish. If a Man in a private Chamber twirls his Band-strings, or plays with a Rush to please himself, 'tis well enough; but if he should go into *Fleet-street,* and sit upon a Stall, and twirl a Band-string, or play with a Rush, then all the Boys in the Street would laugh at him.[67]

Monarchs had written books before (Henry VIII in particular),[68] and they (obviously) wrote poetry from time to time, but no one before James actually published their verse, and the anonymity of the title page demonstrates the tentativeness with which James approached this precedent-breaking move. Even though the book has a royal author, the printer presents it as an anonymous publication; the first page gives us the title—*The Essayes of a Prentise, in the Divine Art of Poesie* (1584; not insignificantly, the type gets progressively smaller and smaller, "Poesie" being nearly unnoticeable, and

---

64. Goldberg, *James I,* 18.

65. Saunders, "Stigma of Print," passim.

66. Wall, *Imprint of Gender,* 26. Wall does not dispute the existence of Saunders's "stigma," but she brilliantly elucidates the gender issues involved with "being a man in print."

67. Quoted in Marotti, *Manuscript,* 228.

68. However, the title page of Henry's book attacking Luther hardly privileges its royal authorship. The first two words of the title, *Libello Huic,* are printed in bold letters and are twice as big as the rest, *Regio Haec Insunt.* Below the title we have a table of contents, but Henry is not mentioned until the fifth item, "Libellus regius adversis Martinum" (the title page is reproduced in Neville Williams, *Henry VIII and His Court,* 86). In this case, the matter supersedes authorship in importance.

certainly subordinated to the more respectable term *Essayes*[69]). We are told that Vaultrollier printed the book "cum privilegio Regali," but nowhere does the title page reveal that the king made (fecit) the book (fig. 18). The introductory sonnets reveal that fact slowly and enigmatically, and even then the book's authorship is apparent only by the third sonnet (by "M. W."), which concludes with this couplet: "O Phoebus then rejoyce with glauncing glore, / Since that a King doth all thy court decore" (sig. *iii).

With the publication, however, of *His Majesties Poeticall Exercises,* in 1591, James more readily announces his responsibility for his text. The title page boldly declares that "His Majesty" wrote this book, with "Majesties" printed in larger type than anything else and in boldface (fig. 19). Even so, the title page of the 1591 edition of the *Lepanto* marks something of a retreat, since it privileges (as so many title pages of playbooks do) the work over the author (fig. 20). Reversing the layout of the initial title page, now the first two syllables of "Lepanto" are printed in large, boldface letters. The reader now knows the name and rank of the text's author ("James the sixt, King of Scotland"), but the work takes precedence over the royal author. What accounts for this change from James's first book?

On the one hand, it could be argued that the shift in title pages proves Goldberg's thesis, that we have an absolute monarch asserting his authority in the domain of authorship, thereby legitimizing authorship and removing, through the fact of his august presence, the "stigma of print." But by 1591 the category of "author" had already started to accrue considerable authority on its own as a middle-class, commercial entity. Marotti suggests that the publication of Sir Philip Sidney's literary works in the early 1590s "fundamentally changed the culture's attitudes toward the printing of the secular lyrics of individual writers, lessening the social disapproval of such texts and helping to incorporate what had essentially been regarded as literary ephemera into the body of durable canonical texts."[70] Yet Marotti also provides evidence of this shift starting earlier. In the first edition of George Gascoigne's *Hundred Sundrie Flowers* in 1573, as in James's *Essayes of a Prentise,* the title page omits the author's name. But in the second edition (1575), the printer gives the work an architectural frontispiece and retitles the work *The Posies of George Gascoigne.* Given that Gascoigne himself likely had no say in this, evidently the *printer* considered it commercially advantageous to make the work's authorship explicit and give it a privileged position. The buying public, in other words, had started to become as interested in who

69. One wonders if James intended a reference to Montaigne's *Essais,* first published in 1580–81.

70. Marotti, *Manuscript,* 229–30.

THE ESSAYES OF
A PRENTISE, IN THE
DIVINE ART OF
POESIE.

Imprinted at Edinbrugh, by Thomas
Vautroullier.
1584.

CVM PR·IVILEGIO
REGALI.

FIGURE 18. Title page, *The Essayes of a Prentise*, 1584 (Reproduced by permission of the Huntington Library, San Marino, California)

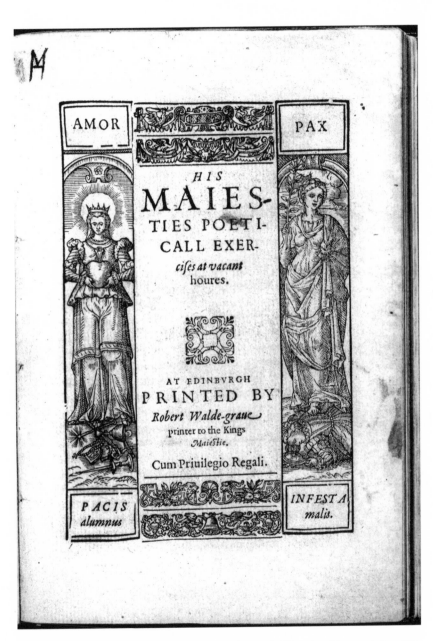

FIGURE 19. Title page, *His Majesties Poeticall Exercises,* 1591 (Reproduced by permission of the Huntington Library, San Marino, California)

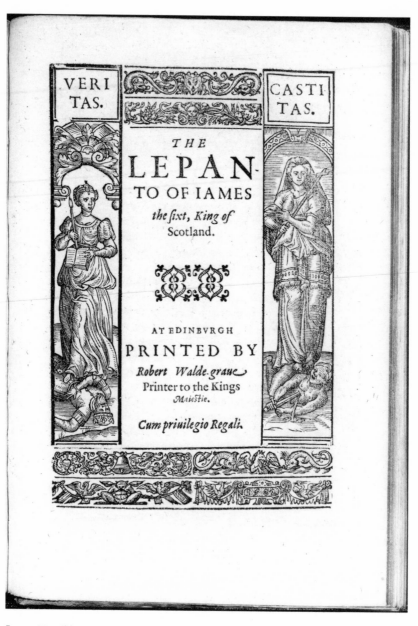

FIGURE 20. Title page, *Lepanto,* 1591 (Reproduced by permission of the Huntington Library, San Marino, California)

wrote the work as in the work itself. This development, however, emanates from the marketplace, not the aristocracy, where the "stigma of print" would continue for some time yet. When, therefore, James allows his Scots printer, Roger Waldegrave, to loudly proclaim the book's royal authorship, he is not so much legitimizing authorship with his royal presence as seeking to appropriate authorship's growing nonaristocratic prestige for himself. In other words, the king does not enhance authorship's authority; rather, authorship enhances the king's authority.

Edmund Spenser's construction of himself in the 1590 and 1596 editions of *The Faerie Queene* especially highlight this shift in authorship's status. On the first edition's dedication page, Montrose points out, "the relations between ruler and subject are graphically manifested," the Queen's name in bold, capital letters and Spenser's "in the lower right-hand corner of the page, in much smaller and italicized type, with only the initial letters capitalized and his given name abbreviated to 'Ed.'"[71] In the 1596 edition, the printer no longer distinguishes between the ruling subject and the ruled author, as he uses the same size and type of font for both, thus signaling the rise in authorship's cultural capital. "For Spenser," Montrose writes, "the material process of reproducing and distributing his poetry in printed books was culturally empowering."[72]

James clearly agreed and, I suggest, wanted to arrogate for himself some of poetic authorship's cultural empowerment upon his ascent to the English throne in 1603. Consequently, in addition to the other festivities, he also reprints the *Lepanto,* this time using the London printers Simon Stafford and Henry Hooke. (A Latin edition appeared one year later.) Several small changes in book layout from the poem's original publication demonstrate that the printers wanted the reader to interpret the 1603 *Lepanto* as a monarchic performance.[73] First, as the title page of the 1603 edition shows (fig. 21), Stafford and Hook print "Majesties" in larger type than anything else, and unlike the title page of the 1591 edition, not even a syllable break draws attention away from the poem's royal authorship. Second, whereas "The Lepanto" appears as the running header on the verso pages of the 1591 edition (fig. 22), in 1603 the printer changed this phrase to "The *Kings* Lepanto" (fig. 23; my emphasis; the running header of the recto pages, "Or, Heroicall Song," remained unchanged).

---

71. Montrose, "Spenser's Domestic Domain," 87.

72. Ibid.

73. Even so, the reception of the 1603 *Lepanto* pales in comparison to the huge success of the 1603 *Basilikon Doron,* which went through eight editions in 1603 alone (Wormald, "James VI and I," 51).

HIS

MAIESTIES

LEPANTO,

Or,

HEROICALL SONG,

being part of his Poeticall exercises
at vacant houres.

Imprinted at London by Simon Stafford,
and Henry Hooke.
1603.

FIGURE 21. Title page, *Lepanto*, 1603 (Reproduced by permission of the Huntington Library, San Marino, California)

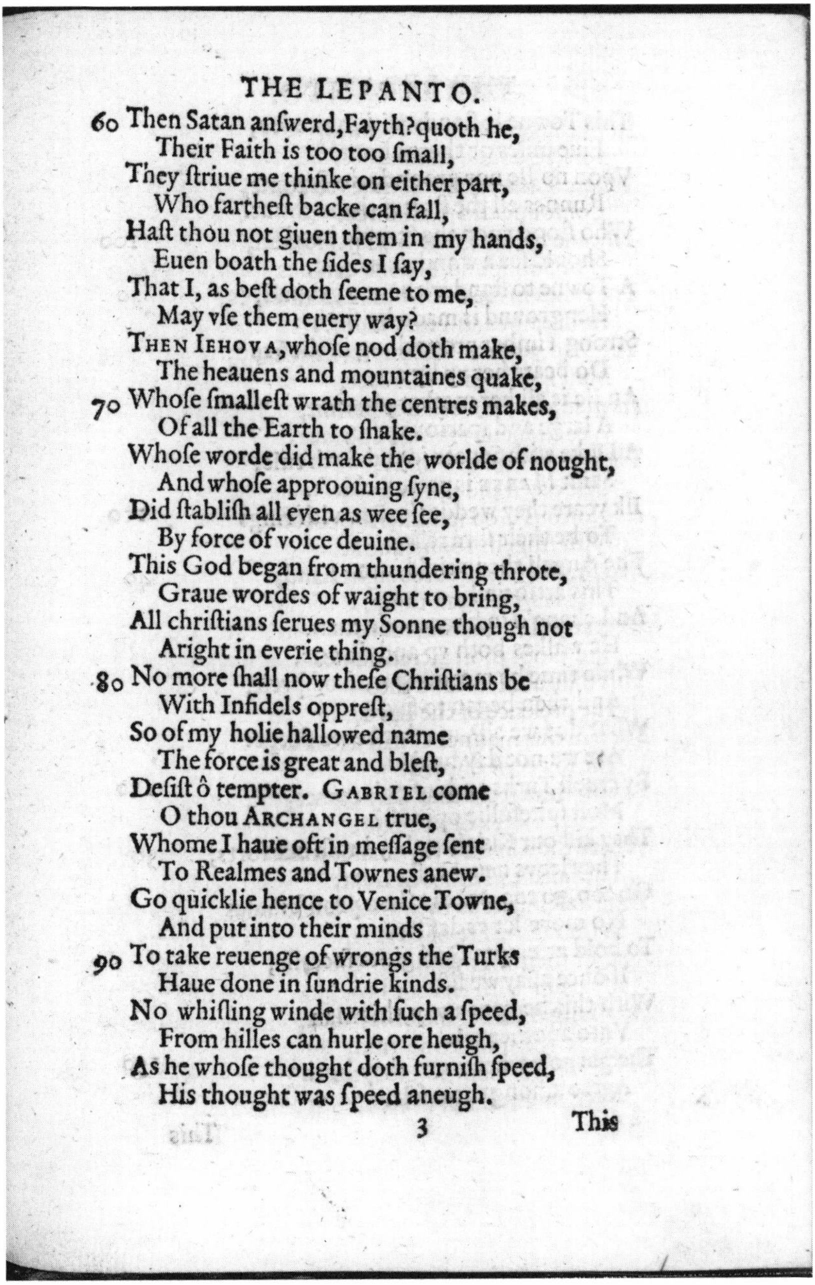

60 Then Satan anſwerd,Fayth?quoth he,
    Their Faith is too too ſmall,
They ſtriue me thinke on either part,
    Who fartheſt backe can fall,
Haſt thou not giuen them in my hands,
    Euen boath the ſides I ſay,
That I, as beſt doth ſeeme to me,
    May vſe them euery way?
THEN IEHOVA,whoſe nod doth make,
    The heauens and mountaines quake,
70 Whoſe ſmalleſt wrath the centres makes,
    Of all the Earth to ſhake.
Whoſe worde did make the worlde of nought,
    And whoſe approouing ſyne,
Did ſtabliſh all even as wee ſee,
    By force of voice deuine.
This God began from thundering throte,
    Graue wordes of waight to bring,
All chriſtians ſerues my Sonne though not
    Aright in everie thing.
80 No more ſhall now theſe Chriſtians be
    With Infidels oppreſt,
So of my holie hallowed name
    The force is great and bleſt,
Deſiſt ô tempter. GABRIEL come
    O thou ARCHANGEL true,
Whome I haue oft in meſſage ſent
    To Realmes and Townes anew.
Go quicklie hence to Venice Towne,
    And put into their minds
90 To take reuenge of wrongs the Turks
    Haue done in ſundrie kinds.
No whiſling winde with ſuch a ſpeed,
    From hilles can hurle ore heugh,
As he whoſe thought doth furniſh ſpeed,
    His thought was ſpeed aneugh.

3   This

FIGURE 22. Running header, *Lepanto*, 1591 (Reproduced by permission of the Huntington Library, San Marino, California)

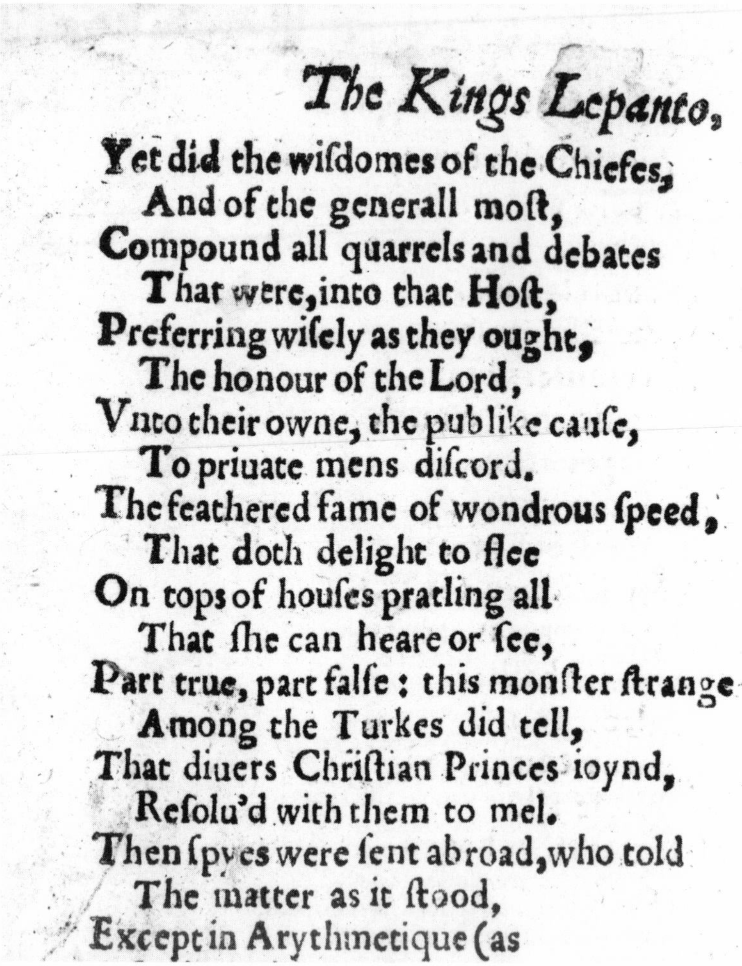

The Kings Lepanto,

Yet did the wiſdomes of the Chiefes,
  And of the generall moſt,
Compound all quarrels and debates
  That were, into that Hoſt,
Preferring wiſely as they ought,
  The honour of the Lord,
Vnto their owne, the publike cauſe,
  To priuate mens diſcord.
The feathered fame of wondrous ſpeed,
  That doth delight to flee
On tops of houſes pratling all
  That ſhe can heare or ſee,
Part true, part falſe : this monſter ſtrange
  Among the Turkes did tell,
That diuers Chriſtian Princes ioynd,
  Reſolu'd with them to mel.
Then ſpyes were ſent abroad, who told
  The matter as it ſtood,
Except in Arythmetique (as

FIGURE 23. Running header, *Lepanto,* 1603 (Reproduced by permission of the Huntington Library, San Marino, California)

The question still remains, why would James take the trouble to reprint this poem as part of his accession celebrations? One reason might be that James considered his accession the right time to appropriate for himself once more the cultural capital of poetic authorship, epic poetic authorship in particular, so as to further legitimate himself in a country not known for its high estimation of Scotland's cultural heritage.[74] James's reputation as a royal poet, as Perry notes, had achieved wide circulation by at least 1600, and so reprinting the *Lepanto* could be seen as an attempt to strengthen this image (the irony being that English poets used James to bolster poetry's sagging reputation in England).[75] In addition, he might have wanted to present something that would further reassure England of his Protestant bona fides, hence his republishing of the 1591 preface asserting the author's allegiance to Protestantism and revulsion toward Catholicism. Doubtless, both are true, and both demonstrate, once more, a monarch using poetry as a vehicle for politics. Yet in 1603, England already had an epic poet, Edmund Spenser, and I would speculate that James may have intended the 1603 *Lepanto* to dislodge Spenser from this position.

Certainly, James had reason for wanting to eclipse Spenser. After the 1596 *Faerie Queene* appeared, Robert Bowes informed Burghley that James wanted action against Spenser:

> The K[ing] hath conceaved great offence against Edward [sic] Spencer publishing in prynte in the second book p[art] of the Fairy Queene and ixth chapter some disnorable effects (as the k. demeth therof) against himself and his mother deceassed. He alledged that this booke was passed with prviledge of her mats [majesty's] Commission[er]s for the veiwe and allowance of all wrytinges to be receaved into Printe. But therein I have (I think) satisfyed him that it is not given with such p[ri]viledge: yet he still desyreth that Edward Spencer for faulte, may be dewly tryed & punished.[76]

To be sure, James's motivation here arises from something other (or less) than filial piety. Impugning his mother means impugning his lineage, and

---

74. In England, according to the Earl of Northumberland, "the name of Scots is harsh in the ears of the vulgar," and the more sophisticated "feared 'swarms of tawny Scots' who, locust-like, would devour office and wealth." The degree of contempt was so great that "the decapitated skull of a Scottish king was used as a flowerpot in the English royal conservatory" (Kishlansky, *Monarchy Transformed,* 78).

75. Perry, *Making of Jacobean Culture,* 23. On antipoetic discourse, see Herman, *Squitter-wits and Muse-haters.*

76. Quoted in Goldberg, *James I,* 1.

James, ever sensitive to anything that might jeopardize his chance to succeed Elizabeth, clearly considered Spenser's poem sufficiently authoritative to be a threat, and so he wanted Spenser punished. Elizabeth never responded to James's request (although perhaps she did when she and her Privy Council urged Spenser's appointment as sheriff of Cork), and so Spenser remained officially unsanctioned, widely read, and England's epic poet.

By publishing his own epic in 1603, James gives notice that England's king is also an epic poet, and just as the monarch sits at the head of the English church, so should the poet-king stand at the head of English poetry. The royal epic poet, in other words, should occupy the place in the canon now occupied by the late (and untitled) Edmund Spenser. Furthermore, while James's *Lepanto* obviously does not approach Spenser's epic in terms of sheer bulk, the two publications share certain formal qualities. Both include letters to the reader explaining the poem's meaning, and both letters complain of previous misinterpretations. Spenser's letter attempts to explain the allegory because the author finds himself misunderstood ("Sir knowing how doubtfully all Allegories may be construed, and this booke of mine, which I have entituled the Faery Queene, being a continued Allegory, or darke conceite, I have thought aswell for avoyding gealous opinions and misconstructions, as also for your better light in reading therof... to discover unto you the general intention & meaning [of this text]";[77] James also writes a preface because he has (ostensibly) been "misconstrued by sundry" (198). While James's preface obviously predates Spenser's by five years, that might not have been immediately obvious to the English reader, since the *Poeticall Exercises* was published in Edinburgh, making it likely that few in London had read it. For the London book-buying audience, therefore, it is at least possible that a reader familiar with both texts would consider James's preface an imitation of Spenser's, and because of James's position as king, his preface would perforce supersede Spenser's.

Furthermore, Spenser's epic begins with a series of commendatory sonnets that are often ascribed using initials rather than full names. In the 1591 version of the *Lepanto,* James includes his own commendatory sonnet at the poem's end, signing it "I.R.S" (for Jacobus Rex Scotorum). But in the 1603 edition, he moves the sonnet from its original place to immediately before the poem and signs the sonnet "I.R." (sig. A3), not "I.R.S." The omission of "S" doubtless signals that he rules more than just Scotland, but it also has the effect of echoing the two initials that Spenser uses to sign his commendatory sonnets: "E.S." The design and the genre of the 1603 *Lepanto,* in sum, recall in enough details Spenser's *Faerie Queene* that one can legitimately wonder

---

77. Spenser, *The Faerie Queene,* ed. Roche, 15.

whether James set out to remind the reader of Spenser's poem. The point, however, would not be homage, since James considered the *Faerie Queene* a threat (perhaps it is lucky that Spenser died in 1599); rather, I suggest, at some level James wanted to replace the *Faerie Queene,* which glorified his predecessor while casting James's mother as a whore, with the *Lepanto,* the king's own Protestant epic. By republishing his poem almost immediately upon his accession, James announces that England's new king is now England's epic poet as well, that he has not only succeeded both Elizabeth and her archpoet, Spenser, but also combined the offices of English monarch and English poet. The 1603 *Lepanto,* in short, announces to James's new kingdom that he, not Spenser, deserves the title of England's Protestant Vergil.

The 1603 *Lepanto* may also mark the the high point for monarchic verse in England, as afterward the fortunes of "royal poetrie" seem to decline. After 1603, James's interest in publishing verse wanes, and so, while the title page of his 1616 collected works constitutes the most elaborate construction to date of James as royal author (the full title is *The Workes of the Most High and Mighty Prince, James*[78]), he conspicuously omits poetry from this text. Yet James did not entirely give up writing verse. In 1622, he wrote and circulated a poetic defense of himself in response to a critical libel (now lost).

James had good reason to feel a bit cranky in 1622. Public opposition to his favorite, George Villiers Duke of Buckingham, as well as anti-Spanish fervor, had continued to grow. King Philip of Spain and his ambassador to England, Diego de Acuna Sarmiento (now Count de Gondomar), continued to temporize concerning the potential marriage of Charles to the Infanta as well as deceive James about their intentions on the continent, where James's Protestant son-in-law, Frederick, had accepted the throne of Bohemia after the Bohemians had deposed the Catholic Archduke Ferdinand, thereby angering Spain and threatening to involve England in a religious war. James did not display a consistent foreign policy toward Spain, which added to the general confusion and frustration (Edward Coke asked with some amazement: "Will he have wars with Spain and a marriage?"[79]). Adding to his troubles, James suffered from a bout of ill-health sufficiently serious that he thought he was dying, and while he recovered, he was so weakened that after he called a parliament in 1621 (for a war subsidy), he had to be brought in to the chamber on a litter for his opening speech. While the parliament started

---

78. Interestingly, the printer uses the same size font for "Workes" and "James," thereby privileging neither one, as is the case in James's previous publications.

79. Quoted in Russell, *Parliaments and English Politics,* 135.

well, it ended in yet another bitter clash between James's absolutism and the Ancient Constitution.[80]

The flashpoint came toward the end of what was generally an amicable session when the Commons presented James with a petition "asking for the enforcement of existing anti-Catholic laws and urging that Charles should be found a Protestant wife."[81] James was furious because it seemed to him that the Commons impinged upon the royal prerogative of conducting foreign policy, and upon the paternal prerogative of marrying off Charles to whomever James wanted. He wrote to the Speaker that his sickness "hath emboldened some fiery and popular spirits of some of the House of Commons to argue and debate publicly of matters far above their reach and capacity, tending to our high dishonour and breach of prerogative royal."[82] For the House, the matter no longer concerned foreign policy, but the fundamental rights of Parliament: if the king could restrict their freedom of speech, then, in Conrad Russell's words, "their institution was not merely obscelescent, but obscelete [sic]."[83] The Commons delivered a "Protestation" to the king, and James responded on 17 December 1621 with a lecture on political philosophy:

> Whereas in our said answer we told them [Parliament] that we could not all of the style, calling it their ancient and undoubted right and inheritance, but could rather have wished that they had said their privileges were derived from the grace and permission of our ancestors and us (for most of them grow from precedents which shews rather a toleration than in heritance), the plain truth is that we cannot with patience endure our subjects to use such anti-monarchical words to us concerning their liberties except they had subjoined that they were granted unto them by the grace and favor of our predecessors.[84]

However, James did not let matters rest with an exchange of words. He decided not only that the protestation needed to be expunged but that he would do it himself. Therefore, he went to the council chamber, got the clerk of Parliament to produced the Commons' Journal Book, and then "His majesty erased it from the Journal Book with his own hand, and ordered an Act of Council to be entered thereof."[85] After keeping everyone

---

80. For an excellent summary of the events surrounding James in 1622, see Stewart, *Cradle King,* 195–214.

81. Ibid., 311.

82. Quoted in Russell, *Parliaments and English Politics,* 135.

83. Ibid., 141.

84. *Commons Debates 1621,* ed. Notestein, Relf, and Simpson, vol. 2: 529.

85. Quoted in Stewart, *Cradle King,* 313.

in suspense for ten days, he finally prorogued Parliament, but the conflict remained unresolved.

In response to widespread criticism of his Spanish policies, the constitutional crisis ending the 1621 Parliament, and a specific libel (now, unfortunately lost), James penned his own poem, "Oh stay your teares you who complaine," which was widely circulated.[86] Several of the manuscripts include the heading "The Kinges verses,"[87] and like Henry VIII's "Though some say that youth rules me,"[88] this poem regularly asserts itself as the product of the royal "I." Addressing the complainers, James asserts: "You cannot judge whats truly myne, / who see noe farther than then the rine" (7–8). But in this poem, James sets forth a hyperbolic vision of absolutist authority that goes well beyond anything Henry VIII or Elizabeth proposed.

In the Whitehall speech of 26 March 1610, James asserted: "The State of MONARCHIE is the supremest thing upon earth: For Kings are not onely GODS Lieutenants upon earth, and sit upon GODS throne, but even by GOD himselfe they are called Gods."[89] Even so, in his speech to Parliament, James says that kings are *like* God, not that they *are* God: "Kings are justly called Gods, for that they exercise a manner or resemblance of Divine power upon earth."[90] In his 1622 poem, kings and the Lord are now peers, and they are equally distant from their subjects: "God & Kings doe passe together / but vulgar wander light as feather" (11–12). True, James qualifies this statement, yet he still asserts a special relationship with God, one previously occupied by poets, and that special relationship means that kings are to be obeyed without question:

> God above men, kings inspires [sic].[91]
> Hoold you the publique beaten way
>   Wonder at kings & them obey.
> ffor under God they are to chuse
> What rights[92] to take, what refuse
>   (14–18)

---

86. All citations from this poem refer to Craigie's edition, *Poems of James VI*, 2: 183–90. On the circulation of this poem, see Craigie, 2: 263. Craigie publishes two versions of this poem (Malone 23 and Harley 367). For the sake of convenience, all quotations in my discussion refer to the Harley 367 version, and substantial variants in Malone 23 will be cited in the notes.

87. *Poems of James VI*, ed. Craigie, 2: 263.

88. See chapter 1.

89. *Political Writings*, ed. Sommerville, 181. I have silently applied modern spelling.

90. *Political Writings*, ed. Sommerville, 181.

91. "God above all men kings inspires."

92. "right."

"Kings," James declares, "ever overreach you all" (142), and therefore, like God, as James once said of Francis Bacon's *Novum Organum,* they "passeth all understanding":[93] "Kings cannot comprehended be / In common mouths"[94] (144, 146). Kings also have God-like power over their subjects' lives. Kings, James writes, "kill even by there sharpe aspecte / the proudest mynde they can dejecte / Make wretched the moste mighty man / though he doth mutinye[95] what he can" (52–55); and later in the poem: "He doth disdaine to caste an eye / of anger on you leaste you die" (148–49). Again like God, James may have the power, but he is primarily merciful: "If I once bend my angry browe / your ruine comes though not as now. / ffor slowe I am revenge to take / & your amendment wrath willd slake" (165–68).

The poem is not an abstract exercise in political philosophy, but a direct intervention into contemporary affairs. Furious at the public criticism of his foreign policy and speculation about Charles's marriage, James issued two proclamations (1620 and 1621) against "excess of lavish and licentious speech of matters of State," in which he warned "all Our lovinge subjects, from the highest to the lowest, to take heed how they intermeddle by pen or speech with causes of state, and secrets of government."[96] These are "matters above their reach and calling," "unfit for vulgar discourse," and engaging in "the inordinate liberty of unreverent speech" will "highly and directly [affront] Us in our Royall commandement." Unsurprisingly, throughout "Oh stay your teares," James reiterates the importance of *arcane imperii* and how no one other than himself and his council are qualified to talk about state matters. "Purblind people," the king writes at the poem's start, "why doe you prate / too shallowe for the depth of State? / You cannot judge whats truely myne" (5–7). The result of public discussion, James warns, is anarchy: "What counsells should be overthrowne[97] / if all were to the people knowne. / & to no use were Counsell Tables / if State affaires were publike bables?" (76–79). Therefore, "meddle not *with* your Princes cares, / For who soe doth, too much he dares" (96–97).

James's assertions of the supremacy of kings in this poem also arise directly from the unresolved constitutional conflict at the end of the 1621 Parliament. From the beginning of James's reign, defenders of parliamentary privilege and the Ancient Constitution often cited the Magna Carta against

---

93. *Letters of John Chamberlain,* ed. McLure, 2: 339.

94. "In Commons circles."

95. "mutter."

96. James issued second editions of both the 1620 and the 1621 proclamations. I will be quoting from the second edition of the 1621 proclamation.

97. "What Counsells would be overthrowne."

the claims of Jacobean absolutism. In 1610, Thomas Hedley declared that the "ancient freedom and liberty of the subjects of England...is confirmed by the great Charter of the liberties of England....For I do not take Magna Charta to be a new grant or statute, but a restoring or confirming the ancient laws and liberties of the kingdom, which by the Conquest before had been much impeached or obscured."[98] Hedley does not state where these "ancient laws" reconfirmed by the Magna Carta come from, and that is because he assumes that their origin lies, to use Sir Edward Coke's phrase, "time out of mind of man,"[99] meaning that "no man then knew the contrarie, either out of his owne memorie, or by any Record, or other proofe."[100] In 1621, faced with James's assertion that the "ancient laws and liberties of the kingdom" are not independent of royal authority, but dependent upon royal grace, the M.P. Thomas Crew, understanding the gravity of this issue, referred back to an earlier protestation by the House:[101]

> We are upon a weighty business. Our privileges are by law from our ancestors and are our due....And by Mr. Chancellor it was said that we declare to his Majesty that the privileges are our inheritances as in the 1 of Jacobi and a protestation upon it and that act to be read. This is of that great consequence. That our liberties must be maintained that they are by inheritance: if we should yield that they are permissive, the walls would witness the contrary as in Magna Carta. We have it granted to their subjects and to their heirs forever, and from us and our ancestors forever, the cities of London and all corporations and all persons, all privileges as they were wont to have which they had afore and franchises and liberties of barons.

Crew was not alone. Sir Edward Coke declared that "the liberties are our inheritance," and, referring to this speech, William Hakewill also maintained that "our privileges are part of the law; not only in my opinion, but in Sir Edward Coke's," and even further: "We may hold our liberties as our ancient privileges by inheritance, used in the protestation in the first session of the first parliament about impositions."[102]

---

98. *Proceedings in Parliament 1610,* ed. Foster, 2: 210.

99. Pocock, *Ancient Constitution and the Feudal Law,* 30–55.

100. Coke, Preface, 1: 62.

101. *Commons Debates 1621,* ed. Notestein, Relf, and Simpson, 2: 525–26. See also Sommerville, *Politics and Ideology,* 98.

102. *Commons Debates 1621,* ed. Notestein, Relf, and Simpson, 2: 530, 533.

James, obviously, held the opposite view. Rights, he told Parliament, flow from the monarch: "Their privileges were derived from the grace and permission of our ancestors and us (for most of them grow from precedents which shews rather a toleration than in heritance)."[103] In "Oh stay your teares," he upends the conventional understanding of English politics in three ways. First, the Magna Carta does not bind the monarchy, as the monarchy created it:

> The Charter *which* you greate doe call
> > Came first from Kings to stay yo*ur* fall.
> ffrom an unjust rebellion movde
> > by such as Kingdomes little loved.
> > > *(118–21)*

Second, laws are not made by Parliament in concert with the monarchy. While it is true, James states, that the monarch calls Parliament into session, once the Parliament has been called, James erases the role of the two houses in making law: "The Parliam*ent* I will appoint / When I see things more out of joint. / Then will I sette wrye things straight" (60–62). Even further, he states: "Kings doe make lawes to bridle you" (114). Finally, and perhaps most portentously, monarchs are not accountable for their actions: "Was ever kinge calld to account?" (66) James asks. The answer James has in mind is obviously no.

But unlike Henry VIII's and Elizabeth's interventions in the political imaginary, James's fails in both its immediate and its longer-term goals. As Curtis Perry notes, the poem may acknowledge "the political importance of manuscript libel," yet at the same time it "acknowledges the crown's failure to contain it."[104] Rather than recuperating "the king's discursive authority,"[105] the poem only serves only to dissipate it further, insofar as the libels did not stop, nor did the king's threats about instant death come to pass. The poem thus rehearses the limits of monarchic power evident in the second proclamation against excess and lavish speech in matters of state, which begins by admitting that nobody is listening: "And yet wee are given to understand, that notwithstanding the strictnesse of Our commandment, the inordinate liberty of unreverent speech...doth dayley more and more increase."

---

103. Ibid., 529.
104. Perry, "'If Proclamations will not Serve,'" 211. I am indebted throughout this section to Perry's fine analysis.
105. Perry, "'If Proclamations will not Serve,'" 211.

Ironically, James complains that his critics would turn monarchy into the very cipher of a function: "O what a callinge were a kinge / if he mighte give or take nothinge / but such as you shall[106] to him bring / Such were a kinge but in a playe / if he might beare no greater[107] swaye" (41–45). But circulating a poem with the futile demand that the "rayling rimes & vaunting verse" (23) cease probably did more to undermine James's authority than the poems about which he complains. The poem's larger goals also failed, as the absolutist vision of English monarchy outlined in this poem, as well as in James's speeches and *The Trew Law of Free Monarchies* (1598; reprinted in London, 1603), would lead ultimately to the English Revolution and the execution of James's son, Charles. As much as they tried, the Stuarts could not impose a theory of monarchy antithetical to the Ancient Constitution and the practice of mixed monarchy.

If the "royal poetrie" produced by Henry VIII and Elizabeth demonstrates the ability of monarchs to alter the political imaginary of authority in the early modern period, the verse by the Stuarts can be said to illustrate the limits. Indeed, the attempts by James (and in the Casket Sonnets, Mary, Queen of Scots) to fashion an image of monarchy fundamentally different from the dominant one in Scotland and England suggest the larger truth of Montrose's argument that the monarch is "a privileged agent in the production of the royal image," but not "its master."[108] James obviously had a tremendous amount of power to fashion his image, and he used verse as one of the means by which he established and maintained authority. But the political imaginary can bend or be manipulated only so much, and James's unsuccessful attempt to impose absolutism upon Parliament and, indeed, the country suggests the outside limits of a monarch's power to shape the royal image. We will now see what sort of poetry is produced in the name of a king who transgresses those limits and finds himself "calld to account."

---

106. "should."
107. "better."
108. Montrose, *Subject of Elizabeth*, 2.

CHAPTER 5

Charles I and the End(s) of Monarchic Verse

When John Milton published *Eikonoklastes* (1649), his point-for-point refutation of the *Eikon Basilike* (Image of a King),[1] he condemned the king's book as a piece of mere fiction, noting that it had recently been turned into verse:

> The Simily wherewith he begins I was about to have found fault with, as in a garb more Poetical then for a Statist: but meeting with many straines of like dress in other his Essaies, and hearing him reported a more diligent reader of Poets, then of Politicians, I began to think the whole Book might perhaps be intended a peece of Poetrie. The words are good, the fiction smooth and cleanly; there wanted onely Rime, and that, they say, is bestow'd upon it lately.[2]

Milton may have had in mind *The Divine Penetential Meditations and Vows of His Late Sacred Majestie in his Solitude at Holmby House, Faithfully Turned into Verse* (London, 1649), attributed to Edward Reynolds, in which the author

---

1. While the book was attributed to Charles I, John Gauden is now generally considered the author.

2. Milton, *Eikonoklastes*, in *Complete Prose Works of John Milton*, ed. Don M. Wolfe et al. (New Haven: Yale University Press, 1962), vol. 3: 406.

presents "a flower plucked out of that most excellent storeyard [*Eikon Basilike*], meanly turned into verse,"[3] but Milton may also have been aware of the clutch of poems circulating under Charles I's name, which included "His Majesties Complaint Occasioned by His Sufferings" (1647) and "A Copie of Verses, Said to be Composed by His Majesty, Upon his First Imprisonment in the Isle of Wight" (1648). Other poems ostensibly by Charles are the Scots ballad "King Charles's Lament" (c. 1650)[4] and "Majesty in Misery; or, An Imploration to the King of Kings," which first appeared in Gilbert Burnet's *Memoires of the Dukes of Hamilton* (1677) and was republished twice thereafter (1681, 1700).[5]

As the qualifications indicate, it is highly unlikely that Charles actually wrote any of these works. Unlike most of his forebears, Charles never evinced any interest in producing verse or writing. In his first speech to Parliament, he stated that it did not "stand with My Nature to spend much time in words,"[6] and indeed, until his death, as Lois Potter writes, Charles I had the reputation of being "a king of images rather than words."[7] But Charles, as Todd Butler notes, lost control over the political imaginary, and while the later Caroline masques constitute an attempt to reassert control over "the imagery of his monarchy,"[8] that attempt obviously failed.

When, therefore, Royalists sought to reassert control over the political imaginary, they abandoned one set of images in favor of others that they hoped would be more successful. Significantly, that meant reasserting the importance of words and the imagination in their constructions of Charles's imagery. Furthermore, these poems not only reflect "a consensus as to what the King ought to have written,"[9] as Peter Davidson puts it, they contribute to the shift in the political imaginary toward including, if not privileging, writing as an instrument of monarchic authority. The ballad *C.R. In a Cloud*

---

3. Reynolds, "To the Reader," in *Divine Penetential Meditations,* n.p.

4. "King Charles's Lament," in *Poetry and Revolution,* ed. Davidson, 325–28. The poem first appeared in *James Watson's Choice Collection of Comic and Serious Scots Poems* (Edinburgh, 1706–11). Peter Davidson informs me that it likely emerged from "Stuart-loyalist circles in the 1650s" (e-mail message to author, 10 March 2008). The lyric is the last in the last volume (117), and there is no editorial apparatus indicating its provenance.

5. *Memoires,* sigs. CCC2r–4r. The full title is "Majesty in Misery; or, An Imploration to the King of Kings, written by his late Majesty King Charles the First, during his Captivity in Carisbrook Castle, Anno Dom. 1648."

6. Quoted in Butler, *Imagination and Politics,* 13.

7. Potter, "Royal Martyr," 157.

8. Butler, 87.

9. Davidson, *Poetry and Revolution,* 541. While Davidson provides edited versions of "Majesty in Misery," "King Charles's Lament," and "His Majesties Complaint," (322–32), I will quote these works from their original editions.

(1647) offered the following evaluation: "Every one doth think / That great Caesars Inke, / Never wrot better. / And as for the matter / We cannot here flatter, / The Royall Inditer, / But say, as true 'tis, / The Pen (as was his), / Is of a ready Writer."[10] What better evidence of the king's literary talent than the poems he supposedly wrote? Especially when one of those poems, "His Majesties Complaint," explicitly rewrites George Herbert's "The Sacrifice," simultaneously demonstrating the king's good literary taste and appropriating for the king's cause Herbert's considerable authority.[11]

And yet, as we have seen, the expectation was that the verse produced by monarchs should reflect their status as monarchs. The question now is, what happens when the monarch (supposedly) writing the poems has been, in a phrase from "Majesty in Misery," "Dis-crowned" (sig. CCC3r)? What kind of verse does a monarch write, or is a monarch expected to write, once he or she no longer occupies the throne, and the traditional properties of absolute monarchy—in particular divine origin and therefore divine protection—cannot be sustained? How does a monarch—or his ventriloquizers—subject to military defeat and execution, recapture lost authority? How do these poems redefine the term "royal poetrie"?

The first answer would be that these poems explicitly point toward their (ostensible) royal authorship in both their titles and their contents. "A Copie of Verses, said to be Composed by His Majesty" contains numerous references to the usurpation of the king's scepter and the king's lost power.[12] Similarly, "His Majesties Complaint" begins, "Are wee your King?" and later reasserts the author's royal identity: "I have been truckt for, bought and sold, yet I / Am King (though prisoner) pray tell me why / I am removed now from Holdenby?" As the reference to Holdenby (one of the places where the king was held prisoner) indicates, these poems are overtly political in their aims. "His Majesties Complaint" is so topical that the printer supplied an extensive note to explain the reference to the "National Covenant" (sig. A3). Most importantly, these poems all seek to intervene in the political imaginary by attempting to reshape the image of the monarch. But whereas earlier instances of monarchic verse sought to intervene in the contests over royal policy, as reflected by the images of monarchy, the verses ascribed to

---

10. Raymond, "Popular Representations," 63.

11. See Gottlieb, "Royalist Rewriting," 211; and Achinstein, "Reading George Herbert," 430–65.

12. E.g., "T'usurpe my *Scepter,* and to make my *power* / *Gnaw* its owne *Bowels,* and it selfe devoure?"

Charles arise out of an almost unprecedented situation: a civil war that the king lost.

Fascinatingly, the poems seek to recapture authority by emphasizing precisely the opposite. In the early 1640s, Royalist propaganda consistently used the language of absolutism to refer to the king. Charles is a "Sacred Person,"[13] an "anoynted King,"[14] and "God's vicegerent."[15] One "J. L" declared in his apology titled "His Sacred Majesty" (1642) that "the King can do wrong" (sig. A3v),[16] and John Taylor called Charles "the Lords anointed."[17] This position obviously cannot be maintained in the face of military loss and captivity. But rather than avoiding the issue, these poems begin by admitting the utter powerlessness of the speaker. The tone of defiance permeating "A Copie of Verses" is unique ("d'ee think my *soule* can be / *Grasp'd,* or infringed, by such low things as ye?"), yet it starts by admitting imprisonment: "Must I be / Your fetter'd Slave, whilst you'r at liberty?" The tone and position of "His Majesties Complaint," however, is sad, even hopeless. The king compares himself to helpless prey ("Causeless they like a bird have chased me," sig. A4v),[18] and the poem's burden alternates between "Never was King so griev'd," "Never was griefe like Ours," and "Never was griefe like mine." Charles was alive when these two poems circulated, but after his death the rhetoric grew even more pathetic. The Scots ballad "King Charles's Lament" has the king declare: "My Griefs and Troubles cannot numbred be: / A hopeless, helpless, harmless Man lies here forlorn, / And held in Scorn" (17–19).

This new emphasis on the monarch's humanity and vulnerability has two purposes. First, as Joad Raymond notes, "Portraits of Charles's deprivations increasingly focused on his separation from family,"[19] but the purpose of such portraits goes beyond increasing pathos or enlisting the reader's sympathies (although both remain important), for the disruption of the family is always juxtaposed with the disruption of the state. In "A Copie of Verses," the king asks: "Was't not enough you made me beare the *wrong* / Of a *Rebellious*

---

13. *King Charles his Defence* (London, 1642), sig. A2v.; see also Samuel Butler, *A letter from Mercurius Civicus to Mercurius Rusticus* (London, 1643), sig. C2. I owe these references and the subsequent ones to Raymond, "Popular Representations," 69 n. 29.

14. A. A., *No Peace,* sig. A3v.

15. Quoted in Raymond, "Popular Representations," 54.

16. *Just Apology,* sig. A3v.

17. *Plea for Prerogative,* sig. A4v.

18. While for the sake of convenience I refer to the speaker of these poems as "the king," I recognize that "the king" is a literary trope, as these poems were, in all likelihood, not written by Charles I.

19. Raymond, "Popular Representations," 62.

Sword, and worser *Tongue,* / To take my *Crowne, State, Children, Friends,* and *Wife* / But will you have my *Liberty,* and *Life?*" In "His Majesties Complaint," the king juxtaposes the fates of his family and his throne:

> Our Scepter's broke, our Lawes lie trodden downe,
> The Revenues belonging to our Crowne
> Are all but purchasers of your renowne.
>   Never was griefe like Ours.
> Our Wif's debar'd us, Our deare Children too,
> Our *Conscience* must be subject unto *you:*
> Why don't you vote to *part our Garments too?*
>   Was ever griefe, &c.?
>
>   (*sig. A2*)

And in "King Charles's Lament," once more rebellion and the destruction of the family are set in parallel: "They raise a deadly Strife, / To separate and breed Debate / Betwixt me and my Wife; / My children also are abus'd, / As to the World is known, / And other they do now enjoy / That which was once my own" (50–56).

If, as has been noted so often, there is a homology in the early modern period between the family and the commonwealth, if the king, as Charles's father, King James, puts it, "towards his people is rightly compared to a father of children," and so, "the style of *Pater patriae* was ever, and is commonly used to Kings,"[20] the fate of one signifies the fate of the other. Consequently, the emphasis on the monarch's personal relations, his portrayal as a man who loves and misses his wife and children, has the paradoxical effect of demystifying Charles (he has a family life like most other people) and *re*-mystifying him by implicitly reminding the reader of the familial relationship between ruler and subject. The rhetorical abandonment of the trappings of monarchy ironically reemphasizes the monarchic position of the poems' speaker as the destruction of political order equals the destruction of the monarch's family, and vice versa.

The image in these poems of a persecuted king, beset by enemies on all sides, calling on God for help (e.g., "His Majesties Complaint," sig. A4v: "Behold, O Lord, looke downe from heaven and see, / Thou that hearest prisoners prayers, hear me / . . . / Thou know'st my wrongs, their vengeance they have wrought, / Their reproaches thou hast heard, and what

---

20. *The Trew Law of Free Monarchies* (1598), in *Political Writings,* ed. Sommerville, 76.

they though, / And now hast all their counsels brought to nought"), also has a purpose beyond stirring up pathos and the reader's sympathy. As Lois Potter has noted, as Charles's political fortunes waned, the king was increasingly associated with David,[21] and again, Charles deliberately fostered the parallel. In the "Penitential Meditations" included in the *Eikon Basilike,* for example, Charles wrote: "I come far short of David's piety; yet since I may equal David's afflictions, give me also the comforts and the sure mercies of David."[22] Thus the poems frequently echo if not the precise words, then the situation of many of the Psalms. Like the speaker in Psalm 3, for example, which begins, "Lord, how are they increased that trouble me! many are they that rise up against me" (King James Version), the speaker in "King Charles's Lament" complains, "Thus am I ev'ry Day most barbarously used, / Basely abused, / By some of them for whom I have done good" (71–73). And just as in Psalm 7, the speaker asks God for vengeance ("Arise, O Lord, in thine anger, lift up thyself because of the rage of mine enemies," 6), so does "His Majesties Complaint" end with Charles asking God to do the same ("Give them rewards, Lord, for their working fit, / Sorrow of heart, thy curse, and with thy might / Follow, and from under heaven destroy them quite," sig. A4v).

On the one hand, the parallels would seem to work against the purposes of this propaganda, since they seem to confirm Charles's position as defeated and his enemies as ascendant. Astute readers of the Psalms might also remember that often as not, David's invocations to the Lord are in the conditional (the Lord has not yet acceded to David's requests for aid). But English monarchs from at least Henry VIII onward have styled themselves as David,[23] and if Cromwell did not foster the connection himself, Andrew Marvell did it for him.[24] They did so because David represents a model of kingship that is not only ideal, but divinely appointed and an instrument of Providence.[25] Consequently, the parallel between King Charles and King David has two purposes that, like the family imagery, work in opposite directions simultaneously. First, the parallel emphasizes the suffering monarch, as literalized by William Marshall's frontispiece to Malvezzi's *David Persecuted*

---

21. Potter, *Secret Rites,* 160–62.

22. *Eikon Basilike,* ed. Knachel, 149. While *Eikon Basilike* was likely put into its final form by Dr. John Gauden, Charles contributed substantially to the book, and the king read and corrected the manuscript before it went to print (xxx–xxxii). In other words, if the precise words are not Charles's, they represent his intentions.

23. See King, "Henry VIII as David," 78–92.

24. Mazzeo, "Cromwell as Davidic King," 29–56.

25. Ibid., 32; Potter, *Secret Rites,* 162.

(1647), which shows a distinctly Charles-like David playing a harp. But in so doing, the parallel reinforces Charles's claim to divinely instituted authority, along with the implied promise of divine retribution. Lastly, the parallel reinforces the primary end of Royalist propaganda: the transformation of Charles I from a divinely appointed absolute monarch to a royal martyr, a process that evidently started several years before Charles's actual execution, with his explicit approval and participation.[26] In a 1642 letter to the Duke of Hamilton, for example, Charles wrote: "I will either be a glorious king or a patient martyr."[27] The phrase finds its way into the conclusion of "A Copie of Verses": "Ile die a *Martyr,* or Ile live a *King."* As we now know, Charles ultimately fulfilled the first alternative.

The last piece of monarchic verse we shall examine, "Majesty in Misery; or, An Imploration to the King of Kings," first appeared in Gilbert Burnet's *Memoires of the Dukes of Hamilton* (London, 1677). Burnet claimed that he got the poem from a servant. Part of his purpose in this work, Burnet writes, is to "publish such Remaines of his [Charles's] Pen as had not been formerly seen or known. I shall therefore insert a Copy of Verses written by his Majesty in his Captivity, which a very worthy Gentleman, who had the honour of waiting on him then, and was much trusted by him, Copied out from the Original, who avoucheth it to be a true Copy"(sig. CCC2).[28] The poem closely follows the pattern established by the earlier examples of the king's verse. It consistently points toward the monarchic status of its author. It begins: "Great Monarch of the World, from whose Power Springs / The Potency and Power of Kings, / Record the Royal Woe my Suffering sings" (sig. CCC3r). Later, the author complains: "With my own Power my Majesty they wound, / In the King's Name the King himself's uncrowned" (sig. CCC4v). As these lines indicate, the poem continually emphasizes the helplessness of its author: even though "nature and Law, by thy Divine Decree" have invested Charles with "the sacred Scepter, Purple Robe, / The Holy Unction, and the Royal Globe, / Yet am I levell'd with the life of *Job"* (sig. CCC3r). "Majesty in Misery" also emphasizes the disintegration of Charles's family. His wife "Is forc'd in Pilgrimage to seek a Tomb," and "Great *Britain's* Heir is forced into *France,* / Whilst on his Father's head his foes advance: / Poor child! He weeps out his Inheritance" (sig. CCC4v).

---

26. Raymond, "Popular Representations," 60; Potter, "Royal Martyr," 242.

27. Quoted in Potter, *Secret Rites,* 173.

28. Raymond refers to this poem as a "1649 ballad" ("Popular Representations," 54), but I have seen no evidence of earlier circulation. Certainly, Burnet presents the poem as if it were published for the first time.

Yet "Majesty in Misery" differs from the earlier poems in two significant ways. First, it expands the use of the carnivalesque tradition of the "world turned upside down." Whereas the earlier poems occasionally alluded to this trope (e.g., "A Copie of Verses": "*Subjects* can have no *safety* but their *graves* / When *Slaves* doe sway, and *Soveraignes* are slaves"; and "His Majesties Complaint," sig. A2: "Wee must obey, that should all you command"), it is a major feature of "Majesty in Misery." Political categories are now inverted: "Tyranny bears the Title of *Taxation* / Revenge and Robbery are *Reformation*, / Oppression gains the name of *Sequestration*" (sig. CCC3v); as are hierarchical relations: "Church-men are chain'd, and Schismaticks are free'd, / Mechanicks preach, and Holy Fathers bleed" (sig. CCC4v). Certainly, the use of this tradition seems contrary to its usual associations of contesting and overturning, if only briefly, hierarchy and authority.[29] One is more used to thinking of the carnivalesque in terms of John Skelton's Elynour Rummyng or Ben Jonson's Ursula, the Pig Woman, than monarchs.[30] And yet, as Lois Potter reminds us, "the definitions of carnival and proper world order depended on one's allegiance. For royalists, a country without a king was a carnivalesque world-turned-upside-down."[31] Thus John Taylor, who calls himself a "well-willer to the King, Parliament and Kingdom" on the title page of *The World Turn'd Upside; or, A Briefe Description of the Ridiculous Fashions of these Distracted Times,* asserts that "this is England's case every day / All things are turn'd the clean, contrary way" (sig. A2). Anticipating "Majesty in Misery," Taylor writes that traditional religious authority is now overthrown: "The felt-maker, and sawcie Stable Groom / Will dare to pearch into the Preachers roome / . . . / *Ignoramus* will his Teacher teach, / And Sow-gelders and Cobblers dare to preach" (sig. A3). That is exactly the position of "Majesty in Misery": "The Church of *England* doth all Faction foster, / The Pulpit is usurpt by each Imposter, / *Ex tempore* excludes the *Pater Noster*" (sig. CCC4v).

Second, "Majesty in Misery" focuses on Charles the royal martyr in a way the other poems do not. Aside from the ending of "A Copie of Verses" ("Ile die a *Martyr,* or Ile live a *King*"), these poems avoid explicit invocations of Charles's execution. "His Majesties Complaint" is exactly that—an extended

---

29. See Kunzle, "World Upside Down," 39–94; Davis, "Reasons of Misrule" and "Women on Top"; and Laqueur, "Crowds, Carnival, and the State." The locus classicus is Bakhtin, *Rabelais and His World.*

30. On Elynour, see Herman, "Leaky Ladies and Droopy Dames"; and on Ursula, see Haynes, "Festivity."

31. Potter, "Royal Martyr," 244.

complaint over how badly Charles has been treated, and the poem ends with the king asking God to avenge the political crimes of the rebels, crimes that do not yet include regicide: "I was their song whether they rise or sit, / Give them reward, Lord; for their working fit, / Sorrow of heart, thy curse, and with thy might / Follow, and from under heaven destroy them quite" (sig. A4v). Similarly, "King Charles's Lament" focuses on the suffering king, "A captive Pris'ner kept is Slavery" (59), and ends with the king's desire "for my Release" (112), not his crucifixion.

Yet "Majesty in Misery" does everything it can to reinforce the image of Charles the martyr. Next to the poem Burnet includes a woodcut (fig. 24) that is clearly indebted to William Marshall's famous foldout illustration for *Eikon Basilike* (fig. 25). In both, the earthly crown lies at the king's feet while he picks up crown of thorns and stares at the heavenly crown. The poem that follows emphasizes, in a way its predecessors do not, the physical harm facing Charles: "With my own Power my Majesty they wound, / In the King's Name the King himself's uncrowned: / So doth the Dust destroy the Diamond" (sig. CCC4v). Even more specifically, we are told "The Crown is crucified with the Creed" (sig. CCC4v). The poem ends, not with a plea for freedom or the destruction of enemies, but with what seems to be a retrospective acceptance of death and a plea for blessings on the state: "Augment my Patience, nullifie my Hate, / Preserve my Issue, and inspire my Mate, / Yet though We perish, bless this Church and State" (sig. CCC4r). Furthermore, Burnet and his Royalist publisher, Richard Royston,[32] do everything they can to call attention to "Majesty in Misery." The poem is introduced by the only woodcut in the *Memoires,* and the text uses a larger, italic font than the rest of the book. Clearly, Burnet wanted to emphasize this poem. The question is why.

"Majesty in Misery" has a very different set of cultural meanings than the earlier examples of poetry ostensibly written by Charles. In the 1640s and 1650s, the point of such texts as *Eikon Basilike,* "A Copie of Verses," "His Majesties Complaint," and "King Charles's Lament" was to increase the political capital of the defeated, then executed king, and to discredit his enemies. By 1677, however, the situation had obviously changed. Charles II was safely on the throne (not that many were happy with his frivolous rule), and the cult of Charles the Martyr had gone into a steep decline. As the civil war and the regicide faded into the past, official remembrances, such as the fast day to commemorate Charles's execution, fell into greater and greater

---

32. For a summary of Royston's career, see Williams, "Richard Royston."

FIGURE 24. Woodcut from Gilbert Burnet, *Memoires of the Dukes of Hamilton*, 1677 (The Burke Library [Columbia University Libraries] at Union Theological Seminary, New York)

FIGURE 25. Woodcut from John Gauden, *Eikon Basilike,* 1649 (By permission of the Folger Shakespeare Library)

disuse.[33] Samuel Pepys, for example, may have done without food that day in 1664, but only because he and his wife had forgotten to stock the larder in advance.[34] We are not yet at the point when someone would say, "After 45 Yeares there ought to be an end,"[35] but we are very close. Yet Gilbert Burnet not only prints "Majesty in Misery" in a format designed to emphasize Charles's image as martyr, but in 1675 he publishes *The Royal Martyr Lamented, in a sermon Preached at the Savoy on King Charles the Martyrs Day* (1674), one year after he had finished writing the *Memoires* and three years before he published the book.[36]

---

33. Potter, "Royal Martyr," 247.

34. Ibid.

35. Quoted in Potter, "Royal Martyr," 248.

36. Martin Greig, "Burnet, Gilbert (1643–1715)" in *Oxford Dictionary of National Biography,* ed. H. C. G. Matthew and Brian Harrison (Oxford: OUP, 2004); online ed., ed. Lawrence Goldman, January 2008, http://www.oxforddnb.com/view/article/4061 (accessed March 20, 2008).

It would seem that Gilbert Burnet is a true believer, striving mightily against the steadily declining interest in the royal martyr. Yet there are additional resonances beyond maintaining his faith in the departed king. After he completed the manuscript of the *Memoires,* Burnet traveled to London, where through the offices of his patron, John Maitland, 2nd Earl of Lauderdale, and Charles II's secretary of state in Scotland, he met Charles II and his brother James, hugely impressing both of them.[37] But Burnet's favor with the royal family was short-lived because of Lauderdale's jealousy, and the young cleric was quickly banished from the court. Both *The Royal Martyr* and, I suggest, Burnet's inclusion of "Majesty in Misery" in the *Memoires* are as much an attempt at restoring his own favor as refurbishing a weakening cult. Thus Burnet casts the subject of his book in terms of merit unrewarded. In the dedicatory epistle to Charles II, Burnet writes: "SIR, You have here a true Account of the Services and Sufferings of two of Your Subjects, who dedicated themselves to Your Majesty's Interests, and became Sacrifices for them.... The Younger survived as long he could serve Your Majesty: but when he saw his Life like to be Unprofitable in Your Service, it became uneasy to himself, which made him so prodigal of it in your own fight." And in his sermon, Burnet reminds the congregants, and by extension, Charles II, of "those who were so generously and nobly loyal as to serve his late *Majesty* of most blessed memory" (sig. A4r).

Given Burnet's own situation at the time, that is, suddenly without the favor he needed to thrive at court, it seems plausible that the late dukes of Hamilton serve the same function that Petrarchism did for Sir Philip Sidney and others—a vehicle for expressing the frustrations of denied courtly service and favor. And while I do not doubt the sincerity of Burnet's royalism, his fervent attachment to the highly attenuated cult of royal martyrdom seems designed as much to curry favor with Charles II as to express devotion to the executed king. "Majesty in Misery" is thus part of a larger project, but the poem does not intervene in the political imaginary of Charles I; rather, its object is the resurrection of Gilbert Burnet's career at the court of Charles II. Thus the end of the early modern genre of monarchic verse— after this poem, there are no others by Charles or any other monarch—also entails a shift in the ends of this verse. "Majesty in Misery" may reiterate the image of Charles as martyr, but the point is less political and more careerist. "Majesty in Misery" is a plea for patronage, an attempt at appropriating Charles's imagery for Burnet's gain by telling his potential royal patron what Burnet thinks Charles II wants to hear.

---

37. Ibid.

Burnet, however, misread the times. Charles II had little interest in promoting the cult of his father (the restored king did nothing to create a monument or tomb until 1678, and even then the plans came to nothing),[38] and in any event, Burnet's career thrived without the help of the Stuarts.[39] The time for monarchic verse, for "royal poetrie," as a potent force within the culture had passed.

---

38. Potter, "Royal Martyr," 252.

39. The plea failed, and Burnet never returned to court. Even so, royal disfavor did not stop him from thriving, and in 1675 he received two prominent positions: "chaplain to the Rolls Chapel, which was conferred on him, much against the wishes of the court, by Sir Harbottle Grimston, master of the rolls" and "Thursday lecturer at St Clement Danes" (Greig, "Burnet, Gilbert"). These appointments plus his writing allowed him to live very comfortably.

❧ WORKS CITED

Primary Sources

A. A. *No Peace 'til the King Prosper.* Oxford, 1645.

Accounts and Papers Relating to Mary Queen of Scots, ed. Allen J. Crosby. Camden Society 93. London, 1867.

The Arundel Harington Manuscript of Tudor Poetry, ed. Ruth Hughey. Columbus: Ohio State University Press, 1960.

Aske, James. *Elizabetha Triumphans.* London, 1588.

Baret, John. *An Alveary or Triple Dictionary, in English, Latin, and French.* London, 1574. In *Lexicons of Early Modern English,* available online at http://leme.library.utoronto.ca/search/results.cfm (accessed 20 February 2007).

Beza, Theodore. *Master Bezaes Sermons Upon the Three First Chapters of the Canticle of Canticles,* trans. John Harmon. London, 1587.

Boccaccio, Giovanni. *Boccaccio on Poetry: Being the Preface and the Fourteenth and Fifteenth Books of Boccaccio's "Genealogia Deorum Gentilium,"* trans. Charles B. Osgood. New York: Liberal Arts Press, 1956.

Bodin, Jean. *On Sovereignty,* ed. and trans. Julian H. Franklin. Cambridge: Cambridge University Press, 1992.

Brantôme, Pierre de. *Recueil des Dames, Poésies et Tombeaux,* ed. Etienne Vaucheret. Paris: Gallimard, 1991.

Buchanan, George. *Ane Detectioun of the Duinges of Marie, Quene of Scottes.* London, 1571.

———. *The Tyrannous Reign of Mary Stewart,* ed. and trans. W. A. Gatherer. Edinburgh: Edinburgh University Press, 1958.

Burnet, Gilbert. *The Memoires of the Dukes of Hamilton.* London, 1677.

Butler, Samuel. *A letter from Mercurius Civicus to Mercurius Rusticus.* London, 1643.

———. *C.R. In a Cloud.* London, 1647.

Camden, William. *The History and Annalls of Elizabeth, Queen of England.* London, 1628.

———. *The History of the Most Renowned and Victorious Princess, Elizabeth.* London, 1630.

Castiglione, Baldesar. *The Book of the Courtier,* trans. Charles Singleton. Norton Critical Edition, ed. Daniel Javitch. New York: Norton, 2002.

Catullus. *Catullus: The Poems,* ed. Kenneth Quinn. London: MacMillan, 1970.

Cavendish, George. *The Life and Death of Cardinal Wolsey.* In *Two Early Tudor Lives,* ed. Richard S. Sylvester and Davis P. Harding. New Haven: Yale University Press, 1962.

Chaloner, Thomas. *De Republica Anglorum.* London, 1579.

Charles I [attr.]. *A Copie of Verses, Said to be Composed by His Majesty, Upon his First Imprisonment in the Isle of Wight.* London, 1648.

——. *Eikon Basilike: The Portraiture of his Sacred Majesty in his Solitudes and Sufferings,* ed. Philip A. Knachel. Ithaca, NY: Cornell University Press, 1966.

——. "His Majesties Complaint Occasioned by His Sufferings." London, 1647.

——. "King Charles's Lament." In *Poetry and Revolution: An Anthology of British and Irish Verse 1625–1660,* ed. Peter Davidson, 325–28. Oxford: Oxford University Press, 1998.

——. "Majesty in Misery; or, An Imploration to the King of Kings, written by his late Majesty King Charles the First, during his Captivity in Carisbrook Castle, Anno Dom. 1648." In Gilbert Burnet, *The Memoires of the Dukes of Hamilton,* sigs. CCC2r–4r.

Churchyard, Thomas. *The Miserie of Flaunders, Calamitie of Fraunce, Misfortune of Portugall, Unquietnes of Irelande, Troubles of Scotland: And the blessed state of Englande.* London, 1579.

Coke, Sir Edward. Preface to "Part Three of the *Reports.*" In *The Selected Writings of Sir Edward Coke,* ed. Steve Sheppard. Indianapolis: Liberty Fund, 2003.

Commons Debates 1621, ed. Wallace Notestein, Frances Helen Relf, and Hartley Simpson. 7 vols. New Haven: Yale University Press, 1935.

Conn, George. *Vita Mariae Stuartae Scotiae Reginae.* Rome, 1624.

Cotgrave, Randle. *A Dictionarie of the French and English Tongues.* London, 1611.

Dekker, Thomas. *The Shoemaker's Holiday.* In *English Renaissance Drama: A Norton Anthology,* ed. David Bevington et al., 483–544. New York: Norton, 2002.

Elegies for Sir Philip Sidney (1587), ed. A. J. Colaianne and W. L. Godshalk. Delmar, NY: Scholars' Facsimiles and Reprints, 1980.

An Elegy Sacred to the Memory of our most sacred Gracious Lord King Charles. London, 1649.

Elizabeth I. *Autograph Compositions and Foreign Language Originals,* ed. Janel Mueller and Leah S. Marcus. Chicago: University of Chicago Press, 2003.

——. *Queen Elizabeth I: Selected Works,* ed. Steven W. May. New York: Washington Square Press, 2004.

Elizabeth I and James VI/I. *Letters of Queen Elizabeth and King James VI. of Scotland,* ed. John Bruce. Camden Society 46. London, 1849.

Fortescue, Sir John. *On the Laws and Governance of England,* ed. Shelley Lockwood. Cambridge: Cambridge University Press, 1997.

François I. *François Ier: Oeuvres Poétiques,* ed. J. E. Kane. Geneva: Editions Slatkine, 1984.

——. *Poésies et Correspondance du Roi François Ier,* ed. M. Aimé Champollion-Figeac. Reprint, Geneva: Slatkine Reprints, 1970.

Frarinus, Peter. *An Oration against the Unlawfull Insurrections of the Protestants.* London, 1566.

Garter, Bernard. *The Joyfull Receyving of the Queenes most excellent Majestie into hir Highnesse Citie of Norwich.* In *Records of Early English Drama: Norwich 1540– 1642,* ed. David Galloway, 247–330. Toronto: University of Toronto Press, 1984.

The Geneva Bible: A Facsimile of the 1560 Edition, intro. Lloyd E. Berry. Madison: University of Wisconsin Press, 1969.

Goodman, Christopher. *How Superior Powers Oght to be Obeyd of their subjects: and Wherin they may lawfully by Gods Worde be disobeyed and resisted.* Geneva, 1558.

The Great Tournament Role of Westminster, ed. Sidney Anglo. Oxford: Clarendon Press, 1968.

Guillet, Pernette du. *Rymes,* ed. Victor E. Graham. Geneva: Drosz, 1968.

Hall, Edward. *Hall's Chronicles,* ed. Sir Henry Ellis. London: J. Johnson et al., 1809.

Harington, Sir John. *Nugae Antiquae: Being a Miscellaneous Collection of Original Papers in Prose and Verse Wirren in the Reigns of Henry VIII, Queen Mary, Elizabeth, King James, &c.,* ed. Henry Harington. 2 vols. London, 1775.

Henry VIII. *The Love Letters of Henry VIII, ed. Jasper Ridley. London: Cassell, 1988.*

——. *The Lyrics of the Henry VIII Manuscript,* ed. Ray Siemens. Renaissance English Text Society. Forthcoming.

——. "Selected Poems," ed. Ray Siemens. In Herman, *Reading Monarchs Writing,* 217–29.

Henry Stanford's Anthology: An Edition of Cambridge University Library Manuscript Dd. 5.75, ed. Steven W. May. New York: Garland, 1988.

Heywood, Thomas. *Gynaikeion; or, Nine bookes of various history, Concerninge women inscribed by ye names of ye nine Muses.* London, 1624.

Historical Manuscripts Commission. Part XVI. London: Her Majesty's Stationary Office, 1933.

"A Homily of the State of Matrimony." In William Shakespeare, *The Taming of the Shrew: Texts and Contexts,* ed. Frances E. Dolan, 171–84. New York: Bedford, 1996.

Inner Temple Library, Petyt MS 538.

James VI/I. *King James VI and I: Political Writings,* ed. Johann P. Sommerville. Cambridge: Cambridge University Press, 1994.

——. *Letters of King James VI & I,* ed. G. P. V. Akrigg. Berkeley: University of California Press, 1984.

——. *The Poems of James VI. of Scotland,* ed. James Craigie. 2 vols. Edinburgh: Scottish Text Society, 1955.

——. *A Proclamation against Excesse of Lavish and Licentious Speech of Matters of State.* London, 1621.

——. "Selected Poems." In Herman, *Reading Monarchs Writing,* 281–323.

——. "A Speech to the Lords and Commons of the Parliament at White-Hall (1610)." In *Divine Right and Democracy: An Anthology of Political Writing in Stuart England,* ed. David Wootton, 107–9. Harmondsworth: Penguin, 1986.

James Watson's Choice Collection of Comic and Serious Scots Poems, ed. Harriet Harvey Wood. 1706–11. Reprint, Edinburgh: Scottish Text Society, 1977.

Jonson, Ben. *Ben Jonson,* ed. C. H. Herford and Percy Simpson and Evelyn Simpson. 11 vols. Oxford: Clarendon Press, 1925–52.

A Just Apology for His Sacred Majestie. London, 1642.

Kendall, Timothy. *Flowers of Epigrammes.* Manchester: Spenser Society, 1874.

King Charles his Defence. London, 1642.

Knox, John. *The First Blast of the Trumpet against the Monstrous Regiment of Women.* Geneva, 1558.

——. *The History of the Reformation in Scotland.* In *The Works of John Knox,* ed. David Laing. 6 vols. Reprint, New York: AMS, 1966.

The Last parte of the Mirour for Magistrates. London, 1575.

Legg, Leopold G. Wickham, ed. *English Coronation Records.* Westminster: Archibald Constable, 1901.

Letters of John Chamberlain, ed. Norman Egbert McLure. 2 vols. Philadelphia: The American Philosophical Society, 1939.

Lorris, Guillaume de, and Jean de Meun. *Roman de la Rose,* trans. Charles Dahlberg. Princeton: Princeton University Press, 1971.

Mary, Queen of Scots. *Bittersweet within My Heart: The Collected Poems of Mary, Queen of Scots,* ed. and trans. Robin Bell. London: Pavilion, 1992.

——. *Letters of Mary, Queen of Scots,* ed. Agnes Strickland. 2 vols. London: Henry Colburn, 1843.

——. *The Letters and Poems by Mary Stuart, Queen of Scots,* ed. Clifford Bax. New York: Philosophical Library, 1947.

——. *The Poems of Mary Queen of Scots.* ed. Julian Sharman. London: Basil Montague Pickering, 1873.

——. *The Poems of Mary Queen of Scots to the Earl of Bothwell.* Haarlem: Enschedé en Zonen, 1932.

——. *Queen Mary's Book: A Collection of Poems and Essays by Mary Queen of Scots,* ed. P. Stewart-Mackenzie Arbuthnot. London: George Bell, 1907.

——. "Selected Poems." In Herman, *Reading Monarchs Writing,* 231–55.

Meres, Francis. *Palladis Tamia.* In *Elizabethan Critical Essays,* ed. G. Gregory Smith, 2: 308–24.

Milton, John. *Eikonoklastes.* In *Complete Prose Works of John Milton,* ed. Don M. Wolfe et al., 3: 337–601. New Haven and London: Yale University Press, 1962.

Montaigne, Michel de. *The Complete Essays of Montaigne,* trans. Donald Frame. Stanford: Stanford University Press, 1965.

——. *The Essayes of Montaigne: John Florio's Translation.* New York: Modern Library, 1933.

Nicot, Jean. *Thresor de la Langue Française.* Paris, 1606. In *Dictionnaires d'Autrefois: French Dictionaries of the 17th, 18th, 19th, and 20th Centuries,* available online at http://www.lib.uchicago.edu/efts/ARTFL/projects/dicos/ (accessed 20 February 2007).

Original Letters Illustrative of English History, ed. Sir Henry Ellis. 3rd ser. 11 vols. London: Richard Bentley, 1846.

Papal Negotiations with Mary Queen of Scots During her Reign in Scotland, 1561–1567, ed. John H. Pollen. Edinburgh: Scottish History Society, 1901.

Petrarch, Francisco. *Petrarch's Lyric Poems: The Rime Sparse and Other Lyrics,* trans. Robert M. Durling. Cambridge, MA: Harvard University Press, 1976.

Plato. *The Collected Dialogues of Plato,* ed. Edith Hamilton and Huntington Cairns. New York: Pantheon Books, 1961.

A Plea for Prerogative; or, Give Caesar his Due. London, 1642. *Proceedings in Parliament 1610,* ed. Elizabeth Read Foster. 2 vols. New Haven: Yale University Press, 1966.

Puttenham, George. *The Arte of English Poesie [1589],* intro. Baxter Hathaway. Kent, OH: Kent State University Press, 1970.

Reynolds, Edward [attr.]. *The Divine Penetential Meditations and Vows of His Late Sacred Majestie in his Solitude at Holmby House, Faithfully Turned into Verse.* London, 1649.

Rhodes, John. *The Countrie Mans Comfort.* 2nd ed. London, 1637.

Ronsard, Pierre de. *Oeuvres Complètes,* ed. Jean Cénard, Daniel Ménager, and Michel Simonin. 2 vols. Paris: Gallimard, 1993.

———. *Oeuvres Complètes,* ed. P. Laumonier. 15 vols. Paris: Société des Textes Français Modernes, 1914–75.

Sidney, Sir Philip. *Sir Philip Sidney: "An Apology for Poetry" and "Astrophil and Stella": Texts and Contexts,* ed. Peter C. Herman. Glen Allen, VA: College Publishing, 2001.

Smith, G. Gregory. *Elizabethan Critical Essays,* ed. G. Gregory Smith. 2 vols. Oxford: Clarendon Press, 1904.

Smith, Sir Thomas. *De Republica Anglorum,* ed. Mary Dewar. Cambridge: Cambridge University Press, 1982.

Smith, Thomas. *Catalogue of the Manuscripts in the Cottonian Library 1696,* ed. C. G. C. Tite. Cambridge: D. S. Brewer, 1984.

Spenser, Edmund. *The Faerie Queene,* ed. Thomas P. Roche. New Haven: Yale University Press, 1978.

Supplement to Volume I and Volume II of Letters, Despatches, and State Papers, Relating to the Negotiations between England and Spain, ed. G. A. Bergenroth. London: Longmans, 1868.

Taverner, Richard. *The Garden of Wysdome.* London, 1539.

Two Tudor Interludes: The Interlude of Youth, Hick Scorner, ed. Ian Lancashire. Manchester: Manchester University Press, 1980.

Van der Noot, Jan. *Theatre for Worldlings.* London, 1569.

Vergil, Polydore. *The Anglica Historia of Polydore Vergil, A.D. 1485–1537,* ed. and trans. Denys Hay. Camden Society 74. London: Royal Historical Society, 1950.

Vives, Juan Luis. "Truth Dressed Up: To What Extent Poets May Be Permitted to Vary from the Truth." In *Selected Works of J. J. Vives: Early Writings,* ed. C. Matheeussen, C. Fantazzi, and E. George, 66–105. Leiden: E. J. Brill, 1987.

Secondary Sources

Achinstein, Sharon. "Reading George Herbert in the Restoration." *English Literary Renaissance* 36.3 (2006): 430–65.

Adler, Doris. "The Riddle of the Sieve: The Siena Sieve Portrait of Queen Elizabeth." *Renaissance Papers 1978* (1979): 1–10.

Anglo, Sidney. *Spectacle, Pageantry, and Early Tudor Policy.* Oxford: Clarendon Press, 1969.

Appelbaum, Robert. "War and Peace in James VI/I's *Lepanto.*" In Herman, *Reading Monarchs Writing,* 179–214.

Archer, John Michael. "Slave Born Muscovites: Racial Difference and the Geography of Servitude in *Astrophil and Stella* and *Loves Labors Lost.*" In *Playing the Globe: Genre and Geography in English Renaissance Drama,* ed. John Gillies and Virginia M. Vaughan, 154–75. Madison, NJ: Fairleigh Dickinson University Press, 1998.

Armstrong Davison, M. H. *The Casket Letters: A Solution to the Mystery of Mary Queen of Scots and the Murder of Lord Darnley.* London: Vision Press, 1965.

Baker-Smith, Dominic. "Great Expectations: Sidney's Death and the Poets." In *Sir Philip Sidney: 1586 and the Creation of a Legend,* ed. Jan Van Dorsten et al., 83–103. Leiden: Brill; Leiden University Press, 1996.

———. "'Inglorious glory': 1513 and the Humanist Attack on Chivalry." In *Chivalry in the Renaissance,* ed. Sydney Anglo, 129–44. Woodbridge, England: Boydell, 1990.

Bakhtin, Mikhail. *Rabelais and His World.* Translated by Helene Iswolsky. Cambridge, MA: MIT Press, 1968.

Beal, Peter, and Grace Ioppolo. Preface to *Elizabeth I and the Culture of Writing,* ed. Peter Beal and Grace Ioppolo, xiii–xiv. London: British Library, 2007.

Bell, Ilona. *Elizabethan Women and the Poetry of Courtship.* Cambridge: Cambridge University Press, 1998.

———. "Elizabeth Tudor: Poet." *Explorations in Renaissance Culture* 30.1 (2004): 1–22.

Bell, Sandra. "Kingcraft and Poetry: James VI's Cultural Policy." In Herman, *Reading Monarchs Writing,* 155–78.

Benson, Larry D. *Malory's "Morte Darthur."* Cambridge, MA: Harvard University Press, 1976.

Bernard, G. W. "Compton, Sir William [1482?–1528]." *Oxford Dictionary of National Biography.* ed. H. C. G. Matthew and Brian Harrison. Oxford: Oxford University Press, 2004. http://www.oxforddnb.com/view/article/6039. Accessed 9 July 2006.

Bingham, Caroline. *Darnley: A Life of Henry Stuart, Lord Darnley, Consort of Mary Queen of Scots.* London: Constable, 1995.

Blevins, Jacob. *Catullan Consciousness and the Early Modern Lyric in England: From Wyatt to Donne.* Aldershot: Ashgate, 2004.

Bowers, Roger. "Cornysh, William (d. 1523)." In *Oxford Dictionary of National Biography,* ed. H. C. G. Matthew and Brian Harrison. Oxford: Oxford University Press, 2004. http://www.oxforddnb.com/view/article/6347 (accessed 17 April 2009).

Braden, Gordon. *Petrarchan Love and the Continental Renaissance.* New Haven: Yale University Press, 1999.

Braudel, Fernand. *The Mediterranean and the Mediterranean World in the Age of Philip II.* Translated by Sian Reynolds. 2 vols. Harper and Row: New York, 1972.

Brown, Georgia E. "Translation and the Definition of Sovereignty: The Case of Elizabeth." In *Travels and Translation in the Sixteenth Century,* ed. Mike Pincombe, 88–103. Burlington, VT: Ashgate, 2004.

Buck-Morss, Susan. *Dreamworld and Catastrophe: The Passing of Mass Utopia in East and West.* Cambridge, MA: MIT Press, 2000.

Burke, Mary E. "Queen, Lover, Poet: A Question of Balance in the Sonnets of Mary, Queen of Scots." In *Women, Writing, and the Reproduction of Culture in Tudor and Stuart Britain,* ed. Mary Burke, Jane Donaworth, Linda E. Dove, and Karen Nelson, 101–18. Syracuse, NY: Syracuse University Press, 2000.

Burns, J. H. *The True Law of Kingship: Concepts of Monarchy in Early Modern Scotland.* Oxford: Clarendon Press, 1996.

Butler, Todd. *Imagination and Politics in Seventeenth-Century England.* Burlington, VT: Ashgate, 2008.

Campbell, Lily B. "The Christian Muse." *Huntington Library Quarterly* 8 (1939): 29–70.

Castor, Grahame. *Pléiade Poetics: A Study in Sixteenth-Century Thought and Terminology.* Cambridge: Cambridge University Press, 1964.

Castoriadis, Cornelius. *The Imaginary Institution of Society.* Translated by Kathleen Blamey. Cambridge: Polity Press, 1987.

Cave, Terence. *The Cornucopian Text: Problems of Writing in the French Renaissance.* Oxford: Clarendon Press, 1979.

Challis, E. *The Tudor Coinage.* Manchester: Manchester University Press, 1978.

Chrimes, S. B. *Henry VII.* Berkeley: University of California Press, 1972.

Corns, Thomas N., ed. *The Royal Image: Representations of Charles I.* Cambridge: Cambridge University Press, 1999.

Cottrell, Robert. *The Grammar of Silence: A Reading of Marguerite de Navarre's Poetry.* Washington, D.C.: Catholic University of America Press, 1986.

Crane, Mary Thomas. "'Video and Taceo': Elizabeth I and the Rhetoric of Counsel." *Studies in English Literature* 28 (1998): 1–15.

Cromartie, Alan. *The Constitutionalist Revolution: An Essay on the History of England, 1450–1642.* Cambridge: Cambridge University Press, 2006.

Cust, Lionel. *Notes on the Authentic Portraits of Mary Queen of Scots.* London: John Murray, 1903.

Davidson, Peter. "New Evidence Concerning Mary Queen of Scots." *History Scotland* 1.1 (2001): 28–35.

——, ed. *Poetry and Revolution: An Anthology of British and Irish Verse, 1625–1660.* Oxford: Oxford University Press, 1998.

Davis, Natalie Zemon. *Society and Culture in Early Modern France.* Stanford: Stanford University Press, 1975.

de Grazia, Margreta, Maureen Quilligan, and Peter Stallybrass. Introduction to *Subject and Object in Renaissance Culture,* ed. de Grazia, Quilligan, and Stallybrass, 1–13. Cambridge: Cambridge University Press, 1996.

Dillon, Janette. *Performance and Spectacle in Hall's Chronicle.* London: Society for Theatre Research, 2002.

Distiller, Natasha. *Desire and Gender in the Sonnet Tradition.* New York: Palgrave MacMillan, 2008.

Doelman, James. "The Reception of King James's Psalter." In Fischlin and Fortier, *Royal Subjects,* 454–75.

Dollimore, Jonathan, and Alan Sinfield. "Introduction: Shakespeare, Cultural Materialism, and the New Historicism." In *Political Shakespeare: New Essays in Cultural Materialism,* ed. Jonathan Dollimore and Alan Sinfield, 2–17. Ithaca, NY: Cornell University Press, 1985.

Donaldson, Gordon. *All the Queen's Men: Power and Politics in Mary Stewart's England.* London: Batsworth, 1983.

Doran, Susan. *Mary Queen of Scots: An Illustrated Life.* London: British Library, 2007.

——. *Monarchy and Matrimony: The Courtships of Elizabeth I.* New York: Routledge, 1996.

Doran, Susan, and Thomas S. Freeman, eds. *The Myth of Elizabeth.* New York: Palgrave, 2003.

Dubrow, Heather. *Echoes of Desire: English Petrarchism and Its Counterdiscourses.* Ithaca, NY: Cornell University Press, 1995.

Dunn, Jane. *Elizabeth and Mary: Cousins, Rivals, Queens.* New York: Alfred A. Knopf, 2004.

Dunnigan, Sarah. "Discovering Desire in the *Amatoria* of James VI. In Fischlin and Fortier, *Royal Subjects,* 149–82.

———. *Eros and Poetry at the Courts of Mary Queen of Scots and James VI.* New York: Palgrave MacMillan, 2002.

———. "Marian and Jacobean Literature." *Literature Compass* 2.1 (2005), http://www.blackwell-synergy.com/doi/full/10.1111/j.1741-4113.2005.00141.x (accessed 9 February 2008).

Ephraim, Michelle Karen. "Jewish Matriarchs and the Staging of Elizabeth I in *The History of Jacob and Esau.*" *Studies in English Literature* 34.2 (2003): 301–21.

Estrin, Barbara L. *Laura: Uncovering Gender and Genre in Wyatt, Donne, and Marvell.* Durham, NC: Duke University Press, 1994.

Farrell, Kirby, and Kathleen Swaim. *The Mysteries of Elizabeth I: Selections from "English Literary Renaissance."* Amherst: University of Massachusetts Press, 2003.

Ferguson, Arthur B. *The Chivalric Tradition in Renaissance England.* Washington, D.C.: Folger Shakespeare Library, 1986.

———. *The Indian Summer of English Chivalry: Studies in the Decline and the Transformation of Chivalric Idealism.* Durham, NC: Duke University Press, 1960.

Ferguson, Gary. *Mirroring Belief: Marguerite de Navarre's Devotional Poetry.* Edinburgh: University of Edinburgh Press, 1992.

Ferguson, Margaret W. *Trials of Desires: Renaissance Defences of Poetry.* New Haven: Yale University Press, 1983.

Figgis, John Neville. *The Divine Right of Kings.* Reprint, New York: Harper Torchbooks, 1965.

Fischlin, Daniel. "'Like a Mercenary Poët': The Politics and Poetics of James VI's *Lepanto.*" In *Essays on Older Scots Literature,* ed. Sally Mapstone, 540–59. Edinburgh: John Donald, 2005.

Fischlin, Daniel, and Mark Fortier, eds. *Royal Subjects: Essays on the Writings of James VI and I.* Detroit: Wayne State University Press, 2001.

Fleming, Morna. "*The Amatoria* of James VI: Loving by the *Reulis.*" In Fischlin and Fortier, *Royal Subjects,* 124–48.

Foucault, Michel. "What Is an Author?" *Language, Counter-Memory, Practice: Selected Essays and Interviews,* ed. Donald F. Bouchard, 113–38. Ithaca, NY: Cornell University Press, 1977.

Fraser, Antonia. *Mary Queen of Scots.* New York: Delacorte Press, 1970.

Freud, Sigmund. *The Basic Writings of Sigmund Freud,* ed. A. A. Brill. New York: Random House, 1938.

Frye, Susan. *Elizabeth I: The Competition for Representation.* New York: Oxford University Press, 1993.

Fumerton, Patricia. *Cultural Aesthetics: Renaissance Literature and the Practice of Social Ornament.* Chicago: University of Chicago Press, 1991.

Geertz, Clifford. *The Interpretation of Cultures.* New York: Basic Books, 1973.

Goldberg, Jonathan. *James I and the Politics of Literature.* Stanford: Stanford University Press, 1989.

Gore-Browne, Robert. *Lord Bothwell and Mary Queen of Scots: A Study of the Life, Character, and Times of James Hepburn, 4th Earl of Bothwell.* New York: Doubleday, 1937.

Gottlieb, Sidney. "A Royalist Rewriting of George Herbert: *His Majesties Complaint to his Subjects* (1647)." *Modern Philology* 89.2 (1991): 211–24.

Greenblatt, Stephen J. "Invisible Bullets." In *Shakespearean Negotiations: The Circulation of Social Energy in Renaissance England*, 21–65. Berkeley: University of California Press, 1988.

——. *Renaissance Self-Fashioning: From More to Shakespeare.* Chicago: University of Chicago Press, 1980.

Greene, Roland. *Post-Petrarchism: Origins and Innovations of the Western Lyric Sequence.* Princeton: Princeton University Press, 1991.

——. *Unrequited Conquests: Love and Empire in the Colonial Americas.* Chicago: University of Chicago Press, 1999.

Greig, Martin. "Burnet, Gilbert (1643–1715)." In *Oxford Dictionary of National Biography,* ed. H. C. G. Matthew and Brian Harrison. Oxford: Oxford University Press, 2004. http://www.oxforddnb.com/view/article/4061 (accessed 20 March 2008).

Guy, John. "The 'Imperial Crown' and the Liberty of the Subject." In *Court, Country, and Culture: Essays on Early Modern British History in Honor of Perez Zagorin,* ed. Bonnelyn Young Kunze and Dwight D. Brautigan, 65–88. Rochester, NY: University of Rochester Press, 1992.

——. *The True Life of Mary Stuart Queen of Scots.* New York: Houghton Mifflin, 2004.

Gwyn, Peter. *The King's Cardinal: The Rise and Fall of Thomas Wolsey.* London: Barrie & Jenkins, 1990.

Halasz, Alexandra. "Wyatt's David." *Texas Studies in Language and Literature* 30.3 (1988): 320–44. Reprinted in Herman, *Rethinking the Henrician Era,* 193–218.

Hannay, Margaret, ed. *Silent but for the Word: Tudor Women as Patrons, Translators, and Writers of Religious Works.* Kent, OH: Kent State University Press, 1985.

Hanson, Elizabeth. *Discovering the Subject in Renaissance England.* Cambridge: Cambridge University Press, 1998.

Harvey, Elizabeth. *Ventriloquized Voices: Feminist Theory and Renaissance Texts.* New York: Routledge, 1992.

Haynes, Jonathan. "Festivity and the Dramatic Economy of Jonson's *Bartholomew Fair.*" *ELH* 51.4 (1984): 645–68.

Hedley, Jane. *Power in Verse: Metaphor and Metonymy in the Renaissance Lyric.* University Park: Pennsylvania State University Press, 1988.

Heisch, Allison. "Queen Elizabeth I: Parliamentary Rhetoric and the Exercise of Power." *Signs* 1.1 (1975): 31–55.

Henderson, T. F. *The Casket Letters and Mary Queen of Scots.* Edinburgh: Adams and Charles Black, 1889.

Herman, Peter C. "Henrician Historiography and the Voice of the People: The Cases of More and Hall." *Texas Studies in Literature and Language* 39.3 (1997): 261–83.

——. "'Is this Winning?': Prince Henry's Death and the Problem of Chivalry in *The Two Noble Kinsmen.*" *South Atlantic Review* 62.1 (1997): 1–31.

——. "Leaky Ladies and Droopy Dames: The Grotesque Realism of John Skelton's *The Tunnynge of Elynour Rummynge.*" In Herman, *Rethinking the Henrician Era,* 145–67.

——, ed. *Reading Monarchs Writing: The Poetry of Henry VIII, Mary Stuart, Elizabeth I, and James VI/I.* Tempe, AZ: MRTS, 2002.

———, ed. *Rethinking the Henrician Era: Essays on Early Tudor Texts and Contexts.* Urbana: University of Illinois Press, 1994.

———. *Squitter-wits and Muse-haters: Sidney, Spenser, Milton, and Renaissance Antipoetic Sentiment.* Detroit: Wayne State University Press, 1996.

Herman, Peter C., and Ray Siemens. "Henry VIII and the Poetry of Politics." In Herman, *Reading Monarchs Writing,* 1–34.

Hill, Christopher. "The Norman Yoke." In *Puritanism and Revolution,* 58–125. London: Panther History, 1969.

Holdsworth, W. S. *A History of English Law.* 17 vols. London: Methuen, 1936–72.

Hopkins, Lisa. *Writing Renaissance Queens: Texts by and about Elizabeth I and Mary, Queen of Scots.* Newark, DE: University of Delaware Press, 2002.

———. "Writing to Control: The Verse of Mary, Queen of Scots." In Herman, *Reading Monarchs Writing,* 35–51.

Howard, Skiles. "'Ascending the Rich Mount': Performing Hierarchy and Gender in the Henrician Masque." In Herman, *Rethinking the Henrician Era,* 16–39.

Howell, Roger. *Sir Philip Sidney: The Shepheard Knight.* Boston: Little, Brown, 1968.

Ives, Carolyn, and David J. Parkinson. "'The Foundation and Very Being of Truth': James VI, Poetic Invention, and National Identity." In Fischlin and Fortier, *Royal Subjects,* 104–23.

Ives, Eric. *The Life and Death of Anne Boleyn, "The Most Happy."* Malden, MA: Blackwell, 2004.

Jones, Anne R. "City Women and Their Audiences: Louise Labé and Veronica Franco." In *Rewriting the Renaissance: The Discourses of Sexual Difference in Early Modern Europe,* ed. Margaret W. Ferguson, Maureen Quilligan, and Nancy J. Vickers, 299–316. Chicago: University of Chicago Press, 1986.

———. *The Currency of Eros: Women's Love Lyric in Europe, 1540–1620.* Bloomington: Indiana University Press, 1990.

———. "The Lyonnais Neoplatonist: Pernette du Gillet." In *Women Writers of the Renaissance and Reformation,* ed. Katharina M. Wilson. Athens, GA: University of Georgia Press, 1987.

Jones, Anne R., and Peter Stallybrass. "The Politics of *Astrophil and Stella.*" *Studies in English Literature* 24 (1984): 53–68.

Jordan, Constance. "Representing Political Androgyny: More on the Siena Portrait of Queen Elizabeth I." In *The Renaissance Englishwoman in Print,* ed. Anne M. Haselkorn and Betty Travitsky, 157–76. Amherst: University of Massachusetts Press, 1990.

———. "States of Blindness: Doubt, Justice, and Constancy in Elizabeth I's 'Avec l'aveugler si estrange.'" In Herman, *Reading Monarchs Writing,* 109–34.

Kallendorf, Craig. "From Virgil to Vida: The Poeta Theologus in Italian Renaissance Commentary." *Journal of the History of Ideas* 56.1 (1995): 41–62.

Kantorowicz, Ernst H. *The King's Two Bodies: A Study in Medieval Political Theology.* Princeton: Princeton University Press, 1957.

Kastan, David Scott. *Shakespeare after Theory,* 109–28. New York: Routledge, 1999.

———. *Shakespeare and the Book.* Cambridge: Cambridge University Press, 2001.

Kennedy, William J. *Authorizing Petrarch.* Ithaca, NY: Cornell University Press, 1994.

———. *The Site of Petrarchism: Early Modern National Sentiment in Italy, France, and England.* Ithaca, NY: Cornell University Press, 2003.

King, John. "Henry VIII as David: The King's Image and Reformation Politics." In Herman, *Rethinking the Henrician Era,* 78–92.

Kingdon, Robert M. "Calvinism and Resistance Theory, 1550–80." In *The Cambridge History of Political Thought, 1450–1700,* ed. J. H. Burns, with the assistance of Mark Goldie, 193–218. Cambridge: Cambridge University Press, 1991.

Kinney, Arthur F. *Continental Humanist Poetics: Studies in Erasmus, Castiglione, Marguerite de Navarre, Rabelais, and Cervantes.* Amherst: University of Massachusetts Press, 1989.

Kipling, Gordon. *The Triumph of Honour: Burgundian Origins of the Elizabethan Renaissance.* The Hague: Leiden University Press, 1977.

Kishlansky, Mark. *A Monarchy Transformed: Britain 1603–1714.* London: Penguin, 1996.

Klein, Lisa M. *The Exemplary Sidney and the Elizabethan Sonneteer.* Newark, DE: University of Delaware Press, 1998.

Kunzle, David. "World Upside Down: The Iconography of a European Broadsheet Type." In *The Reversible World: Symbolic Inversion in Art and Society,* ed. Barbara A. Babcock, 39–94. Ithaca, NY: Cornell University Press, 1978.

Laing, Malcolm. *History of Scotland.* 4 vols. London: J. Mawman, 1804.

Lang, Andrew. *The Mystery of Mary Stuart.* Reprint, New York: AMS, 1970.

Laqueur, Thomas W. "Crowds, Carnival, and the State in English Executions, 1604–1868." In *The First Modern Society: Essays in English History in Honour of Lawrence Stone,* ed. A. L. Beier, David Cannadine, and James M. Rosenheim, 305–56. Cambridge: Cambridge University Press, 1989.

Lee, Maurice. *Great Britain's Solomon: James VI and I in His Three Kingdoms.* Urbana: University of Illinois Press, 1990.

Lerer, Seth. *Courtly Letters in the Age of Henry VIII.* Cambridge: Cambridge University Press, 1997.

Levin, Carole. *"The Heart and Stomach of a King": Elizabeth I and the Politics of Sex and Power.* Philadelphia: University of Pennsylvania Press, 1994.

Lewis, Jayne, ed. *The Trial of Mary Queen of Scots: A Brief History with Documents.* Boston: Bedford/St. Martin's, 1999.

MacRobert, A. E. *Mary Queen of Scots and the Casket Letters.* London: I. B. Tauris, 2002.

Mahon, R. H. *The Indictment of Mary Queen of Scots.* Cambridge: Cambridge University Press, 1923.

Marcus, Leah S. "Queen Elizabeth I as Public and Private Poet: Notes toward a New Edition." In Herman, *Reading Monarchs Writing,* 135–53.

———. "Shakespeare's Comic Heroines, Elizabeth I, and the Political Uses of Androgyny." In *Women in the Middle Ages and the Renaissance: Literary and Historical Perspectives,* ed. Mary Beth Rose, 135–54. Syracuse, NY: Syracuse University Press, 1986.

———. *Unediting the Renaissance: Shakespeare, Marlowe, Milton.* New York: Routledge, 1996.

Marotti, Arthur. "'Love is not love': Elizabethan Sonnet Sequences and the Social Order." *ELH* 49 (1982): 396–428.

———. *Manuscript, Print, and The English Renaissance Lyric.* Ithaca, NY: Cornell University Press, 1995.

Maus, Katherine E. *Inwardness and Theater in the English Renaissance.* Chicago: University of Chicago Press, 1995.

May, Steven W. *The Elizabethan Courtier Poets: The Poems and Their Contexts.* Columbia: University of Missouri Press, 1991.

———. "Recent Studies in Elizabeth I." In Farrell and Swaim, *The Mysteries of Elizabeth I,* 279–94.

May, Steven W., and Anne Lake Prescott. "The French Verses of Elizabeth I (Text)." In Farrell and Swaim, *The Mysteries of Elizabeth I,* 97–133.

May, Steven W., and William Ringler, Jr. *Elizabethan Poetry: A Bibliography and First-Line Index of English Verse, 1559–1603.* 3 vols. London: Continuum, 2004.

Mazzeo, Joseph A. *Reason and the Imagination: Studies in the History of Ideas, 1600–1800.* New York: Columbia University Press, 1962.

McCoy, Richard C. *The Rites of Knighthood: The Literature and Politics of Elizabethan Chivalry.* Berkeley: University of California Press, 1989.

McLaren, Elizabeth. *Political Culture in the Reign of Elizabeth I: Queen and Commonwealth, 1558–1585.* Cambridge: Cambridge University Press, 1999.

Meyer, Barbara H. "Marguerite de Navarre and the Androgynous Portrait of François I er." *Renaissance Quarterly* 48.2 (1995): 287–325.

Middlebrook, Leah. "'Tout mon Office': Body Politics and Family Dynamics in the Verse Epîtres of Marguerite de Navarre." *Renaissance Quarterly* 54.1 (2001): 108–41.

Mignet, François. *The History of Mary, Queen of Scots.* London: Richard Bentley, 1887.

Montaiglon, Anatole de. *Latin Themes of Mary Stuart, Queen of Scots.* London: Warton Club, 1855.

Montrose, Louis A. "The Elizabethan Subject and the Spenserian Text." In *Literary Theory/Renaissance Texts,* ed. Patricia Parker and David Quint, 303–40. Baltimore: Johns Hopkins University Press, 1986.

———. "'Eliza, Queen of Shepherds,' and the Pastoral of Power." In Farrell and Swaim, *The Mysteries of Elizabeth I,* 162–91.

———. "Idols of the Queen: Policy, Gender, and the Picturing of Elizabeth I." *Representations* 68 (1999): 108–61.

———. "'Shaping Fantasies': Figurations of Gender and Power in Elizabethan Culture." In *Representing the English Renaissance,* ed. Stephen Greenblatt, 31–64. Berkeley: University of California Press, 1988.

———. "Spenser and the Elizabethan Political Imaginary." *ELH* 69.4 (2002): 907–46.

———. "Spenser's Domestic Domain: Poetry, Property, and the Early Modern Subject." In de Grazia, Quilligan, and Stallybrass, *Subject and Object in Renaissance Culture,* 83–132.

———. *The Subject of Elizabeth: Authority, Gender, and Representation.* Chicago: University of Chicago Press, 2006.

Mueller, Janel. "Elizabeth I: Poet of Dangers." In *Approaches to Teaching Shorter Elizabethan Poetry,* ed. Patrick Cheney, 202–9. New York: MLA, 2000.

———. "Queen Elizabeth I." In *Teaching Tudor and Stuart Women Writers,* ed. Susanne Woods and Margaret P. Hannay, 119–26. New York: MLA, 2000.

Murphy, Beverley A. "Fitzroy, Henry, duke of Richmond and Somerset (1519–1536)." In *Oxford Dictionary of National Biography,* ed. H. C. G. Matthew and Brian

Harrison. Oxford: Oxford University Press, 2004. http://www.oxforddnb. com/view/article/9635 (accessed 19 July 2006).

Neale, J. E. *Queen Elizabeth I.* London: Jonathan Cape, 1938.

Nelson, William. *Fact or Fiction: The Dilemma of the Renaissance Storyteller.* Cambridge, MA: Harvard University Press, 1973.

Nicolas, Nicholas Harris. *Memoirs of the Life and Times of Sir Christopher Hatton.* London: Bentley, 1846.

Oakley, Francis. "Jacobean Political Theology: The Absolute and Ordinary Powers of the King." *Journal of the History of Ideas* 29.3 (1968): 323–46.

Orgel, Stephen. *The Illusion of Power: Political Theater in the English Renaissance.* Berkeley: University of California Press, 1975.

Patterson, Annabel. *Reading 'Holinshed's Chronicles.'* Chicago: University of Chicago Press, 1994.

Peck, Linda Levy, ed. *The Mental World of the Jacobean Court.* Cambridge: Cambridge University Press, 1991.

Perry, Curtis. "'If Proclamations will not Serve': The Late Manuscript Poetry of James I and the Culture of Libel." In Fischlin and Fortier, *Royal Subjects,* 205–34.

——. *The Making of Jacobean Culture: James I and the Renegotiation of Elizabethan Literary Practice.* Cambridge: Cambridge University Press, 1997.

Phillips, James E. "Elizabeth I as a Latin Poet: An Epigram on Paul Melissus." *Renaissance News* 16.4 (1963): 289–98.

Plowden, Alison. *Two Queens in One Isle: The Deadly Relationship of Elizabeth I and Mary Queen of Scots.* Sussex: Harvester, 1984.

Pocock, J. G. A. *The Ancient Constitution and the Feudal Law: English Historical Thought in the Seventeenth Century.* New York: Norton, 1967.

Potter, Lois. "The Royal Martyr in the Restoration." In Corns, *The Royal Image,* 240–61.

——. *Secret Rites and Secret Writing: Royalist Literature, 1641–1660.* Cambridge: Cambridge University Press, 1989.

Prescott, Anne Lake. "English Writers and Beza's Latin Epigrams: The Uses and Abuses of Poetry." *Studies in the Renaissance* 21 (1974): 83–117.

——. "The Pearl of the Valois and Elizabeth I." In Hannay, *Silent but for the Word,* 61–76.

Quilligan, Maureen. "Elizabeth I: With a Note on Marguerite de Navarre." In *Incest and Agency in Elizabeth's England,* 33–75. Philadelphia: University of Pennsylvania Press, 2005.

——. "Sidney and His Queen." In *The Historical Renaissance: New Essays on Tudor and Stuart Literature and Culture,* ed. Heather Dubrow and Richard Strier, 171–96. Chicago: University of Chicago Press, 1988.

Raymond, Joad. "Popular Representations of Charles I." In Corns, *The Royal Image,* 47–71.

Read, Conyers. *Mr. Secretary Cecil and Queen Elizabeth.* New York: Knopf, 1955; reprint, 1961.

——. *Mr. Secretary Walsingham and the Policy of Queen Elizabeth.* 2 vols. Cambridge, MA: Harvard University Press; Oxford: Clarendon Press, 1925.

Remley, Paul G. "Mary Shelton and Her Tudor Literary Milieu." In Herman, *Rethinking the Henrician Era,* 40–77.

Revard, Stella P. "The Latin Ode from Elizabeth I to Mary II: Political Approaches to Encomia." In *Britannia Latina: Latin in the Culture of Great Britain from the Middle Ages to the Twentieth Century,* ed. Charles Burnett and Nicholas Mann, 156–69. London: Warburg Institute, 2005.

Rickard, Jane. "From Scotland to England: The Poetic Strategies of James VI/I." *Renaissance Forum* 7.1–2 (2004), http://www.hull.ac.uk/renforum/v7/rickard. htm (accessed 9 February 2008).

Rigolot, François. "When Petrarchan Errors Become Political Crimes: Mary Stuart's French Sonnets to Bothwell." In *Writers in Conflict in Sixteenth-Century France: Essays in Honour of Malcolm Quainton,* ed. Elizabeth Vinestock and David Foster, 37–50. Durham, UK: Durham Modern Languages Series, 2008.

Russell, Conrad. *Parliaments and English Politics, 1621–1629.* Oxford: Clarendon Press, 1979.

Saunders, J. W. "The Stigma of Print: A Note on the Social Bases of Tudor Poetry." *Essays in Criticism* 1.2 (1951): 139–64.

Scarisbrick, J. J. *Henry VIII.* Berkeley: University of California Press, 1968.

Schleiner, Winfried. "*Divina virago:* Queen Elizabeth as an Amazon." *Studies in Philology* 75 (1978): 163–80.

Sedgwick, Eve Kosofsky. *Between Men: English Literature and Male Homosocial Desire.* New York: Columbia University Press, 1985.

Sessions, William A. "Literature and the Court." In *The Cambridge History of Early Modern Literature,* ed. David Loewenstein and Janel Mueller, 229–56. Cambridge: Cambridge University Press, 2002.

Sharpe, Kevin. "The King's Writ: Royal Authors and Royal Authority in Early Modern England." In *Culture and Politics in Early Stuart England,* ed. Kevin Sharpe and Peter Lake, 117–38. Stanford: Stanford University Press, 1993.

———. "Private Conscience and Public Duty in the Writings of King James VI and I." In *Public Duty and Private Conscience in Seventeenth-Century England,* ed. J. Morrill, Peter Slack, and Daniel Woolf, 77–100. London: MacMillan, 1994.

———. *Remapping Early Modern England: The Culture of Seventeenth-Century Politics.* Cambridge: Cambridge University Press, 2000.

Shell, Marc. *Elizabeth's Glass.* Lincoln: University of Nebraska Press, 1993.

———. *The End of Kinship: "Measure for Measure," Incest, and the Ideal of Universal Siblinghood.* Stanford: Stanford University Press, 1988.

Siemens, Ray. "'Respect': Verses Attributed to Henry VIII in a Prayer Book Owned by Katherine Parr." *Notes and Queries* 46 (1999): 186–89.

———. "Thomas Wyatt, Anne Boleyn, and Henry VIII's Lyric 'Pastime with Good Company.'" *Notes and Queries* 44 (1997): 26–27.

Smailes, Helen, and Duncan Thomson. *The Queen's Image: A Celebration of Mary, Queen of Scots.* Edinburgh: Scottish National Portrait Gallery, 1987.

Smith, G. Gregory. Introduction to *Elizabethan Critical Essays,* ed. G. G. Smith, 1: xi–xcii. Oxford: Clarendon Press, 1904.

Snyder, Susan. "Guilty Sisters: Marguerite de Navarre, Elizabeth of England, and the *Miroir de l'âme pécheresse.*" *Renaissance Quarterly* 50.2 (1997): 443–57.

Sommerville, Johann P. "James I and the Divine Right of Kings: English Politics and Continental Theory." In Peck, *The Mental World of the Jacobean Court,* 55–70.

———. *Politics and Ideology in England, 1603–1640.* London: Longman, 1986.

Spingarn, Joel. *A History of Literary Criticism in the Renaissance.* New York: Columbia University Press, 1938.

Stafford, Helen G. *James VI of Scotland and the Throne of England.* New York: Appleton, 1940.

Stallybrass, Peter, Roger Chartier, J. Franklin Mowery, and Heather Wolfe. "Hamlet's Tables and the Technologies of Writing in Renaissance England." *Shakespeare Quarterly* 55.4 (2004) 379–419.

Starkey, David. "Intimacy and Innovation: The Rise of the Privy Chamber." In *The English Court: From the Wars of the Roses to the Civil War,* ed. David Starkey, 71–118. New York: Longman, 1987.

———. *The Reign of Henry VIII: Personalities and Politics.* London: George Philip, 1985.

Stevens, John. *Music and Poetry in the Early Tudor Court.* Lincoln: University of Nebraska Press, 1961.

Stewart, Alan. *The Cradle King: The Life of James VI & I, the First Monarch of a United Great Britain.* New York: St. Martin's Press, 2003.

Streitberger, W. R. *Court Revels, 1485–1559.* Toronto: University of Toronto Press, 1994.

Strong, Roy. *The Cult of Elizabeth.* Berkeley: University of California Press, 1977.

———. *Gloriana: The Portraits of Queen Elizabeth I.* London: Thames and Hudson, 1987.

———. *Henry, Prince of Wales and England's Lost Renaissance.* New York: Thames and Hudson, 1986.

———. *Tudor and Jacobean Portraits.* 2 vols. London: Her Majesty's Stationery Office, 1969.

Summit, Jennifer. "'The Arte of a Ladies Penne': Elizabeth I and the Poetics of Queenship." In Farrell and Swaim, *The Mysteries of Elizabeth I,* 67–96.

Szönyi, György E. "Cross-Dressing the Tongue: Petrarchist Discourse and Female Voice in Queen Elizabeth's *Sonetto.*" *Hungarian Journal of English and American Studies* 11.1 (2005): 77–91.

Taylor, Andrew W. "Taverner, Richard (1505?–1575)." *Oxford Dictionary of National Biography.* Oxford: Oxford University Press, 2004. http://www.oxforddnb.com/view/article/27006 (accessed 6 May 2009).

Taylor, Charles. *Modern Social Imaginaries.* Durham, NC: Duke University Press, 2004.

Tennenhouse, Leonard. "Sir Walter Ralegh and the Literature of Clientage." In *Patronage in the Renaissance,* ed. Guy Fitch Lytle and Stephen Orgel, 235–60. Princeton: Princeton University Press, 1981.

Thornbury, Walter. "Henry VIII as a Poet." *Notes & Queries* 5th ser. 1 (1874): 403–4.

Travitsky, Betty, ed. *The Paradise of Women: Writings by Englishwomen of the Renaissance.* Westport, CT: Greenwood Press, 1981.

Le Trésor de la Langue Française Informatisé. http://atilf.atilf.fr/tlf.htm (accessed 15 April 2009).

Vickers, Nancy J. "Diana Described: Scattered Woman and Scattered Rhyme." In *Writing and Sexual Difference,* ed. Elizabeth Abel, 95–110. Chicago: University of Chicago Press, 1982.

Walker, Greg. *Plays of Persuasion: Drama and Politics at the Court of Henry VIII.* Cambridge: Cambridge University Press, 1991.

——. *Writing under Tyranny: English Literature and the Henrican Reformation*. Oxford: Oxford University Press, 2005.

Wall, Wendy. *The Imprint of Gender: Authorship and Publication in the English Renaissance*. Ithaca, NY: Cornell University Press, 1993.

Waller, Gary. "Struggling into Discourse: The Emergence of Renaissance Women's Writing." In Hannay, *Silent but for the Word*, 238–56.

Walsham, Alexandra. "'A Very Deborah?' The Myth of Elizabeth I as a Providential Monarch." In Doran and Freeman, *The Myth of Elizabeth*, 143–70.

Walton, Kristen Post. *Catholic Queen, Protestant Patriarchy: Mary, Queen of Scots, and the Politics of Gender and Religion*. New York: Palgrave, 2007.

Warley, Christopher. *Sonnet Sequences and Social Distinction in Renaissance England*. Cambridge: Cambridge University Press, 2005.

Warnicke, Retha M. *The Rise and Fall of Anne Boleyn: Family Politics at the Court of Henry VIII*. Cambridge: Cambridge University Press, 1989.

Wernham, R. *The Counter-Reformation and Price Revolution, 1559–1610*. Vol. 3 of *New Cambridge Modern History*. Cambridge: Cambridge University Press, 1968.

Williams, Neville. *Henry VIII and His Court*. London: Weidenfield & Nicolson, 1971.

Williams, William Proctor. "Richard Royston." In *The British Literary Book Trade, 1475-1700*, ed. James K. Bracken and Joel Silver, 219–30. Detroit: Gale, 1996.

Willson, David Harris. *King James VI and I*. London: Jonathan Cape, 1956.

Wind, Edgar. *Pagan Mysteries in the Renaissance*. New York: Norton, 1968.

Witt, Ronald. "Coluccio Salutati and the Conception of the *Poeta Theologus* in the Fourteenth Century." *Renaissance Quarterly* 30.4 (1977): 538–63.

Wormald, Jenny. *Court, Kirk, and Community: Scotland 1470–1625*. Toronto: University of Toronto Press, 1981.

——. "James VI and I, *Basilikon Doron* and *The Trew Law of Free Monarchies:* The Scottish Context and the English Translation." In Peck, *The Mental World of the Jacobean Court*, 36–54.

——. *Mary Queen of Scots: A Study in Failure*. London: George Philip, 1988.

Wortham, Simon. "'Pairt of my Taill is Yet Untolde': James VI and I, the *Phoenix*, and the Royal Gift." In Fischlin and Fortier, *Royal Subjects*, 182–204.

❧ INDEX

Absolutism, rejection of, 136–37
Acuna-Sarmiento, Diego de, Count de Gondomart, 189
Ancient Constitution, 135–39, 142–143, 145–46, 190, 192–94
André, Bernard, 5
Anglo, Sidney, 15, 18
Anjou, duke of, later duke of Alençon, François Hercule, 101, 116; and marriage negotiations with Elizabeth, 117–22
Anne of Denmark, 176
Antipoetic sentiment, 4n8, 89–90, 112n51, 141–42, 155–56, 187n75
Armada, English reaction to sinking of, 149–50
Aske, James, 148n182
Authorship, 158
Authorship, authority of, 178–86

Babington Plot, 170
Badoer, Andrea, 15
Baker-Smith, Dominic, 167, 168–70
Baptista, Joannes, 128
Baret, John, 55
Bell, Ilona, 101, 127, 128
Bell, Robin, 55
Bell, Sandra, 157
Bellay, Joachim du, 88–89
Benson, Larry D., 18
Bentley, Thomas, 150–51, 152, 155
Beza, Theodore, 155–56
Blount, Elizabeth, 30
Blount, William, Lord Mountjoy, 40
Boccaccio, Giovanni, 4
Bodin, Jean, 64
Boleyn, Anne, 165
Bowes, Robert, 18, 193
Brantôme, Pierre de, 10n37, 54, 60
Braudel, Ferdinand, 171
Buchanan, George, 9, 69n41, 76, 77, 97–98, 168

Burnet, Gilbert, 197, 202, 206–8;
Butler, Todd, 197

C. R. In a Cloud, 197–98
Camden, William, 119–20, 134
Caroz, Luis, 30–31
Castilgione, Baldesare, 4
Catherine de Medici, 53, 56, 66, 72, 170
Catullus, 128
Cecil, William, baron Burleigh, 65, 107, 108, 118, 119, 122, 125, 187
Chaloner, Thomas, 68, 69n41
Charles I, 189, 192, 195; and absolutism, 199; "A Copie of Verses, said to be Composed by His Majesty," 198, 199–200, 203, 204; "His Majesties Complaint," 198, 199, 200–201, 204; "King Charles's Lament," 199, 200, 203–4; "Majesty in Misery," 198, 202–8; and political imaginary, 197–98; as royal martyr, 202; verses ascribed to, 196–208; woodcut from Memoires of the Dukes of Hamilton, 205
Charles II, 204, 207, 208
Chaseabout Raid, 64
Chateau Vert (spectacle), 26–28
Churchyard, Thomas, 45n72, 142
Clouet, François, 59, 60, 61
Coke, Edward, 189
Conn, George, 69n41
Cornish, William, 2, 5, 51
Cotgrave, Randle, 55, 86, 95
Cranmer, Thomas, 165
Crew, Thomas, 193
Cromwell, Oliver, 201
Cromwell, Thomas, 136

Dante Alighieri, 70
David, 201
Davidson, Peter, 10, 197
Devereaux, Robert, earl of Essex, 147
Devonshire Manuscript, 29

Diane de Poitiers, 53
Distiller, Natasha, 2
Dollimore, Jonathan and Alan Sinfield, 3n7
Donne, John, 35
Doran, Susan, 120
Du Bartas, Guillaume, 167, 170, 171
Dudley, Robert, earl of Leicester, 70, 72,
    114, 126, 145, 170
Dunn, Jane, 53
Dunnigan, Sarah, 58–59, 84n86
Dyer, Edward, 98

Eikon Basilike, 196, 201, 206
Elizabeth I, 1, 3, 58, 66, 195; compared to
    other royal poets, 100–101; circulation
    of poems, 8–9; conflation of private
    and public in prayers, 133n130; as
    embodiment of England, 150, 153;
    and formation of her image, 144–45;
    and gender expectations, 67, 150–52;
    and incest, 164–65; and marriage
    negotiations with Anjou, 117–22,
    124–27; poetic reputation, 6, 99–101;
    and Rainbow portrait 114–15; and
    rejection of absolutism, 136–39; rela-
    tions with Mary, Queen of Scots,
    67–75, 107–12; and Sieve Portraits,
    120–21; as Supreme Head of English
    Church, 152–53
  Letters: to Mary, Queen of Scots (8 June,
    1568), 107; (20 February, 1570), 109–10;
    to Anjou (17 January, 1580), 129,
    (December 1479/January, 1580), 124;
    to Edward Stafford (c. August, 1580),
    129–30, 133; to James VI (March,
    1586), 258
  Poems: "Ah, silly pug" (verse exchange
    with Ralegh), 100, 113, 146–49,
    162; Armada hymn, 101, 149–56;
    "The doubt of future foes," 8, 11–13,
    101–14; "French Verses," 8, 132–39;
    "Genus infoelix vitae" (verse exchange
    with Sir Thomas Heneage), 130n120;
    "On Monsieur's Departure," 8, 13, 101,
    124–32, 133, 148; and provenance,
    114–17; "Reginae Responsum" (verse
    exchange with Melissus), 100, 139–46,
    and view of monarchy, 143–46;
    "When I was Fair and Young," 8, 13,
    101, 114–24, 130; and provenance,
    114–17, as private poem, 116–17
  Speeches: Armada Speech, response to
    Parliament on marriage (28 January

1563), 131; response to Parliament on
    marriage (5 November, 1566), 131;
    response to Parliament's urging execu-
    tion of Mary, Queen of Scots (12 No-
    vember, 1586), 137; Tillbury (1588),
    131; "Golden Speech" (30 November,
    1601), 137
Elizabeth of Valois, 108–9
Erasmus, Desiderius, 40

Ferdinand, King of Spain, 31–32
Ferguson, Arthur B., 26
Field of the Cloth of Gold, 46
Finet, John, 116, 122
Fischlin, Daniel, 157n3
Fitzroy, Henry, duke of Richmond, 30
Fortescue, John, 145–46
Foucault, Michel, 14, 162
Fox, Richard, 16
François I, 52, 54, 69
François II, 54, death of, 56, 65
Frarinus, Peter, 73–74, 75
Freud, Sigmund, 90
Frye, Susan, 100n9

Gascoigne, George, 179
Geertz, Clifford, 14
Gilbert, Humphrey, 136
Goldberg, Jonathan, 2, 101, 178
Goodman, Christopher, 65, 74
Gordon, James, 176
Gordon, Jean, Lady, in Casket Sonnets, 84,
    87, 95
Gosson, Stephen, 142
Gower, George, 120, 121
Greenblatt, Stephen J., 93
Guillet, Pernette du, 92, 92n104
Guy, John, 10, 53, 60n23, 67, 70–71, 75,
    106n33

Hall, Edward, 15, 26, 29, 30, 37, 40,
    47–48, 78; and critique of
    Henry VIII, 26n35
Harington, John, 8, 10n40; letter describing
    circulation of "Doubt of Future Foes,"
    103, 110–12; letter to Prince Henry,
    10–11, 44–45, 156
Hatton, Christopher, 114, 118, 126
Hedley, Thomas, 193
Henri II, 53, 56
Henri III, 101, 118, 125, 126, 170
Henri IV (Henry of Navarre), 170
Henry V, 49

Henry VII, 37, 49; funeral of, 15; iconography of, 18–20, 24; and importation of Burgundian culture, 3–5

Henry VIII, 1, 3, 5, 52, 69, 98, 100, 105, 136, 151, 155, 164, 195; and Anne Boleyn, 45, 49–50; attempt at changing coronation oath, 23–25; council's resistance to policies, 37–41; as David, 201; humanist resistance to policies, 40–41; iconography, 20–23, 25, 47–49; letters to Anne Boleyn, 49n84; performance of lyrics, 8, 50; poetic reputation, 6

Works: "Alac! Alac! What shall I do?" 32–33; *Assertio Septem Sacramentorum,* 49, 178n68; "The Eagle's Force," 8, 44–50; attribution of, 45n72; "Green grows the holly," 28; "Hey Nonny Nonny Nonny No!" 32–35; "Lusty Youth should us ensue," 42–43; "Oh, my heart," 28; "Pastime with good company" ("The King's Ballad"), 34, 36–41, 44, 50, 177; "Though some say that youth rules me," 34, 43–44, 50, 191; "The time of youth is to be spent," 41–42; "Without discord," 29

Henry VIII Manuscript, 7n24, 8, 11, 12, 13, 16n7, 44

Hepburn, James, Earl of Bothwell, 3, 53, 96–97; in Casket Sonnets, 80, 81, 82–83, 84, 86, 87, 92, 93, 95, 123

Herbert, George, 198

Herman, Peter C., 4n8, 89–90, 112n51, 141n156, 155n194

Heywood, Thomas, 99–100

Hill, Christopher, 142

Historie of Jacob (1578), 153, 154

Holbein, Hans, the Younger, 20, 21, 30, 47

Holdsworth, Alan, 135–36

Homily on Matrimony, 131

Hooke, Henry, 183

Hopkins, Lisa, 55

Horenbout, Lucas, 47, 48

Howard, Henry, earl of Surrey, 1, 6, 51

Howard, Skiles, 26, 27

Howard, Thomas, Duke of Norfolk, 108

Howell, Roger, 168–69

Huguet, Edmond, 95–96

Humston, Robert, 149

Imitatio, 88–89

Interfaith marriage, first on record 125n105

Ives, Eric, 49

James VI/I, 3, 98, 100, 136; and absolutism, 146, 158, 168, 178, 190, 191–95; and authorship, 161–62; compared to other royal poets, 157, 194; and incest, 164–65; poetic reputation, 6; publication of verse, 7, 12–13; as royal poet, 157–58

Letters: to Elizabeth I (3 August, 1585), 164; to Elizabeth I (12 December, 1585), 164; to Elizabeth I (1 January, 1586, 164); to Elizabeth I (April, 1586); 159; to Elizabeth (c. 1586), 160–61, 177

Poems: The Essayes of a Prentise, 157, 178–79, 180; "Full many a time" (sonnet to Elizabeth), 158–65; *His Majesties Poeticall Exercises,* 170, 176, 179, 181, 188; *Lepanto,* 157, 170–89; "Oh stay your teares" ("Answer to the Libell called the Commons Tears"), 189–95; and publication history, 158; running headers, 183–86; "Thou might Mars" (Sidney elegy), 158, 165–70; title page, 182; and unauthorized manuscript transmission, 176n63;

Prose: Answer to Parliament (17 December, 1621), 190; *The Trew Law of Free Monarchies,* 195, 200; Whitehall speech to Parliament (26 March, 1610), 191; *Whole Workes of the Most High and Mighty Prince James,* 189

Jones, Anne Rosalind, 81

Jonson, Ben, 6, 203

Jordan, Constance, 132, 134, 138, 153

Katherine of Aragon, 5, 30–32, 49, 164

Kennedy, William, 134

Killigrew, Henry, 70

Kipling, Gordon, 5

Knollys, Francis, 107

Knox, John, 53, 65, 74, 75–77, 80

Labé, Louise, 82

Laing, Malcolm, 102n14

La Mothe-Fénelon, François, 10, 98

Languet, Hubert, 145

Lepanto, Battle of, 171–72

Lerer, Seth, 26, 30

Leslie, John, bishop of Ross, 108, 112

Louis XV, 90, 143

Louise de Savoie, 63

Magna Carta, 192–93, 194

Maitland, John, 170

Maitland, John, earl of Lauderdale, 207
Maitland, William, 110, 112
Marcus, Leah, 9, 10, 45n72
Marcus, Leah, Janel Mueller, and Mary
    Beth Rose, 8, 100, 114, 116, 135n137,
    140
Marguerite de Navarre, 52, 63, 86n90,
    100n6
Marotti, Arthur, 2, 94–95, 162, 179
Marshall, William, 201, 204–5
Marvell, Andrew, 201
Mary of Guise, 58, 64
Mary, Queen of Scots, 1, 3, 100, 105, 123,
    134, 143; and absolutism, 64, 77, 97;
    control over marital affairs, 61–63,
    75–77; deposition, 80, 101–2; educa-
    tion, 53–54; and Elizabeth I, 67–75;
    "en deuil," 58–61; and execution,
    166, 170; poetic reputation, 6, 9–10,
    54; and Scotland, 52–53; and gender,
    52–53, 65, 67–68, 77–80, 81; ico-
    nography, 55–56; images on coins,
    78–80; penchant for cross-dressing,
    70–71; problems faced ruling Scot-
    land, 64–68; and religion, 64–65; and
    subjectivity, 90–98;
    Works: "Adamus Loquitur" (The Dia-
    mond Speaks), 68–75, 106, 163; "Elle
    pour son honneur," 82, 85, 92; "En
    mon triste et doux chant" (elegy on
    François II), 56–63; "Entre ses mains,"
    82, 90, 97–98, 177; "Essay on the Sci-
    ence of Government," 64n31; Latin
    themes in praise of women, 53–54;
    "Et maintenant elle commence à voir,"
    84, 85, 87–90; "Mon amour croist,"
    82, 91; "O Dieux," 81–82, 91, 96;
    "Par vous mon coeur," 92–93; "Pour
    luy aussi," 95; "Quant vous l'aimiez,"
    86–87, 90; and question of forgery,
    9–10, 9n36; "Si ce lieu" (quatrain
    in Mass book), 54–55, 57; Sonnets
    to Bothwell (Casket Sonnets), 9, 53,
    75, 81–98, 124, 143, 195; "Une seul
    penser," 11, 102–3, 105, 106; "De vous
    je dis," 90, 93–95; "Vous la croyez,"
    82, 83–84
Mary Tudor, 65
Maxwell, John, lord Herries, 107
May, Steven and Anne Lake Prescott, 132,
    134–35, 135n137
May, Steven W., 100, 105, 107, 115, 116,
    117, 140n152, 147
McLaren, A. N., 150, 151, 152, 156

Melissus, Paul, 4
Mendoza, Bernardino de, 126
Meres, Francis, 99
Middlebrook, Leah, 63
Milton, John, Eikonoklastes, 196–97
Montaigne, Michel de, 171n49
Montrose, Louis A., 2, 20, 58, 112, 114, 120,
    123, 144, 162, 183, 195
More, Thomas, 40
Morgan, Thomas, 114

Neville, Alexander, 165–66
Nicot, Jean, 55, 134
Nohrnberg, James, 153
Northern Rebellion, 103, 108
Norton, Thomas, 126

Oakley, Francis, 135

Pace, Richard, 8
Pepys, Samuel, 206
Perry, Curtis, 187, 194
Petrarch, Francesco, 70, 86, 128, 129, 132
Petrarchism, 1; and women, 81; and politics,
    162, 207
Philip, King of Spain, 151, 175, 189
Phillips, James E. 139–40, 141
Pigge, Oliver, 149
Plato, 141
Pléiade, 54, 88
Plessis-Mornay, Philippe de, 145, 146n175
Political imaginary, definition, 2–3, 3n7
Potter, Lois, 197, 201, 203
Psalms, 201
Puttenham, George, 2, 9, 51, 99, 103,
    113–14

Rainbow portrait, 114, 115
Ralegh, Walter, 3
Randolph, Thomas, 65, 68, 79–80, 161
Raymond, Joad, 199
Read, Conyers, 118, 147n179
Resistance theory, Protestant, 145, 168
Reynolds, Edward, 196
Richard III, iconography of, 18
Ridolfi Plot, 110
Ritson's Manuscript, 7n24, 6n7, 44
Ronsard, Pierre de, 54, 60, 88, 89
Royston, Richard, 204
Russell, Conrad, 190
Ruthven lords, 170

Sadler, Ralph, 122
Saunders, J. W., 178

Scarisbrick, J. J., 15, 26
Sedgewick, Eve Kosofsky, 84
Selden, John, 178
Shakespeare, William, 84
Sharpe, Kevin, 5n16
Shell, Marc, 165
Sidney, Philip, 70, 86, 89, 119, 128, 142, 143, 145, 179, 207
Siemens, Ray, 44n70
Sieve Portraits, 120–21, 123
Simier, Jean de, 117
Skelton, John, 4, 5, 203
Smith, G. Gregory, 141
Smith, Thomas, 136–37
Song of Songs, 151–56
Spenser, Edmund, 142, 183, 187–89
Spingarn, Joel, 88
Stafford, Simon, 183
Stanford, Henry, 116, 117
Starkey, David, 15
Stevens, John, 26
Stewart, Henry, lord Darnley, 64, 75, 77, 80, 81, 96, 97
Stiles, John, 16
Strong, Roy, 120
Stuart, Esmé, earl of Lennox, 174
Stubbs, John, 119
Summit, Jennifer, 105, 107, 111
Szönyi, Gregöry, 127

Tablet (writing), and "Doubt of future foes," 103, 110–12

Taverner, Richard, 136, 138
Taylor, Charles, 3n7
Taylor, John, 199, 203
Thomworth, John, 77
Throckmorton, Nicholas, 56n18, 58, 61, 62–63, 66–67, 72–73, 95
Topcliffe, Richard, 144
Treaty of Edinburgh, 66, 67, 72, 107, 110

Van der Noot, Jan, 99
Vaultrollier, Thomas, 179
Vergil, Polydore, 17, 18, 37–40
Vickers, Nancy, 86
Villiers, George, duke of Buckingham, 189
Vives, Juan Luis, 141–42

Waldegrave, Roger, 183
Walker, Greg, 26
Waller, Gary, 81
Walsingham, Francis, 118, 125, 126, 168, 169, 170
Walton, Kristen, 76, 80
Wars of Religion, 75
Westminster Conference, 108
Willson, David Harris, 174–75
Windet, John, 166, 167
Wolsey, Thomas, 16, 38, 40–41
Wormald, Jenny, 10n38, 65
Wroth, Mary, 81
Wyatt, Thomas, 1, 6, 29, 32, 51, 70, 95

Youth, 8, 30, 41